SOLVING COACHING PROBLEMS

SOLVING COACHING PROBLEMS: Strategies for Successful Team Development

ROBERT G. HOEHN

Allyn and Bacon, Inc.

Boston   *London*   *Sydney*   *Toronto*

Library of Congress Cataloging in Publication Data

Hoehn, Robert G., 1937–
    Solving coaching problems.

    1. Coaching (Athletics)   I.   Title.
GV711.H63   796'.07'7   82–3920
ISBN 0–205–07818–4   AACR2

10 9 8 7 6 5 4 3 2 1   88 87 86 85 84 83 82

Printed in the United States of America.

To Richard E. Bailie

*For your endless dedication and determination
to make things better for everyone*

Contents

Foreword

This work fills a considerable void that exists in the knowledge and background of inexperienced coaches and more than a few experienced ones.

Written from a practical standpoint, the book deals with problem areas that traditionally have been little considered in the preparation of coaches in our institutions of higher learning.

Most coaches emerge from these colleges and universities very well prepared to deal with the mechanics and strategies of their sports, but become quickly disillusioned when they discover that there is far more to dealing with athletes—especially within the legal climate that exists in our society today—than just the conditioning and technical preparation of a team.

Coach Hoehn writes from the perspective of wide experience. He is an extremely well qualified and gifted teacher-coach. Most importantly he has been through the mill and his comments and suggestions are solidly based in reality—not theory.

This work will be of great value to all coaches and will assist many to avoid and deal with the host of everyday problems that might otherwise plague them and reduce their teaching effectiveness.

Richard E. Bailie
Principal
Roseville High School
Roseville, California

Preface

This book is intended as a practical guide for you, the coach. The purpose of the book is twofold: 1) to offer numerous tips and suggestions for strengthening your particular team program; 2) To show effective ways of handling those facets of coaching that are personally frustrating and disappointing, and notorious for driving coaches out of the profession.

This book is meant to work with you by:

1. Examining high school coaching, past and present. You'll see why the 1980s might be the most challenging time of all. You'll discover why many coaches leave the profession and what you can do to prolong your coaching career.
2. Giving you solid tips and practical suggestions on how to deal positively with athletes, administrators, parents, officials, and community leaders.
3. Showing you ways to communicate effectively with everyone involved with the athletic program.
4. Offering specific guidelines for spotting potential problems and how to handle them. Chapter Two, "How to Handle Problems between Coach and Athlete," gives valuable suggestions on how parents, athletes, and coaches can work together to solve tough problems.
5. Providing excellent advice for handling administrative problems. Chapter Three, "Coaching and the Administration," shows the coach how to work effectively with the administration and build a strong athletic program.
6. Describing successful methods for motivating athletes, publicizing the team's progress, and building a strong rapport with officials.

7. Focusing on preventive strategies—Chapter Nine, "Coaching Burnout," presents those problems that drive people out of coaching and offers suggestions and recommendations for avoiding burnout.
8. Suggesting ways to reduce athletic injury and avoid costly lawsuits.
9. Outlining methods for working effectively with the community and earning money for your athletic program.
10. Offering a step-by-step plan for putting together athletic handbooks and yearbooks.

The book closes with tips on how to bring the season to a smooth finish. Charts and illustrations have been carefully selected to help you prepare a program you, your athletes, and the entire community will be proud of.

Coaching today requires several important attributes: outstanding organizational skills, a thorough knowledge of modern coaching techniques, a willingness to make sacrifices, and the ability to handle tough situations. It is hoped that this book will help the coach master these challenges so that he or she can go on to enjoy a long and productive career.

Acknowledgments

I would like to extend my warmest thanks to those coaches and educators who supplied me with valuable information and advice. Among those who made a special effort are Charles S. Frazier, Dr. Dennis Sparks, Dr. James Garrick, Bill Palmer of the American Sports Education Institute, the Boosters Clubs of America, Richard Bailie, Herman L. Masin, John L. Griffith, Carl Foote, Ed Vasconcellos, Thomas E. Abdenour, Dan Riley, Robert Miller, Bernice J. Goldstein, Joe Gieck, William A. Welker, Paul Gonzalez, Keith Peterson, Marge Drone, and the Roseville High School Boosters Club.

A special thanks is due to Charles R. Wiese, Superintendent, Roseville Union High School District, for allowing me to use the district forms that appear in Figures 3-2, 3-3, 8-1, 11-1, 12-1, 12-2, 14-1a, and 14-1b.

Stepping into the Coaching Scene

*Our progress as a nation can be no
swifter than our progress in education.*

John Fitzgerald Kennedy

Coaching high school sports in the 1980s may be more challenging than at any other time. For the first time in school history, some districts are charging athletes a fee to participate in school sports. In recent years, school districts have been forced to deal with four areas of concern. These are: (1) reduced enrollment; (2) proposed budget cuts; (3) higher costs of operating facilities and buying equipment; (4) sex discrimination in sports.

How well school districts handle these problems may decide the fate of high school athletics. This book will discuss each of these issues and suggest ways athletic programs can cope with these and other significant problems.

COACHING IN THE HIGH SCHOOL TODAY

Let's examine the four major problems and see how they affect a school's athletic program.

Reduced Enrollment

The athletic program suffers when enrollment drops; fewer athletes turn out for sports and less money filters into the school budget. As a result, programs may be eliminated and staff members, including coaches, may be reassigned or terminated. As an example, in Sacramento, California, high school football game attendance has dropped since 1975. School officials say fewer athletes are turning out for the sport as a result of a sharp drop in student enrollment.

Other school districts across the nation are feeling the pinch from declining enrollment. In fact, many schools have closed their doors permanently. Those schools continuing to operate face the possibility of completely reorganizing their athletic leagues to allow outside schools to join.

Proposed Budget Cuts

Budget cuts slice deeply into a school's athletic program. For example, one California school district proposed a $2.3 million budget cut for the upcoming year. This plan included reducing the number of athletic teams at five high schools to four. The school board came up with these recommendations:

- Interscholastic athletic programs at the high schools be limited to participation in four sports—basketball, baseball, football, and track for boys, and the same or equivalent replacement for girls—most likely volleyball, basketball, track, and softball.
- Move the ninth grade to the high school level and eliminate all competitive athletic programs for the seventh and eighth grade schools and replace them with an intramural program.

The district cited reduced income and the uncertainty of future money as reasons for the proposed budget cuts.

What effect do these cuts have on the total athletic program? Some coaches feel that there will be a detriment to community relations; others see great difficulty in explaining to their athletes that one sport isn't as important as another. Also, cuts will increase the amount of free time young people will have. Communities must bear the cost of providing some occupation for young people or the cost of vandalism and juvenile delinquency.

If this district votes to eliminate a sport, three things will happen. One, the sport is no longer sanctioned by the California Interscholastic Federation and athletes can't compete for any reason in a CIF-sanctioned meet. Two, it would also prohibit athletes from competing unattached in post-season championships. Three, the leagues which carry these schools will drop in number.

Higher Costs of Operating Facilities and Buying Equipment

Today, more than ever, coaches are forced to make do while they search for productive ways to earn money to keep their programs alive. Some coaches, along with their athletes, put on jog-a-thons, candy sales, car washes, or run concession stands in order to earn enough money to buy new uniforms or replace expensive equipment. The coach must work hard to organize and direct these projects. Unfortunately, the coach faces many obstacles. There are strict district policies to follow. Often school clubs and community organizations hold money making projects at the same time. Such competition limits the amount of money coming in at one time. However, with the proper management, most of these problems can be worked out in advance.

Here is how one high school raised money to improve its baseball and softball fields:

LAND RUSH . . . On Now!!!

Choice sites still available. Don't be left out on the greatest land deal since the "Sooner Rush." The *sooner* you rush in with your request for a Gold Strike Deed the sooner the fields will be suitable for our Del Campo students and those in the community who use the fields for their softball and baseball games.

The Committee for the Improvement of the Del Campo High School Baseball/Softball Fields is working diligently to achieve its goals. The San Juan School District Maintenance and Operations Department will install a water fountain between the softball and JV baseball fields next month. They have delivered soil which the baseball coaches and players have used to fill some of the holes in the fields. We expect more soil to be delivered this month, if weather permits. Del Campo's baseball coaches and players, together with the parents of a few members of the girls softball team, will combine their efforts to repair Del Campo's fields.

Our fund is increasing—but has not reached a level that will enable us to shop for bleachers or enlarge the backstop fencing. Become a part of this community effort. Make your investment today. Purchase a Gold Strike Deed to honorary ownership of the Del Campo fields—$1.00 per square foot, $2.00 per two square feet, etc. An investment of $10.00 or more will entitle the purchaser to a deed which is handsomely framed. For your convenience use the coupon below. Upon receipt of your check a Gold Strike Deed will be mailed to you.

Mail to:	Del Campo Baseball/Softball Fund
	Del Campo High School
	4925 Dewey Drive
	Fair Oaks, CA 95628
Make Check Payable to:	
	Del Campo Baseball/Softball Fund

Name _____

Address _____

Phone _____

Number of Shares Purchased _____

Amount Enclosed _____

A successful fund raising project can help a struggling program survive during rough times. It also gives community members a chance to work together and get to know the coaches and athletes.

In some school districts fund raising doesn't provide enough money to keep the athletic programs going. A few of these districts are charging athletes from five dollars per student per sport to seventy-five dollars for each sport they sign up for. As expected, parents and students aren't happy with the pay-your-way plan. The fee policy places a hardship on poorer students.

Use of facilities presents a growing problem for girls' and boys' athletics. Crowded gym floors and playing fields can lead to hard feelings between coaches and athletes, especially during inclement weather. Few schools today can afford to build separate playing areas. How, then, can the race for space be settled in an equitable manner? Here are seven suggestions for handling the problem of an overcrowded gym:

1. Decide ahead of time what the practice hours will be. Post these hours so the athletes will know. Start and finish practice on time.
2. Post the practice schedule in advance. If problems arise, there will be time to adjust.
3. Keep the schedule flexible enough to allow other teams to hold early practice. Alternating practice hours with other coaches gives everyone a chance to go home early.
4. When two or more teams use the gym at the same time, divide playing space equally among all teams.

5. Limit activities to those that have a low injury risk to athletes or little chance of damaging the facility. For instance, throwing a baseball or softball in a crowded area poses a danger to others.
6. Use drills and activities that accommodate small groups of athletes.
7. Give athletes a hard workout. Keep them busy at all times. Avoid long-drawn-out practices.

Sex Discrimination in Sports

Title IX became law in 1972 in compliance with the United States Educational Act. It states that any educational institution, private or public, that receives federal funds shall not discriminate on the basis of sex. Title IX prohibits discrimination in:

- Hiring and promotion of staffs.
- Entrance requirements.
- Financial aid programs.
- School policy.
- Counseling and other student services.

Under the new rules, schools will be required to eliminate disparities in the way female and male athletes are treated. These are the new rules:

- List restrictions on the number of approved school sports for either sex.
- Provide, where possible, uniform scheduling of sports by season and allow the sexes equal opportunity to compete in post-season tournaments and championships.
- Equalize the length of seasons for boys' and girls' sports.
- Require schools to schedule an equal number of contests for boys and girls who compete in the same sport.
- Require the same qualifications for officials and the same number of officials at athletic contests.
- Equalize the pay of officials and athletic awards for boys' and girls' sports.

These rules do not force a school to field a team for each sex in each sport. In fact, schools don't have to have sports at all. But the ones they have should reflect comparable opportunities for each sex. Coaches have flexibility. They can still choose team members on the basis of ability.

Here are three reported discriminatory practices in athletic programs:

1. More approved sports for boys than for girls.
2. Longer seasons for boys' sports than for girls'.
3. Higher pay for officials of boys' games than for girls'.

A recent federal court suit against a school system in the Midwest alleged that women coaches were being paid less than male coaches. The complaint alleged that the school system acted unlawfully by establishing lesser wage rates for women coaches in sports such as tennis, track, and basketball. An investigation disclosed that the duties of male and female coaches were equal since job functions required equal skill, effort, and responsibility.

Some school districts give the following reasons for the slow growth of girls' programs:

- Lack of interest on the part of the girls.
- Nonenforcement of discriminatory practices.
- Transportation problems.
- Lack of facilities for practice and play.
- Reduced budget.
- High cost of uniforms and equipment.
- Competition for athletes. As new programs arise, popular athletes are being pressured to play.
- Scarcity of coaches.

HOW COACHING HAS CHANGED OVER THE YEARS

Coaching has and always will be a tough challenge for those entering the field of athletics. Today's coach, to be successful, must have the ability to impart knowledge, the common sense to model socially acceptable behavior, and the enthusiasm to instill confidence in athletes. This philosophy holds true now just as it did in the past. In recent years, however, the coaching picture has changed. Veteran coaches see a change of attitude in athlete and coach.

An informal, two-part survey of veteran coaches (fifteen years or more of coaching experience) listed the following changes in the athlete:

1. Lack of desire. Many athletes have a tendency to be lax in practices and contests. There seems to be less dedication to succeed. Athletes are leaning toward recreational benefits.
2. Lack of self-discipline. Many athletes are not interested in making a total commitment to themselves, fellow players, or coach. Self-improvement isn't a major goal.

3. Conflicting interests. Too many social events going on at the same time. Athlete becomes confused, drops the sport, and does something else.

4. Economic problems. Athlete needs money to buy a car, go out on dates, and be with friends. Finding and keeping a job is extremely important by the time an athlete enters the third year of high school. As the cost of living increases, the athlete is forced to hold onto the job. As a result, keeping present job supersedes going out for sports.

5. Lack of parental support. Less parental pressure on athlete to compete in sports. More than ever, with both parents working, athlete left to make own decisions. Most parents are too busy to watch athletes play. Athlete may lose desire to compete and quit.

6. Overexposure. Many athletes, by the time they reach their second or third year of high school, decide to quit. They grow tired of competing. Some feel the youth programs (Little League Baseball, Bobby Sox Softball, or Pop Warner Football) have sapped them of their energies. Also, overexposure may be caused by too much parental support or pressure.

7. Loss of self-esteem. Athlete honored as "All-Star" in baseball or football prior to entering high school. May see All-Star status crumble as competition increases. Athlete likely to quit rather than accept a second or third string role.

8. Activity preference. Team sports may become less popular than individual out-of-school activities such as tennis, golf, bowling, and racquetball. Many athletes prefer to set their own pace; that is, practice at their convenience and under their own terms—no pressure, no demands. Also, the availability of tennis courts, golf courses, and bowling alleys makes all of this possible.

The second part of the veteran coaches survey revealed this information about the coach:

1. Stress buildup. Coach feels the pressure to win, to show a big improvement over the previous year's record. After four or five years of mounting stress, the coach becomes tense and irritable.

2. Administrative conflicts. When the coach and administration disagree about policies and procedures, the coach may develop a cynical outlook and stop constructive communication.

3. Use of facilities and equipment. Some coaches become disgruntled by having to share facilities and equipment, and may begin to criticize other coaches and the athletic programs.

4. Lack of prestige. Coach feels other sports are receiving more attention from administration, student body, and community. Coach fails to support other sport programs.
5. Discipline of athletes. Coach dislikes disciplining athletes. The energy drain often puts the coach in a negative frame of mind.
6. Lack of financial support. A coach feels major sports are getting lion's share of pie. The coach expresses anger about having to manage on less money than other teams.
7. Lack of community support. Coach displays a lackadaisical attitude in response to passive community interest.
8. General loss of interest. The activity ceases to be fun. Coach no longer looks forward to start of the season. Coach satisfied to settle back and coast through the season.
9. Oversaturated. Coach carries two or more coaching assignments during the year. After a few seasons, the coach loses enthusiasm and starts looking around for something else to do.
10. Low pay. Coach unhappy with pay. Decides not to put forth any extra effort.
11. Lack of appreciation. Coach works hard, spends long hours preparing for practices and contests. Coach begins to feel hostile toward administration and community.

Myriad problems crop up each year between coach and athlete. Chapter 2, "How to Handle Problems between Coach and Athlete," will suggest ways to prevent major problems.

INTERVIEWING FOR A COACHING POSITION

No two school districts are exactly alike. Each has its own unique set of problems. For instance, School District A may have a strong athletic department with a reputation for turning out championship teams. Conversely, School District B seldom produces a winner and receives little or no recognition from the press.

It may be difficult to pinpoint the factors creating the disparity between District A and District B. For this reason, it's imperative that a person find out everything possible about a school's athletic program before accepting a coaching position.

During an interview, the answers to the following questions will help a prospective coach make a decision.

1. How does the school district support the athletic program?
2. How do the student body and the community support the athletic program?

3. What does the school district expect from its coaches?
4. What does the school district expect from its athletes?
5. Do the coaches from the men's athletic department and women's athletic department work well together?
6. What special problems does the district face in relation to athletics?
7. What are the chances for advancement?
8. How does the district view winning?
9. Is there a large turnover in coaching positions? If so, why?
10. How many junior high schools feed into the district? How many athletes come from these feeder schools?
11. Do athletes present any special disciplinary problems?
12. How large is the dropout rate among athletes?
13. Does the district give released time to its coaches?
14. Are coaches evaluated? If so, how?
15. How does the district transport athletes to neighboring schools?
16. Is coaching pay comparable with other nearby districts?
17. What is the general attitude of coaches in the district? Do they attend coaching clinics? Are they willing to share ideas and update their coaching methods?
18. Are coaches expected to organize and run pre-season or post-season programs?
19. Do coaches have to organize fund-raising projects to earn money for their teams?
20. Is there money available for buying new equipment?
21. Are there enough facilities for all the athletic teams?
22. Do teachers and coaches, for the most part, have a harmonious relationship?
23. If the individual has to coach and teach, will the assignments conflict?

Unfortunately, coaching positions aren't as plentiful today as they were several years ago. A coach fresh out of college faces stiff competition. There might be, for example, thirty or more people seeking the same coaching assignment. Under these conditions, a coach may be reluctant to ask too many questions during an interview for fear of antagonizing the interviewer. On the other hand, if the coach doesn't show a genuine interest in the school's athletic program, the interviewer, unimpressed with the coach's passive attitude, may cut off the session with, "We'll let you know our decision within two weeks."

How, then, can coaches prepare themselves for making a strong impression during an interivew? Consider the following seven-step approach:

- Prior to the interview, become familiar with the school's athletic program. Talk to teachers, athletes, and coaches in the community. Get firsthand information about district policies and procedures.

- Dress in a professional manner. Let common sense and good taste dictate appearance.
- Relax, use good posture, and make eye contact throughout the interview.
- Answer questions completely. Come to the point. Avoid boring the interviewer with long, frivolous statements.
- Ask questions directly related to the coaching position. Remember the interviewer has a busy schedule.
- Use the Three B approach: Be enthusiastic, Be confident, and Be assertive.
- Send a thank you note to the interviewer. This courteous gesture adds a professional touch.

PREPARING MENTALLY FOR COACHING

It has been said that coaching is a twenty-four hour job. A slight exaggeration? Perhaps, but most coaches admit that they spend most of the working day—and night—thinking about coaching.

The mental preparation for coaching is important. A successful coach thinks ahead, prepares for the unexpected, and maintains flexibility in handling tough situations. Here are eleven ways a coach can prepare mentally for the coming season.

One, organize practice sessions and meetings well in advance. Have a reason for doing everything. Then set out to accomplish each planned task.

Two, study the rules. Be familiar with new rule changes. Keep athletes informed on school policies, e.g., the expectations of the district and community.

Three, become totally involved with the athletic program. Share in the successes as well as the failures.

Four, keep the lines of communication open. Establish a solid rapport with community leaders and the local press.

Five, set seasonal goals for the team. Help athletes set personal goals for themselves.

Six, attend pre-season coaching clinics. Keep up to date on recent findings in the field. Share ideas and strategies with other coaches.

Seven, help athletes to improve. Take a "one step at a time" approach. Make every effort to strengthen the total athletic program.

Eight, prepare to spend extra time helping athletes, organizing fund-raising projects, setting up tournaments, publicizing coming events, and keeping equipment and facilities in working order.

Nine, keep a positive outlook. Face the challenge of working under adverse conditions.

Ten, support fellow coaches and teachers. Avoid downgrading the efforts of others.

Eleven, remember that desire, discipline, and determination are the working forces behind coach and athlete.

REASONS FOR COACHING

Suppose every coach had to complete a checklist indicating the reasons for wanting to coach. For an example, see Figure 1-1.

	Reasons for Coaching	Yes	No	Maybe
1	Just love to be around sports.			
2	It's an excellent way to stay in shape.			
3	To build a strong rapport with kids.			
4	It keeps a person feeling young.			
5	A step toward bigger and better things.			
6	To improve teaching skills.			
7	For self-satisfaction.			
8	For the money.			
9	Have a strong desire to win, win, win.			
10	Take great pride in watching athletes improve.			
11	Have ex-jock syndrome.			
12	To improve knowledge of sports.			
13	Enjoy socializing with other coaches.			
14	Gives a feeling of importance; prestige.			
15	Generates a feeling of power.			
16	For personal recognition.			
17	An excellent way to expend energy.			
18	Fulfills a need to compete.			
19	Helps improve organizational skills.			
20	To gain special favors from others.			

FIGURE 1-1 Coaching checklist

Now comes the big question: Who decides which of these items are the right or wrong reasons for coaching? The only person who can give an honest answer to this question is the coach.

A recent survey of active coaches throughout the country pinpointed five major reasons for coaching. They are:

1. Self-satisfaction. (Number 7 on the checklist.)
2. To build a strong rapport with kids, especially outside the classroom environment. (Number 3 on the checklist.)
3. Enjoy socializing with fellow coaches. (Number 13 on the checklist.)
4. Take pride in watching athletes improve. (Number 10 on the checklist.)
5. For the money. (Number 8 on the checklist.)

Not everyone coaches for the same reasons. In fact, there may be reasons that are not included in the Coaching Checklist. Regardless of why a person chooses to coach, the athlete must always come first. After all, that's the sole reason athletic programs exist in schools today—for the benefit of those competing in the program.

WHAT TO EXPECT FROM COACHING

There once was a coach named Flynn
who did all he could to win.
He lost every game
and took all the blame,
yet came back again and again.

This may not be the greatest limerick in the world, but it points up one thing: for many, the challenge of coaching provides the impetus to carry on.

With few exceptions, most teams have their share of ups and downs. An experienced coach knows that winning or losing doesn't just happen. For the most part, success comes to those who encourage everyone to pull together. Coaching, like other professions, brings with it times for rejoicing and times for sadness.

Let's examine three situations that put a smile on the coach's face.

Situation One

A high school baseball coach received an unexpected visit from a former player who was kicked off the team for breaking a team rule. Interestingly, the visit came twelve years after the incident. The athlete, now thirty years old, presented the coach with a beautifully engraved plaque which read:

TO (Coach's Name)
IN RECOGNITION OF YOUR
SUPER COACHING
LEADERSHIP
AND FRIENDSHIP
(Athlete's Name)   1980
1964–1968

Why, after twelve years, did the athlete honor the coach? He did it for two reasons: 1) He wanted to say thanks to the coach for not holding a grudge; 2) He felt the coach, by removing him from the team, helped him learn how to cooperate with others. Today the young man makes a successful living selling real estate, and carries a reputation for being a topnotch fast-pitch softball player.

Situation Two

After winning a basketball game in overtime, a parent of one of the players approached the coach, held out his hand, and said, "The kids say you're a good coach. I agree. You give your players one-hundred percent support, win or lose. Thanks, coach."

Situation Three

The principal walked into the dressing room after the football team clinched the league championship. He motioned for silence, then began: "I want all of you to know that we're very proud of the fine season you've had. Your hard work paid off. You deserve to be congratulated. Thanks. Keep it up." The principal followed with a letter of congratulations to the coach.

The word THANKS carries a powerful punch. These six letters can keep a coach—and the program—alive and ticking for many years. Nothing snuffs a team's progress or a coach's spirit faster than a lack of support by significant people in the school and community.

Now let's review three situations that create tension and anxiety for the coach.

Situation One

The Sacramento Bee Newspaper, California, ran an article on a high school football coach whose team hadn't won a game in three years (0–25). The coach gave two reasons for not winning: One, the school didn't have enough talented athletes (smallest school in league); Two, there seemed to be a psychological barrier hovering over the team. And to make matters worse, the principal passed along these words to the coach: "If you have another losing season, the school board will probably make you an administrator."

Situation Two

During a parent conference, a father blasted the coach for not playing his son. His son, according to the father, made every Little League All-Star Team since he was ten years old. The father accused the coach of playing favorites and mishandling the athletes.

Situation Three

The district superintendent, principal, and coach held a meeting. At the meeting the coach received a tongue lashing and a written reprimand for behavior unbecoming a professional. Here are excerpts from the Official Reprimand given the coach:

> During this game (Coach's Name) went on the field to confer with the referee, and after a short discussion the official terminated the conversation. (Coach's Name) attempted to continue the discussion and was asked to leave the field. He refused to do so after being asked three times, and called the referee a "hamburger." The referee then penalized the team five yards for delay of the game.
>
> (Coach's Name) was informed that this conduct is in direct violation of State League rules and school district policy. He was also informed that this type of conduct is unsatisfactory, cannot and will not be tolerated, and further, such conduct will and must result in his removal from coaching.

_____   _____
(Coach's Name)   (District Superintendent)

Date   _____
                                  (Principal)

The coach agreed to talk to his team, to admit that he had been remiss in his conduct, and to re-emphasize the rules of sportsmanship.

Losing seasons, irate parents, and administrative reprimands shake a coach's confidence. In time, a coach may decide to resign, go elsewhere, or try something less frustrating.

In the next chapter we'll study some of the problems that plague coaches and outline some strategies for dealing with these problems.

POINTS TO REMEMBER

A coach leads an exciting life. Each season brings its share of surprises and disappointments. But most coaches know there are no guarantees, no magic formulas for instant success. Success comes only through long hours of preparation, perseverance, and a willingness to make sacrifices.

A knowledgeable coach with the ability to communicate is an asset to any athletic program. An outstanding coach seeks to improve, has a positive outlook, and cooperates with others.

QUESTIONS

1. Why will the 1980s be a challenging time for school athletic programs?
2. What effect does a reduced school enrollment have on an athletic program?
3. Why are school districts across the nation facing budget cuts?
4. What are three advantages of organizing a fund raising project?
5. What things should a coach do before holding a fund raising project?
6. What are the advantages of charging athletes to participate in school sports? What are the disadvantages?
7. What can coaches do to prevent overcrowded gyms?
8. How has the passage of Title IX made coaching in the schools more difficult?
9. In what ways have women's athletics been discriminated against?
10. How have women coaches been discriminated against?
11. According to veteran coaches, how has the athlete changed over the years?
12. According to veteran coaches, how has the coach's attitude changed?
13. How should a person prepare for a coaching job interview?
14. How can a person prepare mentally for coaching? List six ways.
15. In your opinion, what are four wrong reasons for being a coach? Explain each of your reasons.
16. In your opinion, what are the right reasons for being a coach? Explain each of your reasons.
17. What is the purpose of a written reprimand? How can it help a coach improve?
18. Does the future look bright for high school coaches? Explain.

How to Handle Problems between Coach and Athlete

Difficulties are meant to rouse, not discourage. The human spirit is to grow strong by conflict.

William Ellery Channing

It would be nice if every coach could finish a season without any problems. Just think, no unhappy athletes, no budget worries, and perhaps best of all, no conflicts with parents, administrators, or members of the community. But since we live in the real world, problems do exist and will continue to invade the sanctity of the coach for years to come.

Problems and the conflicts they bring test a coach's patience, endurance, and ability to work with people. In this chapter we'll single out some of the problems that confront the coach and athlete.

THE INFLUENCE OF PARENTS ON ATHLETES

Most parents let the coach do the coaching. Furthermore, they give their full support to the coach by helping out whenever possible.

Conversely, a few parents work extra hard to make the coach's job a difficult one.

For example, let's consider the father who gives his son or daughter extra coaching at home. If this coincides with the coach's teaching, then well and good. But if the parent undermines the coach's effort, the athlete may come to believe the coach is incompetent.

William A. Welker, head wrestling coach, Wheeling Park High School, West Virginia, says, "Often a problem between the coach and the athlete begins at home; the parents are trying to coach their child and say negative things about the coach."

The coach must take a stand. Athletes and parents need to understand that only one person, the coach, runs the team and decides how each athlete fits into the total program. Coach Welker goes on to say, "The coach must be aware of such domestic pressures and judge accordingly." Good advice. An inexperienced coach, however, may be confused and not know what to do next.

At this point, the coach must decide what's best for the athlete and the team. If a parent's home coaching offers nearly the same thing, then there's probably no reason to panic. Here's where the coach must use common sense. But suppose an athlete elects to follow dad's advice at the expense of the coach or team, what then? The coach might try the following two-point plan: 1) Remove athlete from competition; 2) Hold a parent conference with the athlete and the administrator present. During the conference, these items should be stressed:

- Explain to parent how interference affects athlete, coaching plans, and team progress.
- Listen to what parent has to say.
- Ask athlete to express feelings.
- Ask for statement from administrator.

If the parent chooses not to cooperate, the coach has little choice but to drop the athlete from the team.

Bernice J. Goldstein, girls' tennis coach, Beach Channel High School, New York, faces a similar problem. She battles outside pressure by coaches or professionals who give contradictory advice to her tennis players. Coaching becomes a challenge under these conditions.

A coach may have little control over outside forces, but the coach can insist upon athletes following a prescribed practice or game plan. This allows the coach to maintain control over athletes during school hours.

What about the parent who attends practice session? What affect does this have on an athlete?

While coaching baseball several years ago, a coach had to deal with a "father factor." The same father appeared at nearly every practice. The father's presence proved embarrassing for his son because the other players would tease the boy about his dad hanging around. The boy, feeling pressure to be "the star athlete," grew tense and irritable. Often he would look in his father's direction, utter a word or two, and lose concentration. According to other players, the boy's father also attended football and wrestling practice sessions.

During a league baseball game the father offered advice to his son by shouting out orders and using hand signals. This situation put the boy, team members, and the coach in an awkward position. Something needed to be done—and quickly.

At the next practice session, the coach spoke with the father. He mentioned how he welcomed the father's support and interest in the team. He pointed out how the boy's desire and dedication added to the team's success. He explained to the father how his presence made the boy feel uncomfortable. The father, acting surprised at the news, wanted to know what he should do. The coach asked the father if he might like to help out, e.g., hit fly balls to the outfielders, umpire a scrimmage or two, and so on. The father accepted, took an active interest in other players, and soon gained favor with everybody. (Note: The coach received administrative approval before allowing the father to assist.)

Did the coach take a chance giving the father an open invitation to join practice? Yes, he did. Fortunately, his decision spawned positive results. The coach wisely chose a diplomatic approach based on experience, common sense, and tact.

Not all parents realize how much pressure they put on their children during the season. For instance, take a mother or father who tries to outholler the loudest fan. These outbursts draw attention away from the athlete and place the parent on center stage.

Few athletes want to be singled out in front of others by a private rooting section. What can a coach do to keep parents from upsetting athletes by yelling out names or embarrassing remarks? Some coaches use this strategy: 1) They speak with parents after the contest. They explain how distractions throw off an athlete's concentration and create confusion. Here's where the coach must use discretion and good judgment. The same approach, however, may not work for every coach. Much depends upon the situation that confronts the coach at that particular time. 2) They ask athletes to urge parents to stay calm during critical moments of the contest. Sometimes a few words at home does the job.

Many coaches throughout the country have their athletes take home a pre-season letter which includes the following item:

How a coach can work effectively with parents:

- A parent can support the program by helping an athlete meet team commitment. For example, do not take athlete on vacation during the season or making routine doctor or dental appointments during practice time.
- Asking parents for their cooperation in refraining from hollering at athletes, the coach, or officials during a contest.
- Outlining a procedure for parents to follow in case they wish to contact the coach. If an unhappy parent wants to speak with the coach, the parent must call the principal and set up a conference.

Few coaches appreciate a parent collaring them after a game or phoning them at home. For this reason, it's vitally important that every parent read and sign the pre-season letter. To assure a one-hundred percent response, the coach should require each athlete to return a signed portion of the letter before allowing the athlete to practice.

ATTITUDE: KEY TO A SUCCESSFUL PROGRAM

An athlete responds favorably or unfavorably to teammates, to the coach, and to the program. And the attitude an athlete holds determines, to a high degree, how much success the athlete and program will have.

Athletes develop attitudes from personal experiences, parental influences, and peer group contact. Athletes, like nearly everyone else, have a tendency to share the same ideas and convictions that are held by members of their peer group.

A wise coach knows that team strength lies in keeping athletes happy, both on and off the field. It only takes one or two sour apples to squeeze the life out of a team. The coach faces a monumental task in trying to isolate those problems that lead to negative feelings. Athletes aren't always willing to open up and say what's on their minds.

It would be useless to try and list all of the factors that bring on problems. Nevertheless, let's examine three events that cause friction for the coach and team.

Athlete Not Playing Enough

An athlete who spends more time sitting than playing may build resentment toward the coach. The athlete complains to parents, teachers, friends, other coaches, team players—anybody who will stop long enough to listen. The athlete loses interest in the program and gives half-hearted support to teammates in the starting lineup. Sadly, many disgruntled athletes keep the fire burning inside of them and never try to find out why they're not playing. They release their frustrations by whining to others and badmouthing the coach. The inability of players to honestly evaluate their skill in relation to other team members leads to resentment that is sometimes directed at other team members and the coach.

Athlete's Reason for Participating

Nothing bothers a coach more than an athlete's nonchalant attitude in practice. The coach fumes over an athlete's lackadaisical response and remarks how such a blasé manner would never be tolerated "when I was playing on a team." A coach must evaluate honestly the reason for such an attitude.

Robert Miller, basketball coach, Rock Valley Community School, Iowa, believes that the coach must understand that every athlete has a different reason for playing and an athlete's goal may not be the same as the coach's.

What do athletes want out of playing sports? According to a recent survey of male and female high school athletes, these are the reasons they participate:

- Wanting to prove to themselves and others that they can succeed in sports.
- A need to do something after school.
- A desire for keeping physically fit.
- An opportunity to make new friends.
- Just for fun.
- To keep out of trouble.
- A desire to compete.
- For self-satisfaction.
- To stay active in school events.
- To avoid boredom.

This survey brought out a major point. The athletes polled view sports participation as a means of improving their social lives. They see sports as a game, a way of obtaining companionship. They show little concern for devoting their lives to it.

Coach Expects Too Much

Some coaches say athletes are too lazy, they don't want to work. Athletes retaliate by accusing coaches of being too demanding in practice. When the coach and athlete trade barbs, problems flare up, and negative clouds drift over the practice field.

It's up to the coach to generate a warm, positive atmosphere. So to start off the season right, a coach should set up a plan that will benefit both coach and athlete. Such a plan might include these ten suggestions:

1. Convince the athletes who aren't playing regularly that they are a contributing factor to the team. This, of course, can be extremely difficult to do. Coach Robert Miller, Iowa, handles the situation by making sure everyone knows who will be playing most of the time. Then he shows the athletes who will be playing next year exactly what they must do and learn. There are no surprises. Athletes know where they stand with the team.

2. At the beginning of the season, give each athlete a written form with the rules and regulations to take home. Require parents and athletes to sign the form. In this way, everyone knows what's expected of them.

3. Leave the door open for discussion. Listen carefully to what athletes have to say. Iron out problems before they spread.

4. Be flexible. Athletes lose respect for a rigid thinker who fails to change with the times.

5. Plan practice around the needs of athletes. Remember, athletes participate for various reasons. As much as possible, include fun activities in practice sessions. Leslie Howell, girls volleyball coach, Roseville, California, has her athletes form teams and compete for "championship" points.

6. Maintain some distance with athletes while encouraging a warm, congenial atmosphere.

7. Assume the role of a strong supporter. Athletes try a little harder for the coach who sticks with them during rough moments. Athletes, in many instances, emulate the actions of the coach. When a coach loses hope, they play accordingly.

8. Show a genuine interest in the program by publicizing team efforts in the school bulletin, school paper, and local press.

9. Encourage athletes to set personal goals. Help athletes set realistic goals within their ability level.

10. Be consistent in handling problems. Follow a specific disciplinary policy when handling problem athletes. Avoid playing favorites.

CUTTING ATHLETES FROM THE TEAM

Cutting an athlete hurts. When an athlete doesn't make the team, everyone suffers. The rejected athlete must face parents and friends not knowing for sure what their reactions will be. The coach, too, may be searching for reassurance that the decision was the right one.

Is there an easy way to cut an athlete from the team? Probably not. Most coaches feel uncomfortable having to tell an athlete, "I'm sorry. We don't have a place on the team for you right now." Some athletes, of course, will take these words in stride and begin thinking about tryouts next year. Also, there's the athlete who falls apart and lashes out with a barrage of insults. No two athletes respond in exactly the same way.

Three common ways of releasing an athlete are: 1) The coach tells the athlete in private; 2) The coach posts the names of successful athletes on the gym bulletin board; 3) After practice, the coach reads the names of athletes who made the roster.

After final cut day, interesting things happen. Here are four situations.

Situation One

An athlete failed to make the basketball team in his junior year. After being cut from the squad, he and his father practiced after school nearly every day on an outdoor basketball court. The boy worked on dribbling and shooting—first with his right hand, then with his left. Before going home he ran several wind sprints up and down the length of the court. The following year he made first string, lead the league in scoring, won All-League honors, and earned a four-year college athletic scholarship.

Situation Two

The day following a final cut announcement, somebody smashed the coach's windshield and slashed two of his tires.

Situation Three

A father, after learning his son didn't make the team, phoned the district superintendent and demanded the coach's resignation. He said the coach ruined his son's life.

Situation Four

A freshman baseball player came out for practice for the first time on final cut day. The coach asked the boy why he hadn't come out earlier. The boy said he didn't know baseball practice had started. The coach explained that would be unfair to other players if he let the boy try out so late for the team. After all, practice had been going on for three weeks.

The following day the coach received a phone call from the boy's mother. She asked for an explanation of the incident. After hearing her son's story and the coach's version, she supported the coach's decision and felt her son should have known when baseball practice started.

In Situation One, it wasn't a question of right or wrong. The boy, with his father's help, decided to work extra hard with one goal in mind—to make the team the following year. Situation Two speaks for itself. Athletes who "get back at the coach" by vandalizing personal property show a lack of respect for themselves and others. Situation Three gives an unreasonable parent room to blow off steam and make a fool of himself in front of his son. The mother, in Situation Four, studied the facts before passing judgment. She showed maturity, excellent judgment, and common sense in handling her son's problem.

There are ways a coach can minimize the agony of cutting athletes from a team. Here are eight considerations:

1. At a pre-season meeting, give each athlete a list of "musts" for making the team. As an example, these items might appear on the list:
    *   Have an athletic clearance card signed by parents and athletic director. Make sure coach receives the card prior to the first practice session.
    *   Show up for practice on time. Have necessary equipment for indoor and outdoor workouts.
    *   Follow school policies and special regulations set forth by the coach.
    *   Make a personal commitment to do the best job possible.
    *   Make a team commitment to show up for all scheduled practices and athletic events.
    *   Speak with the coach about any problem regarding practice time or conflicts in schedule.
    *   Keep parents posted on team activities at all times.
2. Post the practice schedule on gymnasium and teaching station bulletin boards.
3. Run daily announcements in the school bulletin for at least two weeks before the first practice begins.
4. Publish an announcement in the school paper and local press.
5. Post team rules and regulations on gymnasium bulletin board. This will serve as a reminder, as well as inform those athletes who missed the pre-season meeting, of what to expect.
6. Send a list of rules and regulations to school administrators, i.e., district superintendent, principal, vice-principal, and athletic director. Keep the administration informed. This can be done through a systemwide handbook.
7. Alert athletes that rules and regulations are posted on bulletin boards in certain areas.

8. Be upfront with athletes. If it looks like an athlete won't make the squad, let the athlete know as soon as possible. Explain why the athlete didn't make it and offer suggestions for improvement. Always encourage a promising athlete to try out again next year.

A coach knows that there will always be a few soreheads who feel they got cheated out of a chance to play. Whatever the outcome, athletes won't be justified in saying that they didn't know in advance what to expect.

THE PROBLEM OF QUITTING

Some athletes never really get started; that is, they come out just long enough to convince themselves to go elsewhere. In short, they're not ready to discipline themselves or make a commitment at this time.

What about an athlete who tries out, makes the team, then decides to quit half-way through the season? Why do athletes hang on this long before calling it quits? For many it's a question of pride; they don't want to be called a quitter. A quitter, to these athletes, suggests a weakness in a person's character which sets off negative reactions in others.

Propaganda enters the locker room and fills the athlete's mind with anti-quitting slogans. For example:

A QUITTER NEVER WINS. A WINNER NEVER QUITS.

ANYONE CAN QUIT, BUT IT TAKES GUTS TO HANG ON.

Quitting, then, becomes a difficult task for an athlete once the season begins. A tough-minded coach may downgrade an athlete who talks of quitting the team. So, to save face, an athlete may choose to play out the season rather than risk a confrontation with the coach.

It taxes a coach's patience and understanding when a key athlete quits. A wise coach will attempt to find out why the athlete chose to leave and, if possible, will lend assistance in helping the athlete find a solution to the problem.

Case in point: Several years ago following baseball practice, the team's regular second baseman approached the coach in the gym office, held out his uniform, and told the coach he decided to quit. The conversation went something like this:

Athlete: "Here's your uniform back. I quit."
Coach: "What's the problem? You're playing aren't you?"

Athlete:	"Yes, I'm playing, but you won't give me a chance to pitch. Every time I ask to pitch, you smile and point toward second base."
Coach:	"Keep your uniform. If pitching means that much to you, I'll let you throw a couple of innings in tomorrow's intrasquad game, okay?"
Athlete:	"Well, okay. Thanks, coach. You won't be sorry."

The boy pitched to only five batters. He walked the first two, hit the third batter, and the fourth and fifth hitters singled and doubled respectively. The athlete called time, walked up to the coach, handed him the ball, and said, "You're right, coach. I guess I'm not cut out to pitch. Is second base still open?"

By giving the athlete a chance to pitch, the coach avoided losing a player and, at the same time, reassured himself that he didn't misjudge the boy's ability.

Let's turn the situation around and see how a less diplomatic coach might handle the problem:

Athlete:	"Here's your uniform back. I quit."
Coach:	"What for?"
Athlete:	"You won't give me a chance to pitch."
Coach:	"So quit. Tom or Fred can play second base."
Athlete:	"All I wanted was a chance to pitch."
Coach:	"You're no pitcher. You can't throw hard enough to scare a fly. Besides, you'd only make a fool of yourself."

The athlete, stripped of his pride, loses all the way around. Since the coach has no confidence in the boy's playing ability, the athlete decides to quit.

Sometimes an athlete leaves the team for personal reasons. Often, an athlete doesn't wish to discuss the problem with the coach. Consequently, a coach must handle these problems in a discreet manner.

WHY ATHLETES QUIT THE TEAM

Athletes won't always give the real reasons for quitting. For the most part, they try to avoid hurting anyone's feelings. Some believe an honest answer might alienate the coach and fellow teammates. In a few instances, however, a coach pressures an athlete to make a decision regarding the team's welfare. Here are two examples:

One, a volleyball player refused to replace an injured athlete during a game. The player told the coach that she felt dizzy and nauseous. The coach gave her a choice: play or hand in her uniform. The girl left the gymnasium and quit the team the following day.

Two, a wrestling coach asked an overweight wrestler to drop down one weight class. The athlete protested, saying a weight loss would weaken his performance. The coach explained how such a move would benefit the team. Again, the boy refused. The coach moved another wrestler into the boy's slot. Two days later the boy turned in his wrestling gear.

These two cases paint a rough picture of the coach. It shows the coach as a demanding tyrant, a person without compassion or understanding. On the surface, it appears that the coach does more to hurt than to help an athlete. But before passing judgment, take a second look at each case.

In Case One, the reluctant player spent too much time complaining during practice. She antagonized others with her apologetic manner; no matter what happened, she'd have an excuse or reason to cover up her mistakes. In spite of her problem, she played volleyball very well. According to her coach, the girl couldn't relax in a game. She always blamed herself when the team lost a game. As the season went on, she thought up excuses to keep her out of action, especially during close games. The coach, as a last resort, forced the girl's hand and persuaded her to quit.

The girl may tell others that a mean coach or ill health drove her off the team. That's okay. Athletes and coaches alike rely on defense mechanisms to bail them out of tight jams. In this case, however, the player and the coach benefited.

In Case Two, the wrestler goofed off in practice, ridiculed other athletes, and showed little concern for self-improvement. The coach, by asking the boy to make a self-sacrifice, chased him off the mat. Interestingly, the boy made the decision, not the coach.

These are some of the reasons athletes give for quitting a team:

Coach-Related Problems

1. Personality clash with coach.
2. Coach hassles athletes, too demanding.
3. Coach plays favorites.
4. Coach too stubborn, refuses to listen to athletes.
5. Coach can't handle athletes, maintains poor discipline, and doesn't organize practices well.
6. Coach fails to motivate athletes, most practices lack imagination.
7. No confidence in coach's leadership ability.

School-Related Problems

1. The athlete doesn't agree with rules and regulations.
2. Grades falling off, pressure from parents to work harder in class.
3. Poor facilities and equipment.
4. Too many conflicts with other teams and coaches.
5. Practice schedule conflicts.

Personal Problems

1. Can't get along with other athletes.
2. Girlfriend or boyfriend problems.
3. Unsettled home life.
4. Trying to do too many things at once.
5. Job related problems.
6. Loss of interest in sports.
7. Find it difficult to make sacrifice.
8. Too much stress on winning, not enough on having fun.
9. Tired from playing too many sports in one year.
10. No support from parents, relatives, and friends.
11. Parents unhappy with athletic program.
12. Family moving out of area.

A COACH WHO LOST HIS TEAM

A coach might expect one or two athletes to quit during the season, but why would three athletes quit at the same time? Here's what happened to a junior varsity baseball coach at a medium-sized high school.

Coach T. began practice with a nucleus of talented athletes. Everything pointed to a successful year—good pitching, steady fielding, and excellent hitting. Unfortunately, several athletes carried a seedy reputation. Teachers labeled them renegades, goof-offs, and troublemakers.

Within a few weeks the program started to crumble. Several athletes quit. Out of the remaining players, some cut practice while others complained about loose practice organization. The majority of complaints centered around three issues: 1) Coach favored certain athletes; 2) Coach frequently picked on the same two or three players; 3) Coach didn't know how to organize practice in an interesting and meaningful manner.

About half-way through the season, three players quit on the same day. The coach, short of players, had to make a choice: cancel his season or bring up players from the freshmen squad. After conferring with the athletic director and principal, he elected to keep his team together by adding freshmen athletes to the squad. The frosh coach became an assistant junior varsity coach.

How did the coach lose control of his team? It seems a combination of three factors created the problem—a poor team player attitude, the coach's lack of skill in managing practice sessions, and the coach's failure to post specific rules and regulations regarding the code of conduct for athletes.

WHAT TO DO WHEN AN ATHLETE QUITS

Many times there isn't a great deal a coach can do. By the time an athlete decides to quit, the problem may have ballooned beyond repair. Yet it behooves a coach to do more than collect a uniform and erase a name from the roster. A coach may find it useful to ask an athlete these questions:

Athlete/Coach Conflict

1. Do you feel you've been treated unfairly? If so, in what way?
2. How did the coach keep you from performing successfully?
3. Do you think the coach's methods are too harsh? If so, why do you feel this way?
4. Do you feel the coach's policies are too strict? Give an example.
5. Is your decision to quit based on emotion or sound judgment?
6. In your opinion, what changes should the coach make in the program?

School Problem

1. In what way can the coach lend assistance?
2. Are you planning to return next year? If so, do you want a pre-season conditioning schedule?
3. What steps have you taken to solve your problem?
4. How will quitting the team help you solve your problem?
5. Are you sure you're quitting for the right reasons?

Home Problem

1. How does your home problem conflict with school athletics?
2. Have you discussed the problem with your parents? How can the coach help?
3. How do your parents feel about school athletics?

4. How do you feel about leaving the team? Are you coming out again next year?
5. How will quitting the team help you solve your problem?

Coaches ask questions so they may receive important information that will help improve the program and make it more attractive for athletes. Providing a personal touch shows a genuine concern for an athlete and the program.

When an athlete with a negative attitude quits, the coach may be better off to say nothing. In fact, some districts penalize athletes for quitting by declaring them ineligible for other sports. In such cases, the period of ineligibility comes under school policy.

HOW TO KEEP ATHLETES HAPPY

A contented athlete does more to strengthen a program's reputation than any other form of advertising. A good athletic program built around solid educational objectives draws praise, support, and enthusiastic athletes. Let's consider ten ways a coach can bring smiles to the faces of athletes.

One, lace practice sessions with plenty of variety. Change activities often. Make sure everyone stays busy.

Two, include fun activities in practice. An athlete should look forward to practice, not waste energy thinking up ways to escape.

Three, recognize the efforts of athletes. Remember it's tough for an athlete to put out one-hundred percent every day. A pat on the back or smile goes a long way toward showing appreciation.

Four, continue to seek ways to strengthen the program. Keep the lines of communication open and promote a free exchange of ideas between coach, athlete, and community.

Five, realize that athletes aren't perfect. They don't have the coach's experience and will make the same mistake two or three times. Be patient. Throw full support behind every athlete.

Six, stress teamwork. Avoid building the program around "star" athletes. Encourage everybody to pull together.

Seven, hold frequent team meetings. Listen to athletes. Find out what's on their minds. Work hand-in-hand with athletes to keep the program running smoothly.

Eight, be a model of leadership. Leadership is extremely difficult to develop in athletics. It is something that must come from within. Therefore, the example set by the coach will give an athlete a head start toward developing leadership ability.

Nine, urge athletes to help one another. Peer recognition bolsters an athlete's confidence and tightens the foundation of teamwork.

Ten, keep coaching goals within the ability range of athletes. Take each week one day at a time. Forget about reaching the moon until the rocket is ready.

POINTS TO REMEMBER

A coach must constantly strive to build a strong rapport with athletes and their parents. Any problems that develop should be handled in a diplomatic manner. A coach needs the backing of parents as well as athletes.

It's a rare athlete who looks toward sports as a way of life. Most play for the sheer enjoyment of having fun and making friends.

Athletes must know before the season begins exactly what the coach expects. A written policy helps to minimize problems during cut day.

QUESTIONS

1. How do parents influence the behavior of their children?
2. What should a coach do if a parent persists in giving contradictory advice to an athlete?
3. What is meant by a "father factor?" Does the "father factor" help or hinder an athlete's progress? Explain.
4. Sometimes parents become unruly at athletic contests. What steps should a coach take to prevent disturbances?
5. What factors cause some athletes to develop negative attitudes?
6. Listed in this chapter are ten reasons why athletes participate in sports. How many of these do you think develop from peer group contact; from parental influence; from personal experiences?
7. What's one way a coach can begin the season on a positive note?
8. Why do most coaches regret cutting athletes from the team?
9. What can a coach do to reduce the heartache of cutting athletes?
10. Why is quitting a team a problem for some athletes?
11. What are eight reasons some athletes quit a team?
12. What can a coach do to discourage an athlete from quitting?

3

Coaching and
the Administration

*We cannot be separated in interest or
divided in purpose. We stand together
until the end.*

Woodrow Wilson

It has been said that two kinds of coaches give administrators a tough challenge: acceptors and blamers. An acceptor takes full responsibility for everything that goes wrong. For example, if the team has a losing season, the acceptor pleads guilty and apologizes to everyone. Conversely, a blamer points the finger of guilt at others, namely complaining parents, non-dedicated athletes, or a non-supportive administration. An acceptor relies on sympathy for therapeutic relief, while a blamer looks at everything through a negative eye. A blamer views athletes as lazy individuals who couldn't care less if the team wins or loses.

Most coaches are neither acceptors nor blamers. They fall somewhere in the middle. Nevertheless, there are enough problems to keep the coach and the administration busy throughout the season.

In this chapter, we'll see how the coach and the administration can work together in building a strong athletic program.

WORKING EFFECTIVELY WITH
THE ADMINISTRATION

Administrators have their hands full running a school. Supervising personnel, holding parent conferences, and checking student referrals make up a fraction of the day's work. They're in and out of their offices continually. Administrators, unfortunately, aren't always available to lend assistance to coaches. Under these conditions, a coach must either consult the athletic director or handle the problem directly.

A coach who heads for the office every time a problem arises shows a lack of confidence in coaching ability. It's part of a coach's duty to watch for trouble spots and avoid letting problems get out of control. An intelligent coach does everything possible to reduce conflicts that require administrative action.

Let's examine seven areas that create problems for coaches and administrators.

Rules and Regulations

School districts must adhere to state interscholastic rules and regulations. In many cases, administrators are responsible for supplying each coach with a copy of these guidelines. Coaches review and discuss these policies with the athletic director or an administrator during coaches' meetings.

Even with complete coverage at these meetings, a coach could miss these sessions and fail to pick up a policy handbook. Or maybe a coach enters the coaching scene late in the year and neglects to review the guidelines. Also, it's possible a coach simply forgets to cover the policies with athletes. Any of these situations could lead to conflict.

For example, two football players were seen by an assistant coach taking a drink of beer after a game. When the final gun sounded, a man from the stands ran over to the players, handed them a beer cup and said, "Take a swallow. You guys earned it." The assistant coach reported the incident to the head coach and the principal. The principal, after reviewing the matter, declared the athletes ineligible for the remainder of the season.

The athletes and their parents protested, saying the coach neglected to cover training rule violations, which included drinking. The principal upheld his original decision that declared both athletes ineligible, since the Student Handbook provided a section on Code of Conduct for athletes.

Policy problems can be avoided if a coach knows the rules and passes them along to athletes. A coach should go over each policy at a pre-season meeting and answer any questions. Some districts require the coach to pass out an athletic handbook for each sport. The coach goes over the handbook prior to the first scheduled practice. (See Chapter 13, "Putting Together an Athletic Handbook and a Yearbook."

Keeping the Administration Informed

Any special practice session, meeting, or event that requires the services of an administrator should be reported several weeks in advance. An administrator needs time to plan ahead and set up a schedule for personnel to follow.

A coach who waits until the last minute to fill out a request form shows a lack of consideration and builds resentment toward the athletic department.

Filing a Use of Facility Request

Teachers, coaches, and administrators have one thing in common —they all grow tired of filling out forms. Yet without forms a coach would find it tough to survive. For instance, suppose a coach wanted to hold a team banquet in the school cafeteria two weeks after the season ended. If the coach didn't file a use of facility request far in advance, the cafeteria might not be available on that particular night. And to make matters worse, the coach may already have sent out invitations to athletes and parents before checking with the administration.

It's up to the coach to check district policies regarding sign ups for special events. Usually one administrator, e.g., the vice-principal, takes care of setting up an activity calendar for the year.

A smart coach keeps a copy of the request and double checks the activity calendar at least a month before the scheduled event takes place. Busy administrators sometimes forget. A problem discovered early enough can be settled to everyone's satisfaction.

Helping the Maintenance Staff

The maintenance department can be a coach's best friend or worst enemy. A demanding coach who wants everything done immediately usually winds up griping to an administrator about incompetent service. The maintenance crew, complains the coach, waits until the last minute to mow the grass, set up the stands, or wash the courts.

Here's often what happens. A coach forgets to fill out a maintenance request, but does remember talking to "somebody" on the maintenance staff. Days roll by. Nothing happens. The coach flies into a tirade, accuses the maintenance crew of slipping up, and asks the administration to investigate.

Schools are operating on less money today. They're forced to cut back on supplies, staffing, and maintenance service. With fewer employees to keep a school operating, a coach must be willing to cooperate whenever possible. This means employing patience, understanding, and making sure a maintenance request form is properly filed.

Many coaches roll up their sleeves, muster their athletes, and help the maintenance department prepare facilities for athletic events. This gets the job done faster, builds a strong rapport with the maintenance department, and makes life easier for the administration.

Accident Reports

Accident reports can be a big headache for the administration if any, or all, of these things happen: 1) A coach forgets to fill one out; 2) A coach leaves some of the items blank; 3) A coach turns in a form two or three weeks late. (Most districts want reports on file within forty-eight hours after the accident occurred.) It puts a district in an uncomfortable position when an insurance agent or parent calls wanting details of an accident and they aren't on file. A good rule to follow is: report all accidents and injuries fully and promptly.

Several years ago a soccer player called time, limped off the field, and told the coach he twisted his ankle. The coach placed an ice pack around the ankle and told the boy to see a doctor if his injury grew worse. The coach immediately filled out an accident report and turned if into the office. On the following day the boy's parents called the school and said that their family doctor had examined the boy and discovered he had broken his ankle. Thanks to the coach's quick action and prudent manner in handling the situation, the district took care of the paperwork without incident.

Finally, a coach should remind athletes to report any injury that occurred during practice sessions or contests. Insurance companies need and expect fast, accurate information. They frown at playing guessing games. An athlete who keeps an injury a secret may find it impossible to gain sympathy from a coach, the school, or an insurance company.

Athletic Clearance Cards

In nearly every school district an athlete must have an athletic clearance card signed by the athletic director before being allowed to participate in sports. The clearance card usually carries this information:

- Health history
- Medical examination results
- Verification of accident insurance coverage
- Parental permission forms signed by the parent(s) or guardian.

School districts get into hot water when a coach allows an athlete to partcipate in a sport before turning in a card or when a coach accepts an athlete's word for having a card on file with another coach. To avoid problems, the athletic director should work with the coaches to set up a system to check athletes carefully before allowing them to participate. Most coaches carry clearance cards around in a binder or folder. The administration has a duplicate copy on file in the office.

Reporting Unsafe Conditions

A coach must keep a close watch on facilities and equipment that may be defective or in need of repair. The following tips will help a coach and the school district avoid liability problems.

- Be liability conscious. People today waste little time before filing law suits. (We'll discuss liability problems in Chapter 11, "The Coach and the Law.")
- Constantly ask yourself, "Is what I'm doing safe?" If you're not completely satisfied, don't do it! In other words, when in doubt, don't.
- Give proper instruction on how to use equipment and facilities.
- Never allow athletes to experiment with equipment and facilities. Insist that they be used only for the proper purposes.
- Protect athletes at all times.
- Report in writing all unsafe conditions to the administration. Keep a duplicate of the written report on file.
- Immediately follow up on the written report. See to it that somebody takes action.
- Avoid using unsafe equipment or facilities. Your judgment and prudent actions will determine whether the district, and possibly you, may be sued.

SIX MAJOR PROBLEMS THAT HAUNT THE ADMINISTRATION

An administrator may need a calculator to record the number of coaching problems that occur during the year. Problems come in all sizes and shapes; from coaches losing their keys to athletes catching the flu bug. In this section we'll consider six major problems most districts face.

Acquiring New Coaches

With fewer teaching jobs available, districts have a hard time hiring coaches. In some areas, league and state athletic regulations prohibit noncertificated people from coaching. Rather than drop a program, an athletic director may seek special approval from the district to hire outside personnel or he may solicit the services of student teachers.

An ideal situation, of course, would be to have the same coaches run the program every year. But, unfortunately, coaches grow older, lose interest, and move into other challenging areas.

Many coaches balk at the low pay offered by the district. They turn to other sources of income—teaching adult school, teaching driver training, and tutoring home students. In some cases, districts offer released time or an extra prep period to coaches to help compensate for their services. More and more, rising costs and lower budgets are driving outstanding coaches out of the field.

A wrestling coach, in need of an assistant, asked the principal for help. The principal recently had hired three new teachers, two with wrestling experience in college. The district, however, said it didn't have the money for additional coaches. After talking with the new teachers, the wrestling coach asked the district to assign both men as assistant coaches. Did the assistants agree to coach for free? No, the head coach gave the district permission to pay them out of his coaching salary. Each coach received an equal share of the coaching stipend.

Admittedly, few coaches would be so generous. In this case, the wrestling coach felt that building a strong, competitive program overshadowed the amount of money he earned as a coach.

Reduced Staffing

It hurts to lose first and second year coaches. In fact, any time a competent coach leaves, the district suffers a serious setback. Tight money and decreasing enrollments lead to cutbacks which, in turn, mean saying goodbye to needed coaches. The athletic director, working with the administration, must find a way to fill the gaps. Here is the problem: If people aren't available or willing to coach, what will happen to the athletic program? Some educators suggest schools reduce the number of sports, drop interscholastic competition from the program, or switch to a schoolwide intramural program. Whatever course of action a district takes, coaches and administrators will have to pool their energies to keep the athletic program afloat.

Women Not Wanting to Coach

Again, with a reduced teaching staff, the administration struggles to find enough women to coach. Many women teachers are working mothers who leave their children with baby sitters. When school ends, these women pick up their children and go home. They don't wish to spend extra time coaching after school.

Prior to the passage of Title IX (1972), most schools hired women to teach, not coach. As girls' sports grew in popularity, the demand for women coaches increased. Since districts suffered a shortage of women coaches, men were asked to coach women's sports.

Men Coaching Women's Sports

Coaching women's sports has become attractive to men coaches. Here are four reasons men prefer to coach women's sports: (1) Same money as men's sports; (2) New challenge; (3) Fewer hassles; (4) Less stress than coaching men's sports.

Administrators hear an occasional complaint about men who work women too hard or not hard enough in practice. Pacing or gearing practice to the ability level of athletes becomes a problem for men who have never coached women's sports.

Men and women coaches must coordinate their schedules to begin and end practices on time. In this way an adult female will be available to supervise the locker room area. Without adequate supervision, a district leaves itself wide open to lawsuits.

What can a male coach do to build a close working relationship with the women's athletic departments? Here are six suggestions:

- Be open-minded. Listen to the advice of others.
- Share equipment and facilities with fellow coaches.
- Start and stop practice on time.
- Don't be afraid to ask for help.
- Talk with the athletes. Make sure practice drills and activities are commensurate with their needs and abilities.
- Keep the administration informed regarding the team's progress. A considerate coach is a plus factor in any program.

Nondedicated Coaches

A young person fresh out of college might choose to coach for one reason: to gain entrance into a school district. For instance, let's say District X needs an English teacher. Fifty people apply, all with excellent recommendations. Chances are that the person qualified to coach a sport or two will get the job. Applicants know teaching positions are scarce. The ability and willingness to coach gives the teacher/coach a marvelous opportunity.

A few teachers, however, coach for three years, receive tenure, and then quit coaching. They use coaching as a vehicle to secure permanent teacher status. These people might be satisfactory teachers, but they lack the style and compassion of a dedicated coach.

The administration faces the problem of finding a replacement in a district already short of coaches. Some districts are considering ways to encourage coaches to stay, e.g., by signing a long-term coaching contract or making coaching a condition of employment. Since administrator's can't read a coach's mind, they feel a need for some kind of protection.

A coach who anticipates quitting should inform the athletic director or principal as soon as possible. It might take several months to find a replacement. If possible, the coach should be actively involved in the transition.

Complaining Parents

Administrators grow weary listening to the moans and groans of discontented parents. A coach may be doing the best job possible and still be called unfair, ignorant, or incompetent. Regardless of what names a parent calls a coach, an irate telephone call or nasty letter cuts into an administrator's busy schedule. The administrator has to stop, listen to the complaint, and confer with the coach. Often this means a coach/parent/principal conference must be set up to resolve the problem.

A coach can reduce the number of parental complaints by leveling with athletes and letting them know exactly where they stand with the team. Also, a coach should make sure that parents and athletes have a copy of the school's Student Handbook and Athletic Handbook.

Some parents sidestep school personnel and vent their anger through the local press. The following excerpts from a letter written by a disgruntled parent appeared in a small town newspaper regarding the football coach.

Editor:

My son, a senior, is on the varsity team and he diligently attends every practice and works very hard at it.

After attending the games, we come home thoroughly disgusted due to the fact that he and twenty-four other players (who also work hard and attend practice) must sit and warm the bench during the whole game, without so much as playing a few minutes. He and his fellow players are getting pretty disgusted with this game-after-game.

What's with this football coach? Doesn't he know that this is only a game, a mere sport? Or, coach, do you have to be a banker, doctor, or lawyer's son to play in a high school game?

I think it's very unfair to our sons to be treated in this manner by this so-called "coach."

A few days after the letter appeared, the district superintendent responded to the letter. Here are excerpts from his letter:

Editor:

The letter from concerned parents regarding the boys who warm the bench and do not get into football games is one with which I sympathize wholeheartedly.

The coach singled out in this letter is no more to be condemned than should all the public in general. The practice is universal, because the emphasis in competitive athletics is on winning, not the values of the game.

Constructive change will only come when parents become concerned enough to demand that all athletics in schools be solidly placed on an educational foundation. You have to demand an end to the fancy hoopla, uniforms, class interruptions, gate receipts, two-way radios, tournaments, all-stars, long trips, coaching clinics, broadcasts, and other educationally unsound practices. You have to demand high standards of sportsmanship, conduct, ethics, and living up to the spirit and letter of the rules.

Until these things come to pass, the school that gives the boys a chance to play has little chance of winning against the school that only uses its best players.

The series of letters finally ended with a response from a concerned citizen. Here are excerpts from his letter:

Editor:

I have two boys on high school football teams in the city who are not playing regularly, and I have had twelve years of high school varsity football coaching experience.

I am disgusted that well educated, well trained, well qualified, experienced, and sincere people are attacked and ridiculed in such a manner as our high school football coaches were. The reference that a boy's father's occupation had a bearing on his son being played in a ball game is about as ridiculous and uncalled for as anything I have ever seen in print. The "so-called 'coach' " remark is questioning the competence and integrity of people that have been screened many times and devoted at least five hard years in college just to qualify to be hired by conscientious people of this community.

The citizen reminded the "disgusted parent" that every player on the team contributes to the victory or defeat, whether he plays in the game or not, because of his participation in practice all week.

One school district ran an "Attack On Coaches" section in its Coaches' Handbook. It read as follows:

During the past several years we have had several attacks on coaches by disgruntled persons with various motivations. Usually their attacks have been through the mail or letters to the editor's column of the local press.

The District does not in any way condone these vicious attacks and will do everything possible to protect and defend the coaches involved. The District does not and has not yielded to these types of pressure.

In case of these types of attacks, do not do or say anything until after consultation with your principal and the district superintendent.

The success of any educational program depends largely on the support it receives from the district. When a community knows that a district stands behind its coaches, parents hesitate to write caustic letters to the local press. Instead, they're more likely to sit down and talk in a reasonable manner.

CHECKING ON ATHLETIC ELIGIBILITY

Last winter a high school basketball team lost a chance to play in a Tournament of Champions because its roster included two ineligible players. The league's ethics committee decided that both players became ineligible when they moved out of the district. The team had to forfeit nearly all of its games.

Eligibility problems prove embarrassing and costly for athlete, coach, and school. Each athlete should be screened through the main office.

A coach, acting as counselor, has two jobs. One, to make sure every athlete understands the state and district policies covering eligibility. Two, to make periodic checks on each athlete's progress regarding grades, school attendance, and classroom behavior.

Four areas seem to cause the most trouble for athletes. They are:

1. Place of residence. Athlete goes to School A, but lives within the attendance boundary lines of School B. School B officials find out, contact the league president, and file a protest.
2. Behavioral problems in the classroom. Athlete can't get along with the teacher and gets booted out of class. Athlete warned to shape up or suffer a three-day suspension.
3. Poor school attendance. Athlete called into the office for cutting class. The vice-principal notifies the parents. Parents, in turn, tell the coach they've restricted the athlete from play.
4. Failing grades. Coach discovers halfway through the season that two key athletes are ineligible. It seems they flunked too many classes the previous semester. According to interscholastic policy, these athletes must leave the team immediately.

Recently a coach decided to give his athletes a weekly progress checksheet to take around to their teachers. (Figure 3-1.) The coach

Name—					
Date—					
		Athlete Progress Checklist			
Period	Class	Absences	Tardies	Grade in progress	Teachers' signature
1					
2					
3					
4					
5					
6					
Additional Comments:					

FIGURE 3-1 Athlete progress checklist

thought this checklist would make it easier for him to monitor the progress of each athlete.

The checklist, like Frankenstein's monster, stirred up problems for its creator. The coach spent extra time evaluating, recording, and conferring with athletes and teachers. Some teachers began using the checklist as a tool to threaten certain athletes. A math teacher, for example, told an athlete that if his grade didn't improve within a week, she would recommend that he be declared ineligible for two weeks.

After several unhappy incidences, the coach quit sending around checklists. He felt it gave teachers a green light to harass and put extra pressure on athletes.

It's a coach's job to stress to athletes the importance of staying eligible. And it's an athlete's responsibility to tell the coach and school about any change that might effect eligibility.

Some districts include information regarding the ineligibility in a Student Handbook. For instance, Roseville High School, California, prints the following general training rules under a section entitled Code of Conduct for Athletes:

1. An athlete involved in a training rule violation (drinking, smoking, etc.) will be removed from the team for the duration of the season.
2. If the season is less than six weeks away from completion, the period of ineligibility will be six weeks.
3. If the athlete is involved in such a violation while not out for a sport, he shall be declared ineligible for the six week period immediately following the time of his ineligibility.
4. The athlete shall not be permitted to work out with any team during the time of his ineligibility.

EXAMINING A COACH'S HANDBOOK

A school may issue a handbook to coaches to help them run their programs in accordance with district policies. The following outline lists sample items from a Coach's Handbook.

Coach's Handbook

A. The Athletic Program
    1. Role of athletics in the district.
    2. The district's role in supporting athletics.
    3. How the community supports the athletic program.
    4. Goals and objectives of the athletic program.
    5. Justification for a strong athletic program.
    6. Coach's role as a teacher.
    7. The coach as an enforcer of school rules and regulations.
    8. Coach's conduct during practices and contests.
B. Athletic Handbooks (to be issued to every athlete)
    1. Introductory Statement (Athletic Director)
    2. Statement of Parent Responsibility (Athletic Director)
    3. Coach's Statement and Policies (Coach)
    4. Eligibility Requirements (Coach)
    5. Code of Conduct (Athletic Director)
    6. Schedule of games, meets, or matches
    7. Other Matters—Requirements for Letters, School Records, Roster, etc. (Coach)
C. Athlete Disciplinary Policies
D. Rules for each sport
E. A statement concerning equipment and facilities.
F. Insurance Coverage Policy

G. Establishing favorable press relations
H. How to handle protests
I. Miscellaneous (security, physical examinations, awards, attacks on coaches, and so on.)

A Coach's Handbook shows exactly what the district expects from the coach. Going by the book keeps a coach alert and out of trouble with the administration.

EVALUATING COACHING SERVICES

In some areas, a coach's win-loss record serves as an evaluation. After two or three losing seasons, the axe falls. This, of course, holds true for spectator sports, like football and basketball, more than for nonspectator sports, such as badminton or golf.

Many districts exert little pressure on coaches to produce winning teams. They stress maintaining high standards of professional and ethical conduct in coaching methods and personal relationships.

A coach, depending upon the district, may expect one of three things to happen: 1) No evaluation for coaching services; 2) Evaluation by athletic director; 3) Evaluation by principal.

An evaluation usually takes place after the season ends. The principal or the principal and the athletic director sit down with the coach and go over an evaluation sheet. Evaluation of Coaching Services, Form A (Figure 3-2) and Form B (Figure 3-3) are typical examples.

The coaches in one school district, unhappy with Form A, held a meeting with the administration and came up with a revision, Form B. They felt Form A had the following weaknesses:

1. Form A was oriented toward football coaches.
2. Form A included a coach's win/loss record as part of the evaluation.
3. The 5 to 1 rating scale fell short in giving an accurate evaluation of coaching services.

A final point on evaluations—some coaches turn thumbs down on evaluations because they don't believe an administrator, with or without coaching experience, can give a fair evaluation based on one or two observations.

District personnel may never agree on an ideal evaluation instrument since so many variables enter the evaluation process. A dedicated, conscientious coach has very little to fear from any form of evaluation that measures a person's true coaching ability.

Form A

Evaluation of Coaching Services

Coach _____   _____ High School

Sport _____ Season _____ from _____ to _____

Status: 1 2 3   Tenure

	5	4	3	2	1
1. Professional preparation					
a. Knowledge of sport					
b. Knowledge of coaching technique					
c. Plans well for each practice					
d. Efficiently conducts each practice					
e. Shows concern for physical/mental well-being of athletes					
f. Ability to fit athletes to team position or event					
2. Control of emotional involvement					
a. Coaching from sidelines					
b. Protesting officials' calls					
c. Display of temper					
d. Refrains from use of profanity					
e. Stays within restraining lines					
3. Handling of discipline					
a. Keeps teams on the bench & under control					
b. Keeps unauthorized persons off field					
c. Handling of profanity by athletes					
4. Instructs team in rules of sport					
a. Publishes handbook on time					
b. Reviews handbook with athletes					
c. Handbook is complete:					
(1) Introductory statements					
(2) Statement of parent responsibility					
(3) Coaches statement & policies					
(4) Eligibility requirements					
(5) Code of conduct					
(6) Schedule of games					
(7) Other					
5. Maintains good press relations					
6. Maintains good public relations					
a. Handling of Awards Night					
7. Cooperates in administration of school rules, regulations, and policies					
a. Towel program					
b. Locker room security					
c. Travel security					
d. Use of physical facilities					
e. Care of equipment					
f. Enforcement of Athletic Code					
8. Professional relationships					
a. With other coaches					
b. With other faculty members					
c. With administration					
d. With athletes					
e. With officials					

FIGURE 3-2 Evaluation of coaching services

Composite Evaluation of Performance

_____ 5. Excellent—Performs in top 20% of
             coaches in the same sport.

_____ 4. Good—Better than average competence.

_____ 3. Satisfactory—Meets all standards in an
             acceptable manner.

_____ 2. Below Average—Needs to improve.

_____ 1. Unsatisfactory—Not acceptable. Continued
             performance at this level
             will eliminate coaching
             assignment.

RECORD
Won _____
Lost _____
Tie _____

Comments:

_____

_____

_____

_____

_____

_____   _____
           Administrator   Coach

Date: _____

FIGURE 3–2 (continued)

PRE-SCHOOL COACHES' MEETINGS

Pre-school coaches' meetings give every coach, new and old, an opportunity to get together, exchange ideas, and discuss problem areas with the administration. Clearing the air before school begins makes working relationships between coaches and administrators less frustrating.

Administrators use this time to outline those issues that cause problems for everyone. A smart coach will have questions or suggestions ready when the meeting starts. A coach who doesn't bother to attend these meetings puts a strain on the relationship between coaches and administrators. Of course, some coaches must miss these meetings because of practice.

Form B

Evaluation of Coaching Services

Coach _____ _____ High School

Sport _____ Season _____ from _____ to _____

Status: 1   2   3   Tenure

	NA	E	C	I	U
1. Professional preparation					
a. Knowledge of sport & ability to use in coaching.					
b. Knowledge of coaching technique					
c. Plans well for and efficiently conducts each practice					
d. Shows concern for physical/mental well-being of athletes					
2. Control of emotional involvement					
a. Coaching during contests that interferes with individual performance					
b. Maintains self-control					
c. Use of proper language					
d. Observes rules of game (stays within coaching area designated)					
3. Handling of discipline					
a. Keeps team under control					
b. Handling of profanity by athletes					
c. Teaches good sportsmanship					
4. Instructs team in rules of sport (head coach responsibility)					
a. Publishes handbook on time					
b. Reviews handbook with athletes					
c. Passes out completed handbook					
5. Maintains good public relations					
a. Good press relations					
b. Handling of Awards Night					
6. Cooperates in administering school rules, regulations & policies					
a. Towel program					
b. Locker room security					
c. Travel security					
d. Proper use of physical facilities					
e. Care of equipment					
7. Professional relationships					
a. With other coaches					
b. With other faculty members					
c. With administration					
d. With athletes					
e. With officials					
f. With the head coach of the sport					

FIGURE 3-3 Evaluation of coaching services

Composite Evaluation of Performance

E.   Exemplary Performance—Demonstrates exceptional degree
of skill and effort.

C.   Professionally Competent—Meets District standards

I.   Lacks Competence—But is capable of improvement*

U.   Unsatisfactory—Performance is unacceptable*

NA.   Not Applicable

* I and U ratings shall be explained under Comments.

Comments: _____

_____

_____

_____

_____

_____

_____

_____

(   ) I do (   ) do not recommend this individual for re-employment for

_____ for the 19____ - ____ School Year.
    (name of sport)

_____   _____
            Administrator   Coach

                                        (Your signature indicates that you have
                                        seen this report and it has been discussed
                                        with you.)

Date: _____

FIGURE 3-3 (continued)

STRENGTHENING THE BOND BETWEEN
COACHES AND THE ADMINISTRATION

Many coaches believe there are three factors that lead to conflicts between coaches and administrators. One, the administration doesn't show an equal interest in boys' and girls' sports. Two, the administration favors certain sports. Three, the administration avoids issues and delays making important decisions. Administrators, on the other hand, say coaches create problems by failing to follow or support district policies, by not supporting one another, and by lacking consistency in dealing with problem athletes.

Cooperation is the key. According to J. Donald Marks, principal, El Camino High School, Oceanside, California, coaches and administrators should meet on a regular basis and establish a give and take rapport.

Choosing sides and tossing rocks back and forth only serves to widen the gap. An athletic department gains strength when the coaching staff and administration combine forces to solve problems. Through a cooperative effort, then, a district stands an excellent chance to fight off those factors that undermine a school's athletic department.

POINTS TO REMEMBER

A coach can keep problems to a minimum by:

1. Following district and state rules and regulations.
2. Making sure every athlete understands the policies guiding school athletics.
3. Insisting that athletes obey district and state policies.
4. Completing forms on time and turning them into the office.
5. Keeping the administration informed at all times.
6. Cooperating with the administration, other coaches, faculty members, and maintenance staff.
7. Keeping accurate records on all athletes.
8. Keeping athletes under control.
9. Checking the progress of athletes and helping out whenever possible.
10. Working with, not against, the administration.

QUESTIONS

1. How can an "acceptor" restrict the progress of a team?
2. In your opinion, which is worse—an "acceptor" or a "blamer?" Why?

3. What, in your opinion, are three important duties of an athletic director?
4. How does distributing a Student Handbook reduce the number of problems a coach or athlete might face?
5. Why is it necessary for a coach to fill out and turn in an Accident Report on time?
6. How can helping out the maintenance staff lead to problems?
7. Why shouldn't a coach let an athlete participate without a clearance card?
8. Why should a coach keep a duplicate maintenance request on file?
9. Why are coaching positions hard to find in most school districts?
10. How does reduced staffing affect the coaching picture?
11. Some people don't believe men should coach women's sports. Why do you think they feel this way?
12. Why are some school districts short of women coaches?
13. Why do some men prefer to coach women's sports?
14. What are two problems men face in coaching women's sports?
15. Districts report that some coaches quit after three years of service. Is this unfair to the school district? To the athletic program? To other coaches? To the athletes? Explain.
16. What can a coach do to discourage unhappy parents from writing vicious letters to the local press?
17. What things can a district do to support its coaches?
18. In what three ways can ineligibility problems hurt a team and athletes?
19. How do some teachers abuse the idea of using a progress checklist for athletes?
20. What is the purpose of a Coach's Handbook? What items should be included in a Coach's Handbook?
21. Why do you think some districts evaluate coaches?
22. Do you agree or disagree that coaches should be evaluated for each sport that they coach? Explain.
23. How can holding a pre-school coaches' meeting bring the coaching staff and administration closer together?

4

Keeping the Athletic Program Alive and Well

To climb steep hills requires slow pace at first.

William Shakespeare

A successful athletic program, like a chef's favorite dish, contains the right mixture of ingredients. Not everybody, however, can add the same ingredients and burst forth with a winner. There's more to cooking—and coaching—than tossing things together in a mechanical fashion just to see what might happen.

In this chapter we'll see how a coach, with the support of teachers, athletes, and coaching personnel can organize and maintain an educationally sound athletic program.

PLANNING AHEAD FOR THE SEASON

Many coaches begin planning for the coming season the day after the present season ends. This, in most cases, consists of little more than mentally going over ways to improve the program or jotting down ideas that seem worth trying.

Some coaches need to stay busy during the off season. They fear that too much rest and relaxation invites laziness. Yet whatever a coach decides to do, the same thing seems to happen—as the season draws near, stimuli join forces to send a message to the brain: "Hey, it's time to think about coaching." So the coach does. And from this point on fresh ideas tumble about looking for a place to settle. Yes, for the coach it's a brand new season.

Now let's examine those items that require close examination by the coach.

Facility Safety Check

An experienced coach personally inspects facilities several weeks before the first scheduled practice. If any part of a facility needs to be repaired or replaced, a coach should file a maintenance request with the school. Filing a request, however, doesn't always guarantee immediate action. A school district, for example, decided to build a new high school. When the construction people laid out the baseball fields, they put a drinking fountain on the varsity diamond between first base and home plate in the playing territory. The coach complained to the administration, filed a maintenance request, and waited, and waited, and waited. Weeks slipped by. Nothing happened. So he filled out a second form. Three weeks before the season ended, a main-renance crew dismantled the drinking fountain and hauled it away.

Athletes treated the fountain like a shrine calling it the "Fountain of Ruth." On two occasions an umpire threatened to walk off the field and cancel the game because the fountain posed a hazard to players. And to add further insult, the construction workers didn't connect the fountain to the main water line!

This situation left the district and coach wide open to a law suit—the coach for allowing his team to practice and play games on the field; the district for waiting so long before removing the drinking fountain.

A facility safety check should be the number one priority on a coach's pre-season checklist. When inspecting facilities keep these five steps in mind:

- Double and triple check everything.
- If something needs attention, fill out a request and personally deliver it to the principal. Stress the unsafe condition(s) on the report. Remember to keep a duplicate on file.
- Call on the maintenance department. Make sure they know about the problem(s).
- If nothing happens within a reasonable length of time, fill out a second request.
- Do not, under any circumstances, let athletes use an unsafe facility. Refuse to hold practices until the school repairs the facility.

Use of Facility

We mentioned earlier how problems can be avoided by reserving a facility in advance. Some coaches never learn. For example, a wrestling coach brought his team into the boys' gym on the same day the basketball coach scheduled a scrimmage. Rather than call off practice, the wrestling coach held a workout on the stage area of the girls' gym. Three days later the principal reprimanded the coach for holding practice in a limited space, thus risking serious injury to his wrestlers. By not signing up in advance, the coach, feeling pressure to "hold a workout somewhere," displayed poor judgment in his decision.

Signing up in advance holds four advantages: 1) It guarantees a place to practice or play; 2) It gives the maintenance staff time to get the facility ready; 3) It lets others know what facilities are unavailable at certain times; 4) It shows consideration for others.

Equipment Check

When athletes turn in gear, coaches usually mark off each item on an equipment checklist. After everything comes in, a coach takes an inventory, stores equipment in a safe place, bills athletes for lost or damaged items, and orders new supplies.

Heavy losses occur each year when athletes lose their uniforms, abuse their uniforms, damage equipment, or steal numbered jerseys or jackets. A football coach became infuriated when he saw one of his ex-athlete's wearing a football practice jersey at a basketball game. He made the boy give him the jersey and leave the gym.

A coach can hold losses and damages to a minimum by stressing these points with athletes early in the season:

- Treat your uniform like a good friend. Keep it neat and clean.
- Keep your uniform in a safe place.
- Never loan any part of your uniform to anyone.
- Never leave your uniform unattended in the locker room.
- Wear your uniform only on contest days or as directed by the coach.
- If you lose your uniform, tell the coach immediately.
- If your uniform needs repair, see the coach before trying to fix it yourself.
- Following cleaning directions on the label.

Athlete Inventory

Coaches enjoy getting together, comparing notes, and making up tentative rosters of athletes coming out for their teams. That's part of the fun of coaching. And it sends a coach three stories high to learn a super athlete recently checked into school.

A seasoned coach, however, checks out every story or rumor before making serious plans. Nearly every year somebody mentions that an All-State sprinter moved into the district or the baseball team's star pitcher has decided to play tennis in his senior year. Without a doubt, the coach has plenty to think about while preparing for the upcoming season.

How can a coach find out approximately how many athletes will be coming out for the team? Here's a four-step procedure many coaches recommend:

- Post a sign-up sheet on the gym office bulletin board or some other conspicuous place.
- Write a blurb for the school paper informing interested athletes where to go to sign up.
- Run a daily announcement in the school bulletin regarding the sign-up sheet.
- After two or three weeks hold a brief meeting with athletes who signed the sheet. Confirm each signature.

The sign-up sheet won't have everybody's name on the list, but it'll give the coach a fair idea of how many athletes to expect. Some athletes, of course, are busy playing other sports and plan to contact the coach personally.

A pre-season sign-up sheet does two things: One, it lets the coach know approximately how many athletes will be trying out; Two, it gives the coach and athletic director time to check the eligibility of each athlete.

Organizing the Athletic Handbook

The Athletic Handbook sets the pace for action. It takes athletes by the hand and outlines exactly what the coach, school, and community expect from them. The Athletic Handbook, to be effective, must be updated with fresh ideas (including new rules and regulations), well organized, and ready to go when the team meets for the first time.

Some coaches balk at putting together a handbook. To them it's an administrative nuisance which adds one more chore to their already busy schedule. Yet most coaches agree that without guidelines to direct athletes they would be spinning in circles answering questions and explaining procedures related to the athletic program.

In order to save energy, reduce anxiety, and finish the handbook on time, a coach can solicit the help of student aides or the team manager. If the school has a Student Secretary Pool, the coach can see the teacher in charge and arrange to have pages typed, duplicated, and stapled together. Chapter 13 discusses Athletic Handbooks in greater detail.

Attending Coaching Clinics

Chapter One mentioned a newspaper article concerning a high school football coach who lost twenty-five games in three years. The coach attended several coaching clinics and motivation seminars in search of a winning formula. He found clinics confusing because, according to the article, for every set of do's and dont's from one speaker, there is an equal and opposite set from someone else.

Not all coaches hold a dim view of clinics. Many attend for social reasons; that is, they enjoy getting together with fellow coaches and swapping stories. A successful clinic, to these coaches, offers updated, fresh information with practical ideas for improving their programs. Picking up a new idea or two makes attending a coaching clinic worthwhile.

A school's athletic department may set money aside for those coaches wishing to attend workshops and clinics. Other districts, in cooperation with local recreation departments, put on their own clinics for youngsters in the community.

Here are five tips to follow before attending a coaching clinic:

- Carefully study the brochures and available information that describe the clinic.
- Check the background of each speaker.
- Ask coaches who have attended a previous clinic to give it a rating.
- Estimate the total expense for attending. (Not every school provides money for its coaches to attend clinics.)
- If the clinic looks promising, by all means attend.

Coaching Magazines and Books

Some of the same people who appear at coaching clinics write magazine articles and books on coaching techniques. Such magazines as *Scholastic Coach* and *Athletic Journal* publish technical articles devoted to a certain phase or technique of coaching of the various sports. These articles are written by men or women actively engaged in the coaching or administration of high school or college sports.

The coach, by keeping up on the latest coaching methods, stays two steps ahead of those who sleep during the year. A concerned coach, then, spends part of his pre-season time scanning these magazines for innovative ideas. These magazines also do an excellent job reviewing the latest coaching books on the market.

A coach can stay informed throughout the year by doing the following:

- Get to know the school library and the people in charge. Find out what coaching magazines and books are on the shelves.
- Talk to the school librarian. Check to see how much money is available for ordering new books. Then fill out a few orders before the money disappears.
- Before ordering new books, read the reviews in the coaching magazines. If the reviews are favorable, send for them on a free trial basis.
- Be selective. Order the books and magazines most coaches are likely to read.
- Share newly acquired knowledge with others.

Pre-season Get-togethers

Coaches pump themselves up for the coming season in different ways. A pre-season gathering, e.g., picnic, house party or dinner dance gives coaches with winning records an opportunity to squeeze the last bit of breath out of their victories. Even for those coaches who come off a "building year," there's plenty of fun, relaxation, and optimism.

A pre-season get-together should include every coach in the school, the administrators, district superintendent, and board members. A progressive athletic department shares the joys and sorrows of the coaching world with key people in the district. A program gains strength and support by opening its doors to others.

Pre-season Meeting with Athletes

For most coaches a pre-season meeting has four purposes: 1) To find out how many athletes will be coming out for the team; 2) To start athletes on a training program; 3) To pass out district rules and regulations; 4) To discuss any special problems that might arise during the season.

The following tips for holding a pre-season meeting will help a coach start off right and avoid confusion later on.

- Set up a convenient meeting time for most athletes.
- Post meeting time at least two weeks in advance. Run time and meeting place in the daily bulletin and school paper.
- Have Athletic Handbook or information handouts ready to pass out.
- Be organized. Stick to the agenda and move quickly from point to point.

- Emphasize the importance of studying the Athletic Handbook or handouts before the first practice session begins.
- Convince athletes to prepare themselves mentally and physically for a challenging season.

What problem hits most coaches the hardest at pre-season meetings? In a word, absenteeism. For instance, a coach calls for a meeting and four athletes show up. Excuses range from "I didn't know about the meeting" to "I had to work and couldn't come." One coach raised the attendance at pre-season meetings by posting the following information:

ATTENTION SWIMMERS

Interested in staying afloat?
Want to keep your head above water?
If you plan to be on the swim team this year,
you MUST ATTEND ONE of the following meetings:
Feb. 4, Monday morning, 7:30 a.m., Room 214
Feb. 6, Wednesday morning, 7:30 a.m., Room 214
Feb. 13, Wednesday morning, 7:30 a.m., Room 214

The coach increased attendance by doing six things: (1) Emphasizing three key words—Must Attend One; (2) Giving athletes three chances to attend one meeting; (3) Posting the meeting time and place well in advance; (4) Giving athletes a choice of meeting times; (5) Publicizing meeting times in the school paper; (6) Stressing mandatory attendance.

WORKING WITH THE ATHLETIC DIRECTOR

If the coaching staff had to rely on the administration for everything, coaches would be standing in line waiting to see the principal. Fortunately, most schools employ an athletic director to run the athletic program. The coach and athletic director must coordinate their efforts to stay on track and keep things moving smoothly. Here are six ways a coach can effectively work with an athletic director:

1. Help the athletic director schedule practice contests by preparing a list of preferred schools in advance. Ask the athletic director to select only those schools that appear on the list. Also, scan the local paper for schools seeking practice contests. Give the school name, telephone number, and person to contact to the athletic director. Selective scheduling keeps the program in balance and eliminates those schools that carry a questionable reputation.

2. Sit down with the athletic director and go over each athlete's clearance card. Double check any information that might lead to problems later on.

3. Confer with the athletic director before ordering supplies. Find out how much money is in the athletic budget. Then, if given an okay, fill out orders early in the year. Keep track of orders, but allow several weeks for delivery. Don't expect the athletic director to inventory orders for every coach in the school. Be sure, however, to have the athletic director run a check on those orders failing to arrive on time.

4. After the athletic director finalizes the schedule, check the dates and times of away contests. Occasionally a busy athletic director forgets to schedule a bus or accidentally writes down the wrong information. A track team, for example, had a meet scheduled for 3:30 p.m. with a school thirty-five miles away. A bus, according to the schedule, was supposed to pick up the athletes in front of the school cafeteria at 2:00 p.m. At 2:15 p.m. the coach called the bus garage and discovered nobody scheduled a bus for the track team. The team waited forty minutes before the transportation clerk could find an available bus and driver.

   A humorous incident happened a few years back. A basketball team, on its way to play a game, passed another bus filled with basketball players. Athletes from both buses waved and hollered at each other. As the buses passed, one coach jumped up and shouted at the bus driver, "Hey, stop the bus. That's the team we're supposed to play."

5. Prior to each home contest, check with the athletic director to make sure officials have been assigned and contacted. Forfeiting a contest because of failure to assign an official hurts team morale and creates hard feelings.

6. Ask the athletic director to pass along any new rule changes or information concerning tournaments, coaches' clinics, or special athletic events. Frequently mail sent to the athletic director piles up on a desk, tips over, and falls in the nearest waste paper basket. Unless a coach happens by at the right moment, those brochures and circulars may be lost forever. In short, don't expect a busy athletic director to contact each coach personally every time something arrives. An ambitious coach takes the initiative to ferret out this information and use it accordingly.

   A good bit of advice for any coach is: Don't assume anything. Double check times, dates, and locations of all contests. And when in doubt, ask.

PHYSICAL EDUCATION TEACHER/COACH

A physical education teacher/coach holds a definite advantage over the classroom teacher/coach. For instance, the physical educator sees most athletes nearly every day and doesn't have to chase after them like a classroom teacher/coach. In a short period of time, the physical education teacher/coach and athlete get to know each other quite well.

Some classroom teacher/coaches register these complaints against physical education teacher/coaches:

1. Physical education teachers recruit athletes during class. A baseball coach, for example, might protest that the football coach (physical education teacher) puts pressure on baseball players to quit baseball and run track. Why? It turns out the athletes being pressured are also football players. According to the physical education teacher, track will get these athletes in better condition—for football. Unfortunately, an athlete may buckle under pressure just to keep the football coach happy.
2. Physical education teachers control the gym by having first crack at facilities.
3. Physical education teachers receive larger and better located lockers.
4. Physical education teachers hoard supplies and equipment.
5. Physical education teachers give preferential treatment to athletes in their programs.

Most of these conflicts can be resolved if all coaches meet regularly, discuss problems intelligently, and agree to cooperate with each other. These meetings should be held at a time when everyone can attend, including the athletic director and an administrator.

COACH VERSUS COACH

When little problems escalate into major difficulties, coaches wind up yelling back and forth or walking into the principal's office threatening to quit.

Let's look at five situations that cause problems among coaches.

One, a coach uses a facility or a piece of equipment without prior approval.

Two, a coach feels the physical education staff purposely harasses certain athletes. Here's an example: On the day of a league game, the physical education instructor told the starting pitcher to swim laps for twenty-five minutes. The pitcher refused saying the exercise would sap his energy for the game. The instructor gave him a choice—swim or leave on a disciplinary notice to the office. He swam the laps. That afternoon he managed to pitch only three innings before leaving the game.

On the following day the baseball coach complained to the principal. After reviewing the situation the principal sympathized with the coach, but felt the instructor didn't do any real harm to the athlete. Case dismissed.

Three, a coach criticizes the efforts of another coach in the presence of students.

Four, a coach shows special consideration for certain athletes by letting them have the run of the gym office or by putting them in charge of issuing towels and equipment.

Five, a coach works extra hard to build a strong, competitive program. The coach's team consistently finishes high in the league standings. Other coaches, jealous of the team's success, complain and say they're not getting enough publicity and support from the community.

Coaches heading in different directions is similar to a rope pulling contest. If participants yank hard enough, the rope breaks, and nobody wins. Most problems that exist between coaches can be resolved if coaches agree on three points: 1) To stick together and work on resolving conflicts that creep into the program each year; 2) To cooperate with one another and be willing to share a few lumps; 3) To keep the flow going; that is, everyone pools their energy toward a common goal—to build an athletic program the school and community will be proud of.

HOW TO SELECT AN ASSISTANT COACH

First of all, let's assume there's money available to pay an assistant and there are faculty members willing and able to coach. What qualifies a person to become an assistant coach? Most head coaches look for these things:

1. A willingness to learn—A person must have an open mind and a desire to put new concepts into use.
2. Enthusiasm—A person who shows a wholesome interest in the sport.
3. Cooperation—A person willing to share ideas and support the efforts of others.
4. Dependability—A person available to help out at any time, including pre-season and post-season.
5. Desire—A person who goes all out to help athletes improve.

6. Sticktoitiveness—A person who plans to spend two or three or more years in the program.
7. Amiability—A person who is good natured and pleasant to be around.

Few head coaches can afford the luxury of waiting around for the ideal assistant to appear. In many instances, a head coach does handstands just to get a volunteer—any volunteer—to help out. So when a worthy assistant happens by, a coach must do everything possible to encourage the assistant to stay.

HOW TO USE AN ASSISTANT COACH

For one reason or another a coach might accuse an assistant of being nondedicated; an assistant might reply by saying the coach doesn't know how to handle athletes. It really doesn't matter who's right or wrong. What really counts is that a head coach, in order to retain competent assistants, must treat them in an intelligent, thoughtful manner.
Here are three ways a head coach can effectively use an assistant:

1. Set up coaching assignments for assistant several days in advance. An assistant should know where to go, what to do, and when to get it done during each practice session.
2. Assign an assistant coach to areas commensurate with interest, knowledge, and ability.
3. Involve assistant coach in planning daily practice, organizing athletes on contest days, and discussing any problems that spring up during the year.

A head coach must share the ups and downs with an assistant. Leaving an assistant out of any phase of the program shows a lack of confidence, consideration, and sincerity by the head coach. It's a rare assistant who has the patience or stamina to work in an atmosphere of secrecy.

ROLE OF A TEAM MANAGER

Some athletes hold the team manager in low esteem. They see the manager as a person with limited intelligence and poor athletic ability; at best, as a person whose only talent lies in carrying equipment out to the practice field.

Happily, this stereotypical response isn't held by every athlete. In fact, most athletes realize their jobs would be much tougher without a team manager to help out.

Not every coach wants or needs a team manager. A team may not be big enough to warrant the services of a manager. For most coaches, however, a manager saves time, energy, and the embarrassment of leaving equipment behind on long road trips.

A competent team manager, like an assistant coach, isn't always easy to come by. Therefore, when a likely candidate knocks on the door, a smart coach treats the person with kindness and respect.

An active team manager may do some or all of the following:

1. Keep team statistics on all contests.
2. Report contest results to the school paper and local press.
3. Keep track of supplies and equipment, both home and away.
4. Deliver messages for the coach.
5. See to it that supplies and equipment arrive on the practice field on time.
6. Lend a helping hand to the visiting team.
7. Keep the coach posted on the day's events, e.g., athletes absent from school, etc.
8. Help the coach pass out and collect uniforms and equipment.
9. Help the coach inventory supplies and equipment at the end of the season.

A coach looks for an enthusiastic, dependable person to act as team manager. It takes an easy-going, cooperative individual to fit into a large group setting. A person doesn't have to be rugged, but a thick skin and a sense of humor help.

Some coaches, depending upon the sport and conditions, let their managers practice occasionally with the team. (*Note*: In order to work out, a team manager must have a clearance card on file with the coach.) This exercise keeps the manager's spirits up, relieves boredom, and provides a little fun too.

Sometimes a team manager comes to a coach's rescue. For example, several years ago a baseball coach ran into trouble with his team. With three weeks left in the season, he lost four players—two to injuries, two for disciplinary reasons. Being short of players, he let the manager play in the outfield. In this case, by allowing the manager to work out occasionally, the coach had an extra player to call on. Luckily, the manager did a creditable job of playing baseball.

Last point: How athletes treat the team manager is directly proportional to the coach's attitude. For instance, if the coach receives laughs at the expense of the manager, then athletes will feel it's okay for them to do the same thing.

USING A STUDENT AIDE

Many school districts operate a student aide program that allows a student to earn credit by working one hour or more a day for a teacher, coach, or office personnel. An aide, usually selected several months ahead, can reduce a coach's work load by helping gather information for handouts, handbooks, and yearbooks. Most coaches prefer a student who can type, run the copy machine, and talk to people on the phone. An effective student aide must be organized, dependable, and reasonably intelligent.

GETTING ORGANIZED ON CONTEST DAY

All kinds of thoughts race through a coach's mind on the day of a contest. Questions bounce off the inner cerebral walls like race cars out of control—are any athletes sick or unable to play today? Is the team prepared to compete? Am I forgetting anything important?

A coach can reduce contest day jitters by setting up a duty schedule in advance for team personnel (See Figure 4-1). The schedule can be posted for all to see and serve as a reminder of things to do on contest day.

Coaches need a checklist or assignment sheet to help them guide and direct personnel on contest day. No single schedule will satisfy every coach because coaching responsibilities and conditions vary from district to district.

KEEPING PACE WITH THE FACULTY

Not every faculty member shares a coach's enthusiasm for sports. In fact, some teachers feel athletics are detrimental to the welfare of a student. School is for studying and learning, they say, not for playing games and wasting time.

Many teachers turn thumbs down on athletics because they've clashed with athletes and coaches in the past. An athlete, for instance, might take advantage of leaving class early by creating a disturbance before walking out the door, or a coach might forget to give teachers a list indicating which students are members of the team.

The following guidelines for coaches, athletes, and teachers will help keep problems to a minimum:

A. Coach

1. Send each teacher and administrator a list of team members. Keep everyone posted as athletes are dropped or added to the

Personnel	What To Do	
	Home	Away
Head Coach	1. Contact athletic director to see officials have been assigned. 2. Confer with maintenance department. Confirm preparation of facilities for contest.	1. Make sure announcement of bus time appears in daily bulletin. 2. Check with athletic director to see that bus has been ordered. 3. Double check schedule with athletic director.
Assistant Coach	1. Help coach organize and supervise athletes and team manager.	1. Help coach organize and supervise athletes and team manager.
Student Manager	1. Check to see equipment on field and ready to go. 2. Offer to help visiting team. 3. Keep records of contest. 4. Report to coach if any athlete absent from school. 5. Report contest results to school paper and local press. 6. Make sure equipment brought in from field and put away.	1. Make sure equipment gets on/off bus. Bring along first aid kit. 2. Keep record of contest. 3. Report to coach if any athlete absent from school. 4. Report contest results to school paper and local press.
Student Aide	1. If available, assist manager with record keeping and statistics.	1. Not needed at this time.

FIGURE 4-1 Contest day duty schedule

list. An athlete who quits the team can easily hoodwink a teacher by leaving class early on contest days. The teacher, thinking the student is still on the team, smiles and wishes the athlete good luck. Smiles turn to sneers when the teacher discovers the coach neglected to send around a revised team list.

2. Send each teacher and administrator a contest schedule.
3. Announce in the school bulletin the time athletes should be excused from class to compete in away contests. Make these announcements one or two days in advance.
4. Ask faculty members to report any athlete-related problem directly to the coach.

B. Athlete

1. Check contest schedule often. Know ahead of time when team plays away.
2. Remind teachers to check schedule and bulletin on contest days.
3. Leave class in a courteous, orderly manner at the designated time.
4. Don't ask teachers for any special favors like leaving class early to pick up uniform or to make a phone call home.
5. Complete and turn in any missed assignment as requested by teacher.

C. Teacher

1. Allow athletes to leave on time. If problems arise, see coach.
2. Allow athletes a reasonable length of time to make up any missed assignments.

An irate teacher comes running when an athlete stirs up trouble in the classroom. If the teacher goes to the coach, the problem may be resolved without administrative assistance. If the teacher sidesteps the coach and complains to an administrator, the coach might lose an athlete for several days. Therefore, a coach should take a diplomatic approach and establish a harmonious relationship with faculty members long before the season begins.

The secret of gaining faculty support and minimizing classroom conflicts lies in hammering five points into the heads of athletes. They are:

1. Show up for class on time.
2. Be attentive. Show an interest in classwork. Take part in discussions.

3. Complete and turn in assignments on time.
4. Work to the best of your ability.
5. When in doubt, ask for help.

A basketball coach included this short statement in an Athletic Handbook:

BE A STUDENT

Good grades are the key to your future.
Basketball, in its proper perspective, is a
means to an end. Work hard to make your
future a bright and pleasant one.

Finally, at a faculty meeting, thank teachers and administrators for their support. Credit those who helped bring the season to a smooth finish.

POINTS TO REMEMBER

A well-organized coach plans ahead, anticipates problems, and keeps abreast of latest coaching techniques.

A coach learns early to work closely with the athletic director, fellow coaches, and faculty members.

A coach wisely selects team personnel to help the athletic program reach its goals and objectives. A good coach knows how to handle team personnel and keep them happy.

A coach should follow district policy and assess a team's ability before scheduling contests. A contest should be challenging—not too tough and not too easy.

At times coaches and teachers alike expect more from athletes than non-athletes. Some athletes feel pressure to try harder and be a model student for the district.

Courtesy pays. A coach who acknowledges the support of others brings new friends into the athletic program.

QUESTIONS

1. Why is pre-planning important for the coach and the success of the program?
2. Why should a coach personally check facilities and equipment before the season begins?
3. What steps should a coach take to repair damaged equipment?
4. How should a coach go about removing dangerous obstacles from the practice field?

5. What procedure could the coach take to recover most of the gear issued to athletes?
6. How does a pre-season sign-up sheet aid the coach?
7. How can attending a coaching clinic raise the competence of a coach?
8. In your opinion, how can reading and studying available coaching literature upgrade the athletic program?
9. Why do most coaches hold a pre-season meeting with athletes?
10. How can an athletic director make a coach's job easier?
11. Why do some classroom teacher/coaches feel they are discriminated against?
12. What major factors lead to conflicts between coaches?
13. What traits should a head coach look for in an assistant coach?
14. What are some of the duties of an assistant coach?
15. What qualities should a team manager have?
16. What important duties must be performed by a team manager?
17. How can a student aide benefit a team?
18. What are some special problems many coaches face on contest day?
19. Why do some faculty members fail to support athletics?
20. In your opinion, do you feel teachers and coaches expect too much from athletes? Explain.

Strengthening the Program through Effective Practice Sessions

Obviously, the highest type of efficiency is that which can utilize existing material to the best advantage.

Jawaharlal Nehru

Coaches agree that it takes intelligent preparation and plenty of leg work to set up a well-organized practice session. A busy coach, like a thief, often has to steal time during the day to get things ready for practice. For example, a coach may give up lunch to chase down equipment, speak with a teacher, or corner an administrator in the office. Sacrifices, then, must come from coaches as well as athletes.

In this chapter, we'll see how an athletic program benefits from a coach's effort to organize and control practice sessions.

WHAT A COACH EXPECTS FROM ATHLETES

A coach soon discovers how effective practices have been by the actions of those involved, namely athletes. An athlete contributes to the success of each practice by:

1. Showing up on time.
2. Having everything ready to go—practice uniform, any special equipment, and so forth.
3. Being mentally and physically capable of giving a one-hundred percent effort.
4. Showing a willingness to cooperate and share positive experiences with others.
5. Continually striving to improve.
6. Making a commitment to work hard and overcome any weakness that slows down progress.
7. Agreeing to compete as a team member, not as an individual star.
8. Bearing down during rough moments.
9. Having the self-confidence to complete a task.
10. Throwing total support behind the goals and objectives of the program.
11. Seeking positive solutions to problems.
12. Striving to upgrade self, athletic program, and school.

If athletes followed these twelve suggestions, the coach would sail through the season with ease. But coaches seldom do. And, in some cases, the athlete experienced trouble because an unorganized coach allowed too much free time in practice. Therefore, to reduce confusion and increase efficiency, a coach must make practices concise and worthwhile.

WHAT ATHLETES EXPECT FROM THE COACH

Now let's flip the coin over and see what most athletes want in return. They like a coach who:

1. Judges them on desire, potential, and ability—not personality.
2. Allows them to experiment or try something new in practice.
3. Shows enthusiasm by being happy and self-confident; someone full of energy and optimism.
4. Listens to those with problems and helps out if necessary.
5. Has a sense of humor and jokes a bit to help them relax and have fun.

6. Gives them a "breather" by slipping fun activities into practice.
7. Spends extra time helping them improve their skills.
8. Gives full support to every member of the team; a person who shows an interest in everyone.
9. Puts their safety and welfare above anything else.
10. Keeps them busy throughout practice.
11. Livens up practice by changing activities often.
12. Plans practices in advance and lets them know exactly what to do at all times.
13. Gives an honest appraisal of their progress and value to the team.

A COMMON SENSE APPROACH
TO RUNNING PRACTICE

More than ever, a coach needs to plan fast-moving, comprehensive practice sessions. Few coaches can let their teams stay in the gym or on the field for extra long periods of time. Why? Coaches have less time to practice because: 1) They must share facilities with others; 2) They're busy with other school duties and assignments; 3) Athletes, especially the older ones, need additional time to study or work.

Instead of complaining about hard times, a coach should size up the situation and adjust team practices for optimum efficiency. For example, here are eleven common sense tips for keeping practice sessions alive, on the move, and on schedule.

One, keep practice sessions short—two hours or less. Dann Alsheimer, assistant tennis coach, Avoca Central High School, New York, believes an hour of strenuous practice accomplishes a great deal more than two hours of lackadaisical practice. A long-drawn-out session bores athletes and may cause them to develop bad habits.

Two, post a written practice plan one day in advance. This gives athletes an opportunity to make physical and mental preparations.

Three, center daily plans around the needs of athletes. Coach William A. Welker in his article entitled "Organizing Daily Practice Sessions," *The Coaching Clinic*, February 1978, had this to say: "It is important to realize that your daily practices must evolve around the athlete participating in program. For example, if you are working with young or inexperienced athletes you will need to spend more time on the perfection of fundamental techniques before moving on to more advanced skills."

Four, gear practice sessions toward specific goals. In other words, have a reason for everything that goes on in practice.

Five, allow athletes to use their own driving force to help themselves improve; give them free reign to try things on their own.

Six, know ahead of time what equipment is needed, what facilities are available, and what personnel will be doing during practice.

Seven, change activities often so that practices don't become monotonous and boring. Include drills that require athletes to stay active.

Eight, use activities that strengthen the team's weak spots. Jack B. Kaley, lacrosse coach, East Meadow High School, New York, believes the key is to work to improve the areas where the team shows weaknesses. Then design drills to improve them.

Nine, stress drills that teach fundamentals. Whenever possible, inject competition into practice.

Ten, start and stop practice on time.

Eleven, insist on consideration for others and courtesy and promptness from athletes. Then, to show the power of teamwork, give athletes the same treatment in return.

SETTING UP THE DAILY PRACTICE SCHEDULE

How a coach prepares the daily practice schedule depends on such factors as:

- Time of year—Pre-season conditioning program, in-season competitive program, or post-season conditioning program.
- Team's progress—Is the team on a losing streak? Are athletes continually making the same mistakes?
- Health of athletes—Are two or three key athletes out with injuries? Are athletes coming down with the flu?
- Availability of facilities—How long will the team be allowed to use the gym? Will field number three be available on Wednesday afternoon?
- Weather conditions—Is it too windy and cold to practice outside? How many teams will be using the gym at the same time?
- Conflicts with other school functions—How many athletes must attend the Academic Awards Banquet or attend the Ski Club's annual three-day trip to Acorn Valley?

After taking everything into account, a coach schedules the day's activities. Let's examine two sample plans from active coaches.

Sample Plan One

Coach William A. Welker offers the following in-season practice plan for this wrestlers:

ACTIVITY	TIME
Conditioning warm-up exercises	10 – 15 minutes
Wrestling drill work	5 – 10 minutes
Wrestling workout session	30 – 60 minutes
Conditioning finish-up exercises	5 – 10 minutes

Sample Plan Two

Duane Jones, head girls' basketball coach, Joseph City High School, Arizona, offered this plan in *The Coaching Clinic*, March, 1978:

ACTIVITY	TIME
Individual skills	2:45 – 3:00
Circuit training (10-station circuit)	3:00 – 3:25
3-Man weave	3:25 – 3:40
Diamond (running, passing, shooting, and lay ups.)	3:40 – 3:50
Three-on-two	3:50 – 4:00
Scrimmage (either offensive or defensive)	4:00 – 4:30
Wave Drill (defensive drill)	4:30 – 4:35
Run 15 laps (sprint last two)	4:35 – 4:40
Shoot 25-footers (record the number made)	4:40 – 4:45

Notice the similarities between these two sample plans. First, neither session lasts over two hours. Second, athletes move quickly from one activity to another. Third, each plan stresses fundamentals. Fourth, there's a definite time block for each activity.

A coach must balance available practice time with the needs of athletes, and, above all, stay on schedule. After practice a coach should get together with assistant coaches and evaluate the session. This gives the coach a chance to discuss the team's strengths and weaknesses with others before writing plans for the next practice.

PUTTING LIFE INTO PRACTICE SESSIONS

Staleness hits the practice scene when athletes show signs of sluggishness and seem to be standing still. When staleness occurs, a coach must find ways to breathe new life into practice sessions. The following six suggestions are excellent ways to liven up listless athletes:

1. Keep drills short. A fast-moving drill which lasts about fifteen minutes ends when an athlete's interest reaches its peak. Finishing an activity on a high note whets the competitive appetite of athletes. A good rule of thumb is quit before the pace slows down. Use popular drills sparingly. Let the novelty last for the entire season.

2. Dissect two or three popular drills. Find out why athletes select these activities over others. Then isolate the magic ingredients and include them in future workouts. To understand how to dissect an activity, let's examine a perennial favorite among baseball drills known as Champ or Chump.

   Champ or Chump

   Purpose—To provide a fast-paced, interesting drill.
   Location—Baseball diamond
   Technique—Infielders emphasize staying low, keeping their weight forward and bending at the knees with arms outstretched in front of their bodies. The glove hand constantly touches the ground.
   Procedure—All infielders, excluding catchers, line up in a semi-circle between second and third base. The coach stands between the pitcher's mound and the third base line. A pick-up man (catcher) stands to the coach's right. (See Figure 5-1).

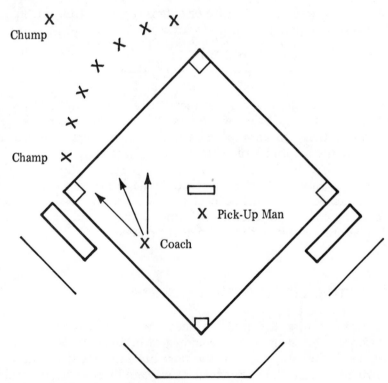

FIGURE 5-1 Champ or chump drill

The chump is a player who commits a throwing error or fumbles the ball. The champ is a player who performs flawlessly during the drill. The objective is to become the champ by playing errorless ball. Clean fielding and throwing are necessary for success in this drill.

The rules are as follows:

1. Infielders must field and throw accurately to the pick-up man. A poorly thrown ball results in the infielder's becoming chump.

2. The coach decides who will become champ or chump before the drill begins. The champ may be the player who won this title in a previous drill.

3. Play begins when the coach hits balls easily, then progressively livens up the drill by adding speed to ground balls. An infielder must play any type of ball hit into his area.

4. The infielder cannot pretend to field the ball or crowd another player. A violation of this rule results in the player becoming the chump.

5. If the ball is mishandled or thrown wild to the pick-up man, the player runs over the second base, touches the bag with his foot, sprints into left field and changes places with the chump.

6. Players move one position at a time from right or left (from second toward third base) only when errors are made.

7. The chump acts as a back-up for any balls hit through the legs or over the heads of the infielders. He can come back to the fielding zone when errors are committed. The chump takes his place at the end of the line (position nearest second base.)

8. The champ can only be dethroned when he makes an error. Then he becomes the chump. The champ is subject to harder-hit balls because his position is so close to the coach. Since he is champ, his right to the title is continually challenged.

9. Sharply hit balls or line drives deemed base hits are not recognized as errors. The coach serves as the judge.

Now let's pinpoint the reasons why athletes favor this drill. One, athletes quickly realize that success comes only through sound utilization of fielding techniques. Two, the drill motivates players because it provides the incentive for becoming The Champ. Three, athletes must concentrate at all times. Four, athletes must follow specific guidelines. Five, everyone must stay alert, there's no room for horseplay. Six, the activity emphasizes sportsmanship. Seven, the coach sets the pace by controlling the speed and type of ball hit. Eight, the activity involves a small number of athletes.

3. Try to include at least one fun activity each practice. Leslie Howell, girls' volleyball coach, Roseville, California, says: "After a good

practice, I like to let the girls choose up sides and play for team points. Sometimes we make up new games with certain rules and go from there."

The key word is *we*. Planning drills with athletes adds zest to the practice session. Letting athletes compete in short, innovative games gives them something to look forward to at the end of practice.

4. Devote one practice to an activity completely unrelated to sport. For instance, let swimmers play basketball or bring football players inside the gym for volleyball. A good time to spring a "play day" on athletes is when they seem tired and restless, usually near the end of the season. A special fun day works best when it comes as a surprise to athletes.

5. Whenever possible, the coach should take an active part in practice. This doesn't mean a coach has to bump heads with athletes unless, of course, the coach elects to do so. A coach need only keep a sharp eye, move about, and help those who are struggling.

6. Give athletes a day off once in a while.

PRACTICE SESSION PROBLEMS
BETWEEN COACH AND ATHLETE

Even the most organized coach can't predict or control the behavior of every athlete. Some practice sessions move along without a wrinkle; others get off to a shaky start and dampen the spirits of everyone. Coaches report that the following problems cause the most trouble for them during the season:

1. Athletes showing up ten to fifteen minutes late for practice.
2. Athletes missing too many practices.
3. Athletes putting forth a half-way effort in practice.
4. Athletes complaining about equipment, facilities, practice activities, and drills.
5. Athletes complaining that the coach is unfair and unwilling to give them a chance.
6. Athletes leaving on vacation in the middle of the season.
7. Athletes showing up for practice without the necessary equipment.
8. Athletes who won't listen to the coach and who prefers to do things one way only—theirs.
9. Athletes who refuse to accept responsibility and blame others when the team loses.
10. Athletes breaking training rules.
11. Athletes creating conflicts in the classroom.
12. Athletes breaking school rules and policies.
13. Athletes who carry personal problems onto the practice field.

Here are three problem cases and how the coaches involved handled them.

Case One

A senior tennis player began arriving late for practice. He told the coach he was staying after class getting extra help from his math teacher. The coach checked the athlete's story. According to his teacher, the athlete left class with other students immediately following the bell. The teacher said she hadn't given the athlete any special help. When confronted by the coach, the athlete admitted spending time with his girl friend after school by keeping her company while she waited for the bus. The coach decided to kick the boy off the squad for breaking a team rule and for lying to him.

Case Two

A football coach, known as a tough disciplinarian, allowed his athletes to miss no more than three practices. One player with three absences missed the next two practice sessions. The coach, thinking the boy had quit the team, checked with the vice-principal. According to the vice-principal, the athlete and two other students were suspended from school for three days. They were caught in the school's parking lot with open containers of beer.

The vice-principal said the boy hadn't actually been caught drinking and didn't have alcohol on his breath, but, unfortunately, he was in the company of those who did.

After discussing the problem with the athlete, the coach decided to give the boy a second chance—any more missed practices or school-related conflicts and the boy would be removed from the squad.

Case Three

After making the final baseball cut, a pitcher began missing practice. He told the coach that he played in the school band and had to attend band practice in preparation for an upcoming concert. The coach gave the athlete a choice: Play baseball or toot his horn full time.

On the following day at practice the boy's father talked with the coach. He told the coach that his son was a sensitive, bright boy (150 I.Q.) who made the Little League All-Star Team two years in a row. He wanted the coach to make an exception in his son's case by allowing the boy to miss a practice or two until the concert was over. The coach explained how he expected every athlete to be totally committed to the baseball program and would not make an exception for any athlete. The boy decided to quit the band. He never missed another baseball practice.

The following tips will help a coach hold practice problems to a minimum:

1. Set up specific rules for tardies and absences. Athletes must know what the coach expects.
2. Stick to the rules, but keep an open mind and study a situation thoroughly before coming to a decision. Under certain conditions, a coach can justify making an exception.
3. When an exception arises, handle the situation in a positive, prudent manner. Try to seek a solution that will benefit the individual, team, and school.
4. After making an exception, let team members know exactly why that particular decision was made. Keeping athletes informed prevents rumors from spreading about how the coach treats each athlete differently or how the coach bends rules for certain athletes.

POINTS TO REMEMBER

The practice session, heart of the athletic program, must be well-organized, with challenging activities to keep athletes interested.

A coach must key each practice session to the needs and abilities of athletes. Also, whenever possible, a coach should change activities often so that practices do not become drudgery.

Short, concise workouts seem to work best for everybody. Comprehensive activites which stress fundamentals prepare athletes for stiff competition.

All practice sessions should point to one major goal: self-improvement. Through self-improvement every athlete contributes to the team's overall success.

Athletes must know before the season begins what is expected of them.' Athletes shouldn't have to wonder what will happen if they goof around in practice, cause trouble for their teachers, or miss too many practices.

A practice filled with short, fast-paced activities keeps athletes moving and doesn't give them time to think about anything but practice.

QUESTIONS

1. In what ways do athletes contribute to the success of daily practice?
2. Why do some coaches lose control of their athletes during practice?

3. In your opinion, what are the three most important things an athlete looks for in a coach?

4. Why do many coaches restrict their practice sessions to two hours or less?

5. What problems do coaches who hold extra long practices run into?

6. Common sense means using good judgment. How does common sense guide a coach in organizing practices?

7. List two factors that are not mentioned in this chapter that influence how a coach prepares the daily workout. How important are these for carrying out a successful practice?

8. How can a coach tell when athletes become stale?

9. What can a coach do to prevent staleness in athletes?

10. What can a coach do to eliminate staleness in athletes?

11. How can "taking apart" a popular drill help the coach plan better practices?

12. Why do some coaches, more than others, have trouble handling athletes? List four reasons.

13. Which coach, in your opinion, organizes the most effective practices—the strict coach or the lenient coach. Explain.

14. What specific practice problems do strict coaches have with athletes? What problems do lenient coaches have?

15. How can a coach keep practices running smoothly throughout the season?

6

Practical Ways
to Publicize the
Team's Progress

*Things don't turn up in this world
until somebody turns them up.*

James A. Garfield

The coach can do more than anyone else to attract attention to a team. A basketball coach, for example, who runs up and down the court shouting at the referee draws a mixed reaction from spectators. Unfortunately, in many instances, a team suffers from the bad publicity generated by an emotional coach. Negative publicity can slow a team's progress and limit the number of schools willing to compete against it.

We'll see in this chapter what a coach can do to bring positive publicity to the team and how a coach can share ideas and techniques with others.

ADVERTISING THROUGH
THE DAILY BULLETIN

A coach, like a smart business person, must advertise to get the most exposure for the team. A coach needs to create a strong, positive image that will grab and hold the interest of others. In short, the coach who works the hardest to spread the word will leave the deepest impression.

How can a coach keep the student body informed? Let's begin with the daily bulletin. Many schools issue daily information to its students through a printed bulletin which may be read over an intercom and/or posted in strategic places around the school.

Reading the bulletin aloud, however, doesn't always succeed in getting the message across. For instance, students may be talking, shuffling papers, sharpening pencils—anything but listening to the bulletin. Therefore, a coach's important announcement encouraging students to come out and support the team falls on deaf ears.

Here's what a coach can do to increase the effectiveness of advertising through the school bulletin:

- Run the same announcement three or four days in succession.
- Keep announcements brief and to the point.
- Whenever possible, flavor themwith bits of humor using athletes as main characters.
- Check to see bulletins are posted around the school.
- Urge athletes to spread the word in their classrooms. Most teachers won't object if an athlete makes an announcement before class begins.

PREPARING AN ANNOUNCEMENT
FOR THE DAILY BULLETIN

It doesn't take a college education to write a simple announcement, but it does require a pinch of imagination with a creative touch to titillate the psyche of students. After all, few students cling to their desks waiting to hear the bulletin.

Try this experiment. Read the following two announcements. Which one has the greatest appeal?

First Announcement

Come out today after school and watch our great Girls' Varsity Basketball Team play Oakhurst. We need your support.

Second Announcement

Who runs, jumps, and shoots today after school at 3:30 p.m. in the girls' gym? Give up? Okay, it's the Girls' Varsity Basketball Team. Come out and watch the girls dribble Oakhurst into submission. You'll be glad you did. Just wait and see.

The first announcement carries a clear nineteen-word message, but packs as much punch as a fistless boxing glove. Conversely, the second forty-four word message smacks of suspense and humor designed to hook the students.

There isn't a set formula for writing an announcement. A simple, straightforward approach works fine for most coaches. A lively announcement, however, backed with enthusiasm sticks in the listener's mind longer than a lifeless three-lined message.

Here's how a soccer coach reported his team's victory in the daily bulletin:

Soccer team beat Meadowview last week, 4 to 1.

Obviously, the coach doesn't wish to dwell on past conquests. Yet such a cold, terse message serves only to chill an athlete's enthusiasm. On the other hand, athletes perk up when they read an announcement like this:

The Bayside Soccer Team stomped Meadowview last Tuesday by a score of 4 to 1. Jim "Snapper" Gillis scored twice in the first half. John "Shorty" Frudall speared the ball past the goalie with ten seconds left in the game. Bill Thomas and Gary Devine turned in outstanding defensive plays by blocking shots near the goal line. Congratulations, team. What an outstanding team effort! Let's do it again.

Here are seven tips to help a coach prepare an announcement:

1. Turn in announcements on time. Meet the bulletin deadline.
2. Take the time to write a complete and concise message.
3. Set a positive tone.
4. Recognize the special efforts of athletes, but credit the entire team.
5. Double check contest statistics. Accurate reporting is a must.
6. Be consistent. Publicize both winning and losing efforts. A coach who reports only wins becomes known as a front runner.
7. Spell athletes names correctly. This seems like a small point, but parents don't always agree.

A DAILY BULLETIN PROBLEM

Sometimes the simplest message stirs up a beehive of controversy. For example, the following announcement created problems for the administration.

> There will be a special rally tomorrow honoring
> our top sports team. Make sure to come out and
> support our fantastic team.

The message appears innocent enough except at this particular time three teams had perfect records: girls' tennis team, girls' gymnastic team, and the varsity football team. Coaches from all three teams converged on the principal demanding to know which team would be honored. The principal said that the school intended to honor all three teams, not one certain team. He pointed out how the "s" was left off of the word "team."

RELEASING INFORMATION
TO THE LOCAL PRESS

Will Rogers hit home when he said: "All I know is what I read in the paper." And for many members of a community, all they know is what appears in print. Period.

A newspaper reporter, for the most part, gathers information from interviews with school officials, coaches, and athletes. To a degree, a coach controls the slant or direction a particular story takes. A coach, for example, who "talks down" the press or favors one newspaper over another or fails to supply timely information upon request opens the athletic program to severe criticism. A reporter, miffed at being overlooked, may "forget" to report any encouraging team news. A coach owes it to the athletes, school, and community to establish an honest working relationship with the press.

A coach who fails to keep the press informed cheats the athlete and the community. It's easy to see how—an athlete receives little recognition for long, hard hours of work and the community loses contact with the team's progress.

A small local newspaper may not have the staff to cover every contest. Therefore, a coach must supply the paper with the latest developments. Here are twelve suggestions to help a coach establish a solid rapport with the local press:

1. Send a roster of team athletes along with a contest schedule to the sports editor before the season begins.
2. Supply the sports editor with fresh, updated information.
3. Be available for interviews and pictures.
4. Be optimistic. Keep a positive, but sensible outlook on the team's chances of success. Never, never undersell opponents or degrade athletes for a poor performance.
5. Speak in favor of the press. Never downgrade the press, especially in front of athletes.

6. Keep the sports editor's name and phone number handy. Call in scores on time. *Note:* Some people in the community mistakenly blame the press for not reporting contest scores. Often the coach fails to call in the scores on time.
7. Phone in winning and losing scores.
8. Report the facts. The press isn't interested in publishing alibis or complaints about poor officiating.
9. Stress the high points of the contest. Have them ready to go when calling in scores.
10. When something newsworthy happens inform the press immediatley.
11. Single out individual play. Then commend the team for an overall, super effort.
12. Courtesy counts. Show team appreciation by inviting the sports editor to attend sports banquet or athletic awards assembly.

A LOCAL PRESS PROBLEM

A varsity basketball coach, with a mediocre team, fell into good fortune by picking up two junior transfer players shortly after the season began.

Surprisingly, both boys turned out to be superior athletes; that is, they could shoot with razor-sharp accuracy and outjump any player on the team. The local press ran several picture-laden articles featuring the two new athletes. Prior to their arrival, another outstanding senior player grabbed most of the headlines. Now he had to settle for third place.

The senior player's father, displeased with the press coverage, castigated the coach, principal, and local newspaper. The father accused the coach of favoring the new players by giving them the lion's share of publicity. He blamed the principal for not asking to screen statements in articles about athletes. He criticized the newspaper for drawing reader attention to the new transfers.

The father reasoned that his son, a graduating senior, should receive most of the publicity in order to strengthen his chances of winning a college athletic scholarship. Did dad win? No. The coach countered by saying that he only reported game results to the press and didn't write the story. The principal said he didn't have the time, energy, or authority to proofread every article a paper printed on school sports. The sports editor felt he treated athletes fairly and had no intention of purposely giving one athlete more publicity than another.

The father calmed down after his son and the two transfers made the All-City Basketball Team. All three players received plenty of press as the team won the league championship and regional playoffs.

SUPPLYING INFORMATION
TO THE SCHOOL PAPER

Many coaches criticize the school paper for giving their teams and athletes minimum coverage. Often it's the same old story: the coach fails to supply the paper with information. Let's say, for instance, a student reporter wants to interview the soccer coach. Every time the reporter drops by, the coach, who also teaches competency english, is busy correcting papers or tutoring slow students. As a result the reporter leaves without a story. It's critical, then, that the reporter and coach agree on a meeting time and place convenient for both. If not, an excellent story might be lost.

A coach can keep the student body informed on the team's progress by doing the following:

1. Cooperating with student reporters by helping them to meet their deadlines.
2. Treating student reporters in a courteous, easygoing fashion. Many young, inexperienced reporters shy away from interviewing certain coaches. They're afraid these coaches might embarrass them in front of other students or athletes. Therefore, a coach should be sympathetic and patient during an interview.
3. Keeping the paper current by furnishing the sports editor with short articles, newsclips, or summaries regarding important team events.
4. Encouraging athletes to cooperate with the paper staff by giving accurate, timely information.

A SCHOOL PAPER PROBLEM

A school paper in a medium-sized high school featured the male and female athlete of the month. The newspaper staff selected those athletes they felt turned in outstanding performances in the preceding month.

A physical education teacher/coach blasted the paper's girl athlete selection of the month in front of several students. The teacher said the girl didn't deserve to win because she was mediocre at best and needed help tying her shoe laces. The teacher also remarked how the girl had sympathetic friends on the newspaper staff. After learning from a friend what the coach said, the girl became upset and told her parents.

The girl's father called the principal, registered a complaint, and set up a meeting that included principal, teacher, and daughter. The father passed along these comments at the meeting: One, the teacher showed poor judgment by making caustic remarks in front of other students. Two, the teacher's remarks upset the girl emotionally. Three, the teacher damaged his daughter's reputation by causing others to doubt her athletic ability.

The father requested that the teacher apologize to his daughter and in the future refrain from broadcasting personal opinions when a student's welfare is at stake. He also suggested that the school paper review its athlete selection procedure. He favored the idea of honoring top athletes, but felt the selective process should be above reproach.

It's tough to spotlight every deserving athlete. There will always be those who disagree with the selections for any number of reasons. But if the school paper practices impartiality, there won't be any legitimate reason for people to complain.

SETTING UP ATHLETIC RALLIES AND ASSEMBLIES

Rallies and assemblies honoring the efforts of athletic teams give the student body an opportunity to meet athletes, hear them speak, and share in their long-range plans.

The success of any rally or assembly depends on 1) Student body and faculty support of athletic program; 2) Administrative support of athletic program; 3) Overall student behavior; 4) Attitude of athletes and coaches; 5) Extent of pre-planning by coaches and administration.

Some administrators think twice before taking on too many special rallies or assemblies. Why? They know from past experience how teachers grumble about schedule changes that upset their classroom plans. Also, it's difficult to provide adequate seating for a large student body. Many students, rather than jam together in a small gym or auditorium, skip the program and mill around in the halls. Gathering crowds require extra supervision.

Coaches interested in holding a rally or assembly should keep these things in mind:

1. Become familiar with district and school policies regarding special programs.
2. Discuss planned events and times with the administration. Make sure the administration approves each activity before finalizing the program.
3. Make arrangements far in advance (two or three or more months) with the administration.
4. If necessary, fill out a use of facility form.

5. Arrange with the maintenance department to set up the necessary equipment.
6. Let athletes take an active part in the program.
7. Load the program with fun activities. Move quickly from one activity to another.
8. Stay on schedule.
9. Remember, there's no substitute for a well-planned program.

SOLICITING THE TALENTS OF CREATIVE STUDENTS

Thank goodness for art departments. They've done more to pull coaches through rough seasons than most people realize. For example, a varsity football coach at a first year school knew his green squad would be doormats for the rest of the league. He decided to run a fun campaign by having art students design banners advertising team spirit. The banners, taped along the hallway walls, said things like:

WINNING ISN'T EVERYTHING, BUT SHOWING UP
TO PLAY IS.
WE'VE GOT DESIRE AND PRIDE. TWO OUT OF TWO
ISN'T BAD.
WHY WAIT UNTIL NEXT YEAR? WE PLAY TONIGHT!

Each week different messages appeared. These fresh, enthusiastic expressions gave the student body the kick in the pants it needed to support a struggling football team.

According to the coach, team morale remained high in spite of losing every league game. A clever student came up with the following banner at the close of the season:

WHY WAIT UNTIL NEXT YEAR? 'CAUSE THE SEASON'S
OVER.

Art departments spawn talented, creative students. Often these students finish their classroom projects early and search about for new ideas. An energetic coach can contact these students through the art department and set up the following projects:

1. Design handbook or player program covers.
2. On contest days decorate the lockers of team athletes with spirit-boosting messages.
3. Create cartoons, caricatures, or animations showing athletes in a positive light.

4. Design humorous posters to be displayed in the gymnasium, classrooms, main office, cafeteria, and library.

A coach, of course, must check beforehand with the administration and obtain permission to display art projects around the school. This helps prevent the circulation of offensive material. Also, a coach should make arrangements to reimburse the art department for the cost of supplies and materials.

Art students appreciate recognition too. When the season ends, a coach should write a short letter to the head of the art department thanking everyone for helping to build team spirit and student body support. Here is an example:

Dear Mr. James:

Members of the McKinley High School Varsity Football Team and coaching staff wish to thank you and your art students for helping us survive a challenging year.

Your creative efforts gave us a steady transfusion of hope during many, many tense moments. The signs, banners, and posters lifted everyone's spirit and strengthened team morale.

Thanks again for a super job.

Sincerely,

_____

Varsity Football Coach

The coach should ask the newspaper staff to publish a copy of the letter. Finally, everybody who supported the team should be mentioned at rallies and assemblies.

A coach and team can repay the art department by supporting money-making projects like art shows and craft sales. When everyone pulls together programs gain in confidence and strength.

SHARING IDEAS WITH COACHES EVERYWHERE

Coaches cut their teeth on the trial-and-error learning process. Coaches are famous for experimenting until the right combination of ingredients blend together. Then, after years of experimentation, a coach settles on a specific way to organize practice sessions, teach fundamental skills, or set up offensive and defensive strategy.

A young coach may wish to speed up the process by reading books or magazine articles written by experienced coaches. In time, this young coach may develop a unique coaching style sought after by others. So the coach may decide to write a technical article or two showing fellow coaches how to improve their programs.

For coaches interested in writing a technical article, here's what John L. Griffith, Publisher of *Athletic Journal*, has to say:

Our editorial guidelines are relatively simple. First, we require that the articles be of a technical nature devoted to a certain phase or technique of coaching of the various sports. Second, the article must be written by a man or woman actively engaged in the coaching or administration of high school or college sports. Third, we like to have the articles about five double spaced typewritten pages in length and accompanied by as many diagrams and/or pictures as are necessary to clarify the text. The diagrams should be just rough drawings as we will have our artist put them into finished form.

If quotes are used from other publications or books, this should be clearly indicated. We do require that the article be submitted only to our publication until advised regarding its acceptance or rejection. This is usually done within two weeks' time, depending upon our staff that evaluates the articles and checks for repetition of material.

Finally, we would ask that the article be accompanied by a short resume of the author's athletic or teaching history for use in the author's block.

In January, 1979, Herman L. Masin, Editor of *Scholastic Coach* magazine, wrote an article entitled "Writing for Publication (One More Time"). He outlines the procedure for writing and submitting technical articles to Scholastic Coach. Here, in its entirety, is Mr. Masin's article:

WRITING FOR PUBLICATION
(ONE MORE TIME)

Coaches who want to write a technical article usually fall into one of two categories:

Those who've never been published . . . and are, hence, hesitant and humble. Those who have been published (even if it only was a doctoral dissertation on Biddy Basketball) . . . and are cocky and confident.

For the beginner, we say despaireth not. For the published "writer," we say stick around—you may learn something.

Writing a technical article can be rough—if you don't know how to go about it. It can be easy—if you have an orderly mind and an organized approach.

We can't supply the mind, but we can supply the approach. In fact we did it once before. Back in January 1971, we published an article on "Writing for Publication." The readers loved it. Many of them told us it was fabulously helpful and that they were filing it away for permanent reference.

Terrific. For a year or two, our manuscripts showed a distinct improvement. But time and readers move on, and a lot of new customers move in. And so here we are back where we started in 1971.

'Tis frustrating—about 75% of our contributors—being amateur writers —don't know how to prepare a manuscript. They commit the cardinal sin of going into a "ballgame" without enough preparation.

That's no way to coach . . . or do anything else in life. Everyone needs a game plan, and we'd like to pass along a little playbook on the fundamentals of writing for publication. if you think you know it all, splendid. You can move right on to "Coaches' Corner" or you can begin diagraming the 1,000 best volleyball plays of 1978—there are magazines that love this kind of stuff.

First move: Pick a subject that you know, that you haven't seen many articles on. It doesn't have to be an entire offense or defense. It can be a little gimmick or twist or just a different approach to something.

Commonplace subjects that have been written to death are off-season weight training programs, football drills, basketball's motion (or passing) game, the triple option, defensing the triple option, baseball pick off plays, defensing the first and third double steal, the dangers of weight reduction in wrestling, etc.

Point: Even a commonplace subject can be made interesting and useful with a few personal twists.

If you're not sure of your subject, write to the editor. Ask him how he feels about your idea. Or list a few ideas and ask for an expression of interest in any of them.

Never ask the editor for a topic, unless your name happens to be John Wooden or Bear Bryant. What does the editor know of your capabilities? You can't expect him to dream up a hot topic for you. If there's anything special he wants, he's going to go to someone he knows.

If you've never written before, you may ask for guidelines. Nobody can tell you actually how to write, but you can get some helpful suggestion on how to prepare a manuscript.

O.K., we're now ready to get down to the specifics of writing for publication.

What do you get out of writing a technical article? First, great personal satisfaction. Second, the discipline of articulating your ideas clearly and logically, and discovering how much or how little you know about a subject.

Third, professional aggrandizement; remember, every coach of consequence will read your article, and it will be a big plus on your resume when job hunting.

This is the reason most coaches write. Following are some of the coaches whose careers were enhanced by writing for *Scholastic Coach* as beginning coaches: Ben Schwartzwalder, Frank Leahy, Al Davis, Chuck Knox, Jack Ramsay, Sam Rutigliano, Lee Corso, Ken Meyer.

Money? Forget it. Technical magazines pay a pittance. If you're looking to get rich by writing, try Playboy. (P.S., you'll never make it—unless you're a former longshoreman, of course.)

How many magazines are there in the technical field? Three or four, depending upon what you call a magazine. *Scholastic Coach* is the only professionally edited publication. Every article receives a complete overhaul or rewrite before it is published. Reason: Our authors are not professional writers, and we believe in offering our readers clear, concise, easy-to-follow, authoritative, and completely grammatical articles. No other technical magazine can make that claim.

Though one or two others may look like *Scholastic Coach*, just read carefully and the difference will become immediately apparent. You don't even have to be an English major to see it.

How long do you have to wait for publication? Anywhere from one to six or seven months, depending upon the subject matter and the magazine. Since we try to publish our articles several months before the start of their respective seasons, coaches can't wait until the opening of their season to submit their piece. (Classic statement: "Dear Editor, the basketball season is about to begin and I thought you might be interested in an article on my stratified transitional man-to-man defense with psycho-cybernetic zone principles.")

By the time the season actually begins, we're way into the next sport season. So submit your material several months before the season for which it is intended.

How about photos? Great. If you intend to take them yourself, make sure you have the right kind of camera and a competent photographer. You can't take movie sequences with anything but a 35-mm camera. It's almost impossible to get adequate enlargements (prints) from 16-mm film. For still photos, you can use almost any camera.

Tips:

1. Make sure the players are completely uniformed. The pictures look "bush" when you let your players wear sweat clothes or perform without helmets or shoulder pads.

2. Make sure the players wear contrasting uniforms—dark and white to denote offense and defense. See that all shirts are tucked in, socks pulled up, shoes are the same.

3. Check the background. Pick a spot without a lot of cars, trees, fences, buildings, and other distracting elements. If you can't find that kind of spot, get yourself a ladder or platform, move up about five or six feet and shoot down at your subjects. That should eliminate much of the bad background.

4. Check the lighting. If you're shooting indoors, you'll probably need supplementary lighting. Have your photographer check the light level for you. It's foolish to shoot in poor light. Unless you love shadows and ghosts.

5. The best kind of enlargements are $3''$ by $5''$ black-and-white prints on heavy gloss stock. Don't shoot in color without first querying the editor. Check your enlargements. If they're too dark or too gray, shoot them over or just forget about them.

Another thing: Never use ink on a picture. In fact, other than inserting numbers in the corners, don't mark the pictures at all. You may ruin them. If you must make markings, do it with a grease pencil—such markings can be removed with the swipe of a cloth or tissue.

How about "style" in writing? Avoid it like a N.Y. Mets double-header. Amateurs sound stilted and foolish when they try to write with "style." Write as simply and directly as possible. Avoid over-adjectivizing, cliches, 10-buck words, and redundancies.

Keep your sentences and paragraphs short. Long sentences tend to become tortuous and confusing. Big blocks of words also discourage the reader. Write good, short, punchy sentences—just the way you talk on the field (unless you're a former longshoreman, of course.)

Remember, your purpose is not to entertain, but to explain. So let the funeral directors like Humble Howard orate or write with style. You observe the K.I.S.S. principle.

Absolutely the best aid on the subject is "The Elements of Style" by Strunk and White (Macmillan): a fabulous little goldmine of tips that can be purchased for a couple of bucks at any college bookstore.

The authors main thrust is the elimination of excessive verbiage—a curse —and writing simply and directly.

One other thing: If you're submitting a survey, remember that you're not writing for Research Quarterly. Avoid formulas like C89 . 12 VR the inverse ratio of bivalent quorums. (Translated: A Rolling Stone gathers no Beatles.)

Also, avoid terms that only a statistician, a laboratory researcher, or a high priest of medicine can understand: and don't submit nine-page bibliographies that everyone knows you never read and that nobody cares about anyway.

In short, if you have a great article for the Research Quarterly, send it there. Scientific researchers write for other scientific researchers, never for people.

Scholastic Coach is written for coaches, athletic directors, trainers, physical education instructors—people interested in sound, lucid, hard-core information they can use in their everyday jobs.
Write?

Mr. Masin offers these guidelines for writers:

1. If you have doubts about your topic, write to the editor for an expression of interest.
2. Write on ordinary paper: avoid that gummy, erasable stuff.
3. Double-space the entire manuscript.
4. Allow plenty of space at top, bottom, and sides.
5. Avoid excessive underlining and capitalization to emphasize certain points.
6. Place all charts and diagrams on separate sheets and draw them large. Don't squeeze a dozen diagrams on a single sheet of paper.
7. Include a brief sketch of your professional career—pictures of yourself are unnecessary.
8. Before mailing the article, check the magazine's masthead for the editor's name and the address.
9. Mail the article flat in a 9″ x 12″ envelope, don't fold it once or twice and stuff it into a small envelope.
10. Never send the article to more than one magazine at a time. Every magazine insists on initial publication rights. Wait until your article is returned before submitting it elsewhere. If you prefer to keep the original copy of the article, let the editor know that no other copies are floating around.

POINTS TO REMEMBER

Most coaches work long, hard hours to develop competitive teams. Their efforts require the support of everybody in the school and community. Therefore, in order to build a strong following, a coach must keep people up to date on the team's progress.

How? Simply by providing fresh, timely information for the school bulletin, school newspaper, and the local press.

A coach can also spread the news by working with the administration to set up athletic rallies and assemblies. In this way students can share in the joys and sorrows of team athletes.

Not all students desire to compete in athletics. Some prefer to express themselves in an artistic manner. Yet these same students play a big part in a team's success by designing banners, posters, and signs that stimulate team spirit and promote student body interest.

Coaches grow professionally by sharing knowledge and seeking new ways to improve their programs. Some coaches pass along their ideas by writing technical articles for coaching magazines. Coaches who are considering writing an article or two should take the time to learn what a publisher wants.

QUESTIONS

1. How effective is the school bulletin in disseminating information regarding a team's progress?
2. How can a coach make sure students receive information concerning the team?
3. What special problems occur when someone reads the daily bulletin over an intercom?
4. What guidelines should a coach follow in writing a daily bulletin announcement?
5. Why do you think some coaches criticize the press?
6. In what ways does the press help an athletic program gain support?
7. A coach must be a good public relations person. How can a coach build a strong rapport with the press?
8. How can a busy coach keep the school paper informed on the progress of a team?
9. Why do some teams receive more publicity than others?
10. How can rallies and assemblies help students get to know their athletic teams?
11. Why is it important for a coach to work closely with the administration in planning a rally or assembly?
12. Why do some athletic rallies fall flat?
13. How can a coach increase the chance of producing a successful rally or assembly?
14. In what way can the art department help a coach build team morale and student body support?
15. Why would a coach seek the help of art students?
16. Why do some coaches write technical articles for coaching magazines?
17. How can writing articles help a person improve as a coach?
18. How can writing technical articles enhance a coach's career?

Getting the Most
Out of Athletes

*Every human mind is a great
slumbering power until awakened
by a keen desire and by definite
resolution to do.*

Edgar F. Roberts

Coaches continually face the challenge of "pumping up" their athletes. Factors such as player experience, health, and desire determine the quality of performance at any given time.

This chapter will show how a coach's talent for developing athletes is directly proportional to the motivational forces within the athletic program. We'll see how motivational devices, like the main spring in a watch, keep athletes moving forward.

Psychologists define motivation as the activating of behavior that satisfies the individual's needs and enables the person to work toward a goal. A motivational device, then, is the tool or mechanism a coach uses to attain a goal.

Let's examine how today's coaches inspire their athletes and prepare them for competition.

THE COACH AS A PRIME MOTIVATOR

Perhaps the greatest motivator is an athlete's affection and respect for a coach. We've discussed how regard must be earned, primarily through an intelligent training program and well-organized practices.

This in itself will motivate an athlete to train conscientiously and intelligently.

In a recent survey, coaches were asked this question: What motivating devices work well for you in girding athletes for action? Here are their responses:

- Developing team strength through group pressure; that is, depending on athletes to help each other. For example, if an athlete goofs around in practice, then team members join forces and prod the athlete into working harder.
- Seeking ways to help athletes develop self-confidence. Insisting that athletes keep a personal performance chart along with a list of goals to be attained by the end of the season.
- Playing up team strength, not dwelling on weaknesses.
- Praising the performances of athletes by saying the right things at the right time. Also, by using constructive criticism to help athletes improve.
- Keeping a sense of humor through difficult moments.
- Developing a mutual respect between coach and athlete.
- Showing a genuine concern for athletes by being open, honest, and sincere.
- Continually looking for fresh ideas to include in practice sessions.
- Encouraging certain athletes to assume a leadership role.
- Pointing the total team effort toward winning.
- Rewarding individual successes in practices and contests.
- Scheduling tough competition.
- Seeking ways for athletes to reach their full potential.
- Shedding an occasional emotional tear.
- Inserting fun activities into practice sessions.
- Acknowledging a job well done at the time it occurs, not two or three days later.
- Giving athletes an occasional day off.
- Using coaching aids to spice up practice sessions.

These eighteen motivating devices have the same thing in common, each one has the coach as the main driving force. Clearly, the direction athletes take lies squarely on the coach's shoulders. Coaches must develop motivational techniques that fit their particular school and setting.

EXAMINING EXTRINSIC MOTIVATIONAL DEVICES

An athlete who performs for a prize or an award rather than the personal satisfaction it brings is said to be extrinsically motivated; for instance, an athlete who works extra hard to win the "Most Improved Athlete" trophy.

Extrinsic (artificial) rewards aren't directly related to the task. Trophies are extrinsic rewards. These awards have proliferated tremendously in recent years, creating a danger. When distributed promiscuously, they tend to cheapen performance.

Stressing extrinsic rewards undermines the intrinsic values of an activity. For instance, if a basketball player practices shooting for the sole purpose of becoming the team's leading scorer, then the fun of playing may be lost.

A carefully controlled award program can, however, be most beneficial. It motivates athletes and makes them aware of their progress.

What motivational devices are popular among coaches and athletes?

1. Charting an athlete's performance in practices and contests. Awarding points accordingly (Figure 7-1).

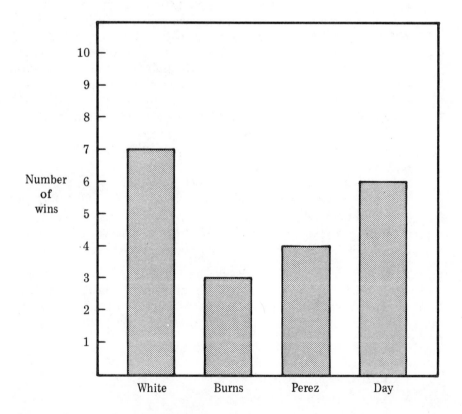

*Athlete receives five points per win.

FIGURE 7-1 Free throw contest

2. Trying to talk to every athlete every day. Congratulating and encouraging them, reserve players as well as starters. *Note:* A coach who gives praise for everything an athlete does may lose credibility. A coach builds trust and confidence by showing genuine interest in a task well done, not by indiscriminately praising every move an athlete makes.

3. Preparing athletic handbooks with sections on individual and team records, awards, and seasonal objectives.

4. Preparing team yearbooks that highlight special events and outstanding individual and team performances. John C. Hemmer, track coach, Oak Ridge High School, Orlando, Florida, issues a "name shirt" to his outstanding athletes. According to Coach Hemmer, when an Oak Ridge athlete appears on the track wearing his last name on the back of his shirt, the other competitors will know that he is a quality performer and the man to beat.

5. Publicizing individual and team accomplishments.

6. All-League teams, scholarships, and varsity letters.

7. Publishing a team calendar, including individual and team pictures, records, and schedules.

8. Organizing booster clubs and pep clubs to help publicize the team's progress.

9. Posting news clippings on bulletin boards.

10. Setting aside bulletin board areas for special recognition, e.g., honor roll (list of top performers each year), school records, league records, motivational slogans.

11. Sending out press releases—publicizing meetings, tryouts, and team or athlete honors.

12. Organizing annual alumni contests, parent/child contests, competition night, etc.

13. Organizing an incentive system by awarding a coke, hamburger, or candy bar for outstanding individual performances on a daily or weekly basis.

14. Setting up challenges; that is, giving athletes times or distances to beat. These are excellent motivators for swimmers, cross country, and track and field athletes.

The bond between team members can be a powerful extrinsic motivator. Not just peer pressure—which is an obviously important motivator—but a sense of belonging and responsibility to one's team-mates, and concern for the wellbeing of teammates. As Larry Chapman, head basketball coach at Auburn in Montgomery, has said, "The best motivator is *love*."

Athletes who equate winning trophies or medals with stardom may run into trouble after leaving school. Why? With fewer individual trophies available, an athlete may quickly lose interest and shy away from participating in recreational activities.

Coaches realize that few athletes can press a magic button and summon self-motivation. So, in order to make practices and contests more exciting, a coach looks for ways to reward athletes for their superlative efforts.

A reward must be physically challenging, yet within the grasp of every athlete. When rewards come easily, athletes may lose interest and seek other ways to gain status.

HELPING ATHLETES DEVELOP
INNER MOTIVATION

An athlete who plays sports for fun, not for prizes, is said to be intrinsically motivated. Such an athlete experiences joy and self-fulfillment from being around other athletes.

The advantages of intrinsic motivation are evident from everyday experiences. No special rewards for performance are needed to teach a girl how to dribble her new basketball or a boy to throw his new baseball. The learning and the end result have an intrinsic relationship.

Athletes who recognize their own achievements need no further incentive. They have the battle half-way won. A mere handshake, a pat on the back, or an encouraging word gives these athletes all the support they need.

How can coaches help their athletes develop self-motivation? First, coaches must motivate themselves before attempting to motivate others. A disinterested coach quickly snuffs an athlete's desire to compete. Second, by setting up a program that feeds the self-motivating mechanism.

Coaches throughout the country use many of the following intrinsic motivational devices:

1. Encourage athletes to do their best. Instill confidence by giving them an opportunity to improve their playing skills and learn all they can about their respective sports.
2. Communicate freely with athletes. Make sure athletes know the direction of the program and how each one fits into the master plan.
3. Be a disciplinarian. Most athletes want and respect a coach who establishes specific guidelines for them to follow. This stresses the value of making personal and team commitments.
4. Help each athlete set up a personal goal chart (Figure 7-2). First-year athletes would write their own prescriptions, then work during the season to reach each goal. A returning athlete outlines the previous year's accomplishments and prepares a list of new goals.

Name: <u>Carol Johnson</u>

Sport: <u>Softball (Position: Shortstop)</u>

Date: <u>February, 19</u>

Personal Goal Chart

(Batting Averages)

Junior year record							
ab	r	h	2b	3b	hr	rbi	avg.
52	15	18	3	1	1	9	.346
Senior year goals							
ab	r	h	2b	3b	hr	rbi	avg.
60	20	24	5	2	3	15	.400
Senior year record							
ab	r	h	2b	3b	hr	rbi	avg.

FIGURE 7-2 Personal goal chart

5. Set up a relaxed, unhurried atmosphere in practice. A well-organized coach can guide athletes through practice without building stress and tension. Smart coaches have little trouble staying on schedule if they tell athletes ahead of time what to expect.

6. Stay active during practices by giving instruction, watching, and recording the actions of athletes. Most athletes try to please their coaches. A coach who offers advice and then walks away kills an athlete's desire to excel. An athlete experiences self-satisfaction by demonstrating those tasks favored by the coach. A thoughtful coach praises an athlete's effort, makes any necessary corrections, and then encourages further practice.

7. Encourage each athlete to set up a progress chart (Figure 7-3). This shows an athlete's progress throughout the season. It also helps pinpoint strengths and weaknesses.

8. Strive to keep facilities (indoor and outdoor) clean and equipment in good shape. Nothing tears down morale more than a lazy coach who maintains an office littered with papers, basketball pumps, and old paint peeling from the walls.

Name: Steve Nichols

Sport: Track and Field (shotput)

Progress Chart for Shotput
Measurements in Practice

March, 19 _____

Date	Measurements		Comment
Tuesday 3/4	1) 38.2 3) 40.5 2) 39.1 4) 39.6 AVG. 39.35		TENDENCY TO DROP ELBOW
Thursday 3/6	1) 37.5 3) 40.2 2) 39.6 4) 40.6 AVG. 39.325		GET DOWN RHYTHM IN GLIDE
Tuesday 3/11	1) 41.0 3) 39.5 2) 38.7 4) 40.7 AVG. 39.975		OKAY, BUT MUST CONTINUE TO CONCENTRATE
Thursday 3/13	1) 41.5 3) 38.6 2) 40.3 4) 39.6 AVG. 39.85		SLIGHT PROGRESS, BUT STILL DROPPING ELBOW

FIGURE 7-3 Progress chart for shotput

9. Provide a cheerful, positive atmosphere. Some coaches pipe music into the locker room or play records between innings or before the start of a swim meet.
10. Spend the majority of practice time teaching skills, showing athletes the correct way to perform. A knowledgeable coach is a great asset to an athlete, especially a marginal player. Why? These athletes develop a stronger self-image when a coach helps them improve. Coaches are most effective as teachers, not judges.
11. Provide a program for athletes built around desire, dedication, determination, and discipline.

WINNING AS A MOTIVATIONAL DEVICE

Many coaches agree that winning supersedes anything else for motivating athletes. A winning program, they say, provides an incentive for most athletes to reach down deep and pull out something extra. Winning combines self-satisfaction with extrinsic reinforcement to coax athletes into winning—again and again.

Let's examine the positive side of winning.

One, winning nudges a coach into working harder and seeking effective ways to strengthen the program. Once coaches taste the fruits of victory, they develop a craving for more.

Two, winning is an excellent way to advertise the health of a team. A team's win-loss record, for many people, says it all: A good team wins, a poor team loses. Also, coaches with winning records attract top athletes.

Three, winning brings recognition, slaps on the back, and mile-wide grins. Winning puts nearly everybody in a happy mood.

Four, winning supplies proof that hard work pays off.

Five, a winning program signifies power and strength.

Six, a winner doesn't have to supply excuses for failure.

Seven, people tend to throw their support behind a winner.

Eight, a winner collects top awards and prizes, invitations to banquets, and the lion's share of publicity.

Nine, the majority of athletes selected to All-Star squads come from winning teams.

Ten, winning helps build and maintain a competitive team spirit.

In some instances, critics lambaste the athletic program for putting too much emphasis on winning. Here are their complaints.

One, hard feelings and jealousy develop because one team gets more fan support and money than another.

Two, a coach may bend the rules or resort to trickery to gain an advantage.

Three, winning may become an obsession with the coach. Family life and/or teaching responsibilities may suffer.

Four, stress on winning may cause an athlete to resent the program, quit the team, and try something else.

Five, reserves seldom see action; coach plays the same athletes in every contest.

Six, coach may drive athletes too hard in practice. Athletes complain that practice sessions are too tedious and demanding.

Seven, coach plasters gym walls and bulletin boards with "must win" material. He may spend more time on brainwashing than teaching. Note: Slogans can be valuable motivational devices, but they must be used judiciously.

Eight, an athlete may let studies slide in favor of practicing.

Some coaches have been accused of winning at all costs, using star athletes as a stepping stone to further their careers. Fortunately, most districts weed out these coaches before they turn athletes against school sports.

Coaches who constantly criticize do more harm than good. Few athletes will work to please these coaches. Athletes cannot be continually downgraded or exposed to super-competitive situations. They will eventually break down, lay down, quit, or rebel.

The sincere, realistic coach is rarely "destroyed" by the team's showing. Such a coach keeps correcting, motivating, and organizing. Most big upsets can be attributed to a coach who convinced the team that they could win.

Winning, of course, is worth pursuing because of the effort it takes to become a winner. Coaches must teach athletes how to cooperate in a competitive context and, above all, keep winning in perspective; athletes first, winning second.

THE PROBLEM OF OVERMOTIVATING ATHLETES

A coach may bombard athletes with a potpourri of praise, slogans, and high hopes until they buckle under strain. Too much of anything wears thin after a while.

Occasionally a frustrated coach loses contact with reality and makes the mistake of doing any of the following:

1. A coach may "good, good" athletes to death. In other words, no matter how poorly an athlete performs, the coach reinforces every move with expressions like: "Shake it off, you're doing fine" or "Hang in there. You'll get 'em next time." Now there's nothing wrong with positive reinforcement. After all, it's the driving force behind team spirit. But when a coach resorts to back slaps and handshakes instead of meeting a problem head-on, the athlete stands little chance of improving.

2. A coach may develop "sloganitis" and paper the locker room walls with messages designed to fire up athletes. Here are some examples:

    NEVER ACCEPT DEFEAT. IT'S A SIGN OF WEAKNESS.

    SOMEONE HAS TO LOSE. LET IT BE THE OTHER PERSON.

    WIN. THEN GRIN.

    THE THREE D's OF A CHAMPION ARE DETERMINATION, DEDICATION, AND DESIRE. THE THREE D's OF A LOSER ARE ALGEBRA, HISTORY, AND ENGLISH.

    IT'S BETTER TO BE A SYMPATHETIC WINNER THAN AN APOLOGETIC LOSER.

    Today's modern sophisticated athlete realizes there's more to life than throwing a ball, jumping a hurdle, or winning a wrestling match. Therefore, a wise coach doesn't rely totally on slogans to mentally gird an athlete for competition.

3. A coach, euphoric over winning a close contest, may give false hope to others. For example, after a basketball game, an elated coach says to the team, "You were great! Everyone plays in the next

game." Unfortunately, the coach "forgets" the promise and plays only nine athletes. The reserves, embarrassed and disappointed, lose faith in the coach and interest in playing.

4. A coach, infected with a life-long dedication to sports, may expect athletes to feel the same way. Such a coach goes overboard by encouraging athletes to eat, sleep, and think sports—twenty-four hours a day. The coach fails to realize that most athletes aren't ready or willing to devote their lives to sports.

How can a coach avoid overmotivating athletes? Here are four suggestions:

- Reward only those actions that conform to an approved style of play. If an athlete experiences trouble, locate the problem, and prescribe a plan to help the athlete recover. Offer praise only when an athlete makes an honest effort to improve.
- Slogans are good examples of positive propaganda. They help boost team morale. But watch out for "oversloganizing" athletes with pithy catch-phrases and dim-witted messages that can make a coach look ridiculous. Make every effort to keep slogans fresh and intelligent.
- Think first, speak second. Never make a definite statement when emotion controls the tongue. A sincere gesture activates the adrenaline system and sparks enthusiasm; a false promise does nothing but alienate athletes.
- Dedication can't be taught. It must come from within an individual. The best thing a coach can do is share experiences, spread enthusiasm, and model exemplary behavior.

COACHING AIDS AS MOTIVATIONAL DEVICES

Coaches are famous for seeking new ways to teach old skills. Each year sporting goods companies flood the market with motivational gadgets "guaranteed" to make every athlete a champion. But how can a coach tell if these special aids inspire athletes and improve their playing ability as well? One way is to test each aid by asking these questions:

1. Do athletes request to use the aid?
2. Is the aid accessible to all athletes?
3. Is the aid simple to use and fun to operate?
4. Does the aid provide a challenge?
5. Can the aid be adjusted to different levels of difficulty?

If athletes respond enthusiastically to an aid, the answers to Questions 1, 2, and 3 will be yes. If the aid shows promise in developing certain skills, the answers to Questions 4 and 5 will also be yes.

It's easy to see, then, that any aid which polls a unanimous decision deserves a place in the athletic program.

GOAL-SETTING FOR MOTIVATING ATHLETE AND COACH

Athletes try harder when they see themselves improve. So do coaches. Therefore, both athlete and coach should monitor their progress by setting daily and seasonal goals.

A goal, according to Webster, is the end to which a design tends; objective; aim. In short, the incentive. And everyone needs incentives to feed the desire to succeed.

Before a person sets goals, the following criteria must be considered:

1. Evaluate self. Do you have the ability and desire to reach goals?
2. Know ahead of time exactly what you hope to gain.
3. Set realistic goals. Don't shoot for the moon before your space ship is ready.
4. Make goals challenging and worthwhile. Seek major goals that are not easily attainable, and minor goals to allow for success on the way.
5. Constantly evaluate goals. Keep things moving on schedule.
6. Don't expect too much too soon. Let improvement develop at a natural pace.
7. Write everything down so you won't forget.

A daily goal for an athlete might be to throw fifty pitches (baseball), run ten 440's (track), win nearest-to-the-pin contest (golf), make three tackles in scrimmage (football), or score two goals in practice (soccer). It can be almost anything, but the action should serve to meet a specific goal. For example, a pitcher tosses fifty pitches in order to sharpen control or a football player wants to make three hard tackles to impress the coach.

A daily goal for a coach might be to teach the single leg takedown (wrestling), back-stroke (swimming), or dribbling (basketball). Daily goals give meaning to practice and guide athletes and coaches.

Seasonal goals require an athlete to make a definite commitment to excellence. A soccer player, for instance, might list these seasonal objectives:

1. Be selected to the All-City team.
2. Lead the team in scoring.
3. Win a college athletic scholarship.

Dedicated athletes know goals provide the incentive or extra push necessary to do the best job possible.

A coach's long-range plan for reaching seasonal goals hinges on the individual effort of every athlete on the team. One or two costly injuries can throw a team's hope for a thirty-yard loss. Luck plays a vital part in the success of any program. So it's imperative that a coach allows for the unexpected while assessing a team's chances of meeting seasonal goals.

For instance, it would take optimism, confidence, luck, and darn good athletes to reach these objectives:

1. Break three league records in girls' track.
2. Break five league records in boys' track.
3. Win the girls' sophomore league title.
4. Win the boys' varsity league title.
5. Place no lower than third in the sub-sectional track meet.
6. Place no lower than fourth in the sectional track meet.
7. Qualify at least eight athletes in the state track meet.

Finally, a coach should post seasonal goals. This will serve as a reminder to the coach and athletes to bear down when the going gets tough.

POINTS TO REMEMBER

Some athletes are easier to motivate than others. What "fires up" one athlete might not trigger another into action.

Athletic programs are rife with motivational devices offering both intrinsic and extrinsic rewards. Nevertheless, a coach's actions, on and off the field, largely determine how athletes will respond.

Satisfied athletes need no further incentive. They find pleasure and joy from participating. Unfortunately, some coaches lean heavily toward awards and prizes to bribe athletes into giving their best.

Winning will always be the Number One prize among competitors. The question is: How much stress should a coach place on winning? The answer, of course, depends on the attitude of those involved with athletics, including parents and the community.

Coaching aids such as pitching machines, tennis machines, batting tees, blocking dummies, swimming kick boards, and conditioning units serve to motivate athletes and get them ready for competition. A coach should test the efficiency of each aid by carefully scrutinizing their use in practice.

A coach can instill pride, boost team morale, and inspire athletes by setting a good example. In order to motivate athletes, a coach must be respected. Coaches, therefore, must possess and display the very same exemplary character traits they want their athletes to develop.

QUESTIONS

1. Why do coaches use motivational devices? Give three reasons.
2. Why are some coaches respected more than others? Give five reasons.
3. In your opinion, what motivational devices seem to work best among athletes? Give a reason for each.
4. What is meant by the statement "extrinsic rewards aren't directly related to the task?"
5. What are the main differences between an extrinsic and an intrinsic reward?
6. Why do some athletes lose interest in sports shortly after leaving school?
7. How can inner motivation help an athlete succeed?
8. Can inner motivation be self-taught? Explain.
9. Why must coaches be self-motivated before they can inspire others?
10. As a coach, how would you develop self-motivation in your athletes?
11. How is winning a motivational device?
12. In what ways can winning bring positive results?
13. In what ways can winning stir up problems?
14. How have external forces caused some coaches to win at any cost?
15. How can a coach overmotivate athletes?
16. How can overpraising athletes cause problems?
17. In what ways can a coaching aid be detrimental to athletes?
18. How can a coach be reasonably sure a coaching aid is effective?
19. Why should athletes and coaches set goals?
20. What should a person do before finalizing a goal plan?

Building a Strong Rapport with Officials

It is with our judgments as with our watches: no two go just alike, yet each believes his own.

Alexander Pope

Contests have been won or lost based on an official's call. That's a part of sports. A coach's last minute decision may decide the final outcome of a contest. That's also a part of sports. Take away any of these ingredients and fans would holler loud enough to register 9.5 on the Richter Scale.

Officials bring excitement to sports by making key calls, discussing rule interpretations with coaches, and assigning penalties to overzealous athletes and coaches.

Officials have their hands full trying to keep fans from stampeding, coaches from suffering permanent brain damage, and athletes from saying anything that might affect their playing time.

In this chapter we'll see how officials and coaches can work effectively to hold problems to a minimum and keep contests moving along smoothly.

A GATHERING OF OFFICIALS

It's not uncommon to hear an anxious fan yell out, "Hey, ref, try it again . . . this time with both eyes open." People laugh, coaches throw up their hands in disgust, and athletes walk away shaking their heads.

This seamy reaction, of course, paints a negative picture and suggests officials can't please everybody. They don't. They're trained to make decisions based on knowledge of the rules and sound judgment. People don't always agree, but one thing is clear: Without officials to control the tempo of a contest, there would be utter chaos.

In many areas, a person goes through a rigorous program before becoming an official. A local group may train officials by having them attend regular meetings and clinics, join discussion workshops, take written and practical tests, and officiate practice contests or pre-season tournaments without pay. Each newcomer is evaluated by a veteran official and rated on a score sheet (Figure 8-1).

Official's Rating

Official's Name _____

Date _____

Event _____

(Circle One)

4 Excellent   2 Fair

3 Good   1 Poor

Comment: _____

_____

_____

_____

_____

Evaluator's Name _____

FIGURE 8-1 Official's rating

Rating sheets and recommendations are sent to the section commissioner. The commissioner may pair up a newcomer with a veteran official or start the newcomer on the freshmen or junior varsity level.

An official gains recognition, status, and better assignments when high ratings pour in from coaches and fellow officials. It takes patience, hard work, and determination to reach the top in any organization.

OFFICIALS' CODE OF ETHICS

Most organizations provide guidelines for their personnel to follow. The Collegiate Commissioners Association, for example, provides the following Code of Ethics for its officials:

A good official shall:

Not officiate any game after having had any alcoholic drink that day.

Not converse with crowds at any time before, during, or after game, intermissions included.

Not request to officiate a game or games from any coach, league, or official thereof. (No official should obligate himself to any person affiliated with any game he might be assigned to officiate.)

Be in good physical condition.

Be prompt for appointments.

Not be over-officious.

Not accept league assignments for any school he has attended or coached, or has any relationship with the affiliates or coach thereof.

Not become intimate with coaches or affiliates of teams for whom he might be assigned league games.

Not criticize or attempt to explain other official's judgment on decisions to either coach, team, or affiliate thereof.

Never argue with players. If a player asks a question, he should listen to it, then give a definite and decisive answer, but should not quibble about any situation.

Assist players in the interpretation of rules when such request is made at a proper time.

Give each team his best efforts, as he is the representative employed to administer the rules of the game.

Enthusiastically adhere to the ideals of sportsmanship, qualities of loyalty, courage, unselfishness and self-control; desire for clean and healthful living and respect for wise discipline and authority. Officials' actions both on and off the court should be a credit to the profession of officiating.

It can be seen, then, that officials aren't dragged off the street and tossed inadvertently on the playing field. With few exceptions, by the time the season starts, officials are ready to call a respectable contest.

AS THE SEASON NEARS

Many official associations provide a pre-season service that benefits coaches, athletes, and officials. In Sacramento, California, for example, a referee organization puts on a free clinic for athletes and coaches. At these clinics, referees explain new rule changes, discuss major problem areas, and give demonstrations to help clarify rule interpretation. All a coach need do is phone the commissioner and set up a date.

A coach, carrying a grudge from the year before, may refuse to work with officials in any way. In fact, such a coach may criticize any program that attempts to bring coaches and officials together. Unfortunately, this attitude filters into the athletic program and influences how others think, namely athletes.

As the season approaches it becomes extremely important that coaches drill their athletes on rules and regulations. A coach or athlete who calls time out two or three times a contest for a rule interpretation tests the patience of everyone. A pre-season officials' clinic can clear up most of these problems.

Officials goof on occasion. They either misinterpret a rule or show outright ignorance. For instance, during a high school baseball game several years ago a batter hit a pitch down the right field line. The ball landed on the foul line, kicking up a cloud of powder. The umpire hollered "foul ball" and called the batter back to home plate. The batter's coach called time and ran up to the umpire. The conversation went something like this:

Coach: "Hey, ump, didn't you see the ball hit the foul line marking?"

Umpire: "Yah, I saw it."

Coach: "Well, then, why did you call the ball foul?"

Umpire: "Because it landed in foul territory."

Coach: "That's crazy. A ball that hits the line is a fair ball."

Umpire: "Wrong. The ball landed on the foul side of the line."

The offended coach didn't file a protest because his team won the game in extra innings.

Ironically, two weeks later the same umpire showed up to call a game for the offended coach. The umpire admitted his mistake, shook his head, and said, "I can't believe I made that call. You can bet it'll never happen again."

Here, then, are the advantages of holding a pre-season officials' clinic:

- It helps clarify rules for coaches and athletes.
- It identifies and isolates problem areas before they escalate into major conflicts.
- It gives everyone a chance to work together in a spirit of co-operation.
- It emphasizes the key role an official plays in athletics.
- It helps officials get into shape for the upcoming season.

Officials' organizations try hard to keep the peace. Many send out a pre-season official's form to coaches (Figure 8-2). If coaches wish to scratch officials before the season begins, this form allows them to do so. Coaches who fail to give reasons for scratching officials may wind up having those same officials call their contests. A rating system only works when everyone cooperates.

DEALING WITH PROBLEM OFFICIALS

Why do some officials have so much trouble with coaches, athletes, and fans? There could be several reasons, but let's look at three giant ones:

1. Attitude. An official takes an authoritarian stance; that is, seldom lets another person's opinion influence a ruling. Even if the official is wrong, the decision stands. This official becomes known as a tyrant, a hard-nosed ogre who eats gravel for breakfast.

2. Inconsistent Calls. A coach loses patience with an official who makes erratic calls. For instance, an umpire might call a knee high pitch a strike for three or four innings, then for some unknown reason, begin calling the same pitch a ball.

   Many coaches complain about "yellow light" officials. These are officials who approach the coach before a contest and wave caution flags. They tell the coach that they will be calling certain penalties during the contest. The coach knows from experience what to expect. An official, for example, tells a football coach to warn his athletes about clipping. The coach acquiesces, then girds himself for a rash of clipping penalties.

Pre-Season Volleyball Official's
Rating Sheet
(Date)

_____ School

_____ Principal   _____ Coach

Your cooperation is needed to assist us in pre-season information of our volleyball officials. Please rate these officials whom you have either seen work or have had last year. The Sac-Joaquin Section of C.I.F. Constitution and By-Laws state: "Ten percent is the maximum of names that coaches may delete from the list of officials sent out by the Commissioner at the beginning of the season. Officials not scratched shall be graded as to choice 1-2-3-4. *Specific and detailed reasons must be given for scratching the official.* Scratch list information shall be available, through the commissioner, to the official concerned upon his request."

Please return this form to Don Tipton, 5052 Deerpark Circle, Fair Oaks 95628. If the ratings are not returned before the first assignment sheet is to be made, the Assistant Commissioner for Women's Athletics will have to send out officials as he sees fit.

Ratings: (1) Superior   (2) Very Good   (3) Good   (4) Fair   (5) Scratched

( ) Abram, Margo	( ) McKim, Warren
( ) Bennet, Nancy	( ) Meyer, James
( ) Bradley, David	( ) Madson, Millie
( ) Brent, Virgil	( ) Pentz, Judy
( ) Bunley, Ron	( ) Phillips, Jean
( ) Clayborn, Alice	( ) Pride, Anne
( ) David, Cory	( ) Sanchez, Mary
( ) Englehardt, Butch	( ) Sandoval, Rudy
( ) Flagg, Paula	( ) Tilbert, Bob
( ) Hanson, Chris	( ) West, Murray
( ) Hartley, Brenda	( ) Wilcox, Sandra
( ) Johnson, Shirley	( ) Williams, Carl
( ) Kirk, Ronald	( ) Young, Chris
( ) Manley, Andrew	( ) Zen, Dana

FIGURE 8-2 Pre-season volleyball officials' rating sheet

3. Prejudice. An official may harbour a preconceived notion that Coach X or School Y is bad news. When this official meets Coach X or works a contest at School Y, problems may arise. Mr. Official may be itching to slap a penalty on Coach X for one main reason: to show Coach X who's boss.

Let's take the example of School Y. Prior to a basketball playoff game, the coach of School Y met an official from another league. As they shook hands, the official said, "Oh, yes, you're from the school that takes five weeks to pay its officials."

A lousy official, like an incompetent coach, seldom hangs around too long. Official Associations ask for assistance from coaches and school administrators to weed out poor officials.

The Collegiate Commissioners Association passes along certain guidelines to its members that apply to officials at every competitive level.

Here are the "Officiating Requisites" from the Collegiate Commissioners Association:

Courage, knowledge of the rules and mechanics, hustle, and tact are indispensables of a good official. But none of them is of any more importance than another prime requisite—good judgment.

Rules and Mechanics

Unfailing familiarity with the rules and full understanding of mechanics are necessary for the proper conduct of a game, but are no guarantee of optimum performance. The intent of each rule must be kept in mind. Every official should seek the happy medium between excessive strictness and undue laxity. Situations arise in a game which cannot be foreseen and which cannot be covered in a manual.

Courage—But Not Belligerence

A smooth running game can suddenly get out of hand as a result of an overly officious attitude toward players and coaches. Conversation with coach or player should always be courteous without sacrifice of dignity. If something is said or done that warrants a penalty, penalization should be done unobtrusively, and without dramatization. A game is kept under control by proper administration of the rules, which can be best accomplished if no impression of militant supervision is created.

Tact—But Not Submission

Tact is necessary but should never be a justification for retreat from a position properly taken on a decision correctly rendered.

Poise—But Not Indifference

"Staying loose" is an asset in officiating, as in any other phase of sport where fast reflexes are required. A relaxed appearance is a great help if it gives the impression of confidence. However, care should be taken to avoid the appearance of indifference. The poised official is able to remain inconspicuous as he moves to the right place at the right time.

A coach can help eliminate inferior officials by doing the following:

1. Scratch unwanted officials on a pre-season rating form. Give specific reasons for deleting officials.
2. If the officials' organization doesn't send out scratch sheets, set up your own "black list" of officials (with reasons for doing so).
3. If an official consistently causes problems, present the principal with a list of grievances. Then meet with the principal, discuss the matter, and ask for the report to be sent to the commissioner's office.
4. After every contest write down comments about the officials. Record specific incidents, both positive and negative. Underline strengths and weaknesses. Make comments immediately following the contest or the next day. A good place to register these remarks is on the back of the scorebook.

DEALING WITH PROBLEM COACHES

There are times a coach's halo slips. Officials, too, kick up their heels about the behavior of certain coaches.

Let's see what some coaches do to antagonize officials.

1. Intimidation. An intimidator bugs officials before, during, and after a contest. An intimidating coach enjoys pointing the finger of guilt at the opposition.

   For example, a football coach, known for his intimidating manner, pulled the same routine on every new official. Before each game he would walk up to the official and say, "I've studied films of the other team. You won't believe it. Those guys clip like hell. You'll really have to watch them closely."

Complaints from officials began to pile up on the commissioner's desk. So officials banded together and came up with this strategy —the next time the coach mentioned "clipping films," they would suggest that he summon the opposing coach and repeat his charges.

It worked. This reaction hit the coach like a rake handle between the eyes. He soon dropped the "clipping film" scheme. After all, he wanted to harass only one person—the official. He certainly wasn't interested in starting a feud with the opposing coach.

2. Personality Problems. A rough-talking coach who downgrades athletes puts added stress on officials. An irritated official may lose concentration when athletes take out their frustrations on opposing players.

A contest may easily get out of hand. Usually this coach collects several warnings or penalties in a short time and builds a reputation for putting on a "better" show than the athletes.

In time, irate parents, complaining athletes, and "fed up" officials muster forces to drive this individual out of coaching.

3. Lack of Organization. Officials grit their teeth when they are assigned contests involving "hit-or-miss" coaches. These are coaches who seldom have things ready to go. They are always searching for something—a piece of equipment, the first aid kit, a maintenance person, or a stray athlete. They wait until the last minute to hand in their starting lineup. And perhaps worst of all, they sometimes forget to unlock the dressing room for the visiting team. Naturally, the coach blames everyone else for delay of contest.

An official can help rectify this situation by discussing the problem with the coach. If the coach ignores the problem, the official should file a written complaint with the commissioner's office. The commissioner can pass the grievance along to the school principal.

In most instances, a meeting between the coach and principal is all it takes to clear up any difficulties the coach might be having.

WHAT OFFICIALS WOULD LIKE COACHES TO KNOW

Nobody knows for sure what another person is thinking. But coaches don't have to be soothsayers to know what pleases officials.

Here are eight points officials would like coaches to keep in mind at all times:

1. Treat officials in a polite, friendly manner. However, don't come on like college pals meeting for the first time in fifteen

years. Being overly friendly creates problems when close calls go against the opposing team.

2. Keep negative comments about coaches, athletes, or other officials to self. A coach who ridicules others in front of strangers displays poor judgment and shows a lack of good sense.

3. Have everything ready to go so the contest can start on time. Provide a safe and secure place for officials to store their valuables.

4. Pay officials on time. Either pay them the day of the contest or mail checks out on the following day. A great way to strain a relationship is to wait four or five weeks before mailing checks.

5. Refrain from reminiscing about last week's contest. Officials are concentrating on today's menu, not yesterday's leftovers.

6. Hold conversations to a minimum. Don't distract officials with needless chatter.

7. Know the rules. Read the rule book. Study any new rule changes. Avoid wasting an official's time with needless rule interpretation.

8. Let officials know in advance the preferred line of communication; that is, a specific way to relay messages between coach and official. Some coaches like to approach officials by using athletes as messengers; others prefer to use hand signals or speak directly to an official.

It's a coach's duty to provide a clear path for effective officiating. This requires a coach to plan ahead, watch for trouble spots, and attend to the immediate needs of officials.

WHAT COACHES WOULD LIKE OFFICIALS TO KNOW

Coaches and officials need to zero in on the same wave length. That's not too difficult because an official who follows a reasonable code of ethics will do those things most coaches find admirable.

Here are eight points coaches would like officials to consider throughout the season:

1. Act in a professional manner. Treat coaches and athletes with respect.
2. Know the rules.
3. Be consistent when making a call or decision.
4. Keep athletes moving at a brisk pace.

5. Keep a watchful eye for dangerous play. Alert coaches when an athlete runs the risk of injury.
6. Demonstrate a positive attitude toward athletics, not one of supreme authority.
7. Refrain from prejudging a coach, school, or athletic team. Give people a chance to prove themselves.
8. Don't cover up a mistake. Nobody expects perfection. If an error occurs, admit to it, and try not to make the same mistake again. Also, avoid coaching an athlete at the coach's expense. Never make a coach look foolish by correcting athletes in a condescending manner.

A VETERAN OFFICIAL SPEAKS OUT

Don Tipton, veteran high school and college official, serves as Commissioner of Girls' Sports, California Interscholastic Federation, in Sacramento, California.

Don says this about today's official: "Officiating is a state of mind. If you want to do a good job, you will. Some officials lack dedication. They officiate for the money or to impress somebody. They don't study the rules."

Don believes officials should let sound judgment guide them as they approach potentially explosive situations. He feels officials, especially the younger ones, will stay out of trouble if they practice these guidelines.

Before Contest

1. Interpret a rule or demonstrate anything unique only when coaches from both teams are present.
2. Carefully check equipment, facility, and playing area before starting a contest. See that everything conforms to the rules.
3. Hold all conversations with coaches and athletes to a minimum.

During Contest

1. Follow the rule book throughout the contest.
2. Hustle. A hard working, fast-moving official draws raves, not criticism.

After Contest

1. Leave. Go home. Forget about the contest. Coaches love to smother lingering officials with "what-if's."

2. Make only constructive comments. It's the best way to stay on a coach's good side.

CHOOSING A DIPLOMATIC APPROACH

A frustrated, inexperienced official might toss an athlete out of a contest before sizing up the situation. Often this reaction compounds a problem and draws fire from parents, coaches, and, of course, athletes. An official might say something like, "What else could I do? The athlete kept riding me."

The following two cases illustrate how a diplomatic approach worked for the officials involved.

Case One

During a high school varsity footbal game, a lineman swore every time he missed a tackle, lost his balance, or moved in the wrong direction. After several incidents, the referee walked up to the athlete and said, "Son, I'm a very religious man. I'd appreciate it if you'd stop your swearing." It worked. The athlete saddled the rough language for the rest of the game. (Incidentally, the official wasn't known for his religious training. In fact, he seldom went to church.)

The official could have penalized the team or kicked the athlete off the field. But he didn't. Instead he wisely chose to handle the matter in a calm, sensible fashion.

Case Two

For three straight innings the visiting team's catcher criticized every pitch the umpire called a ball. He would say things like, "C'mon, ump, shake yourself" or "Open your eyes, ump, you're missing a great game."

Finally, the umpire reached his saturation point. He bent over the catcher's shoulder and whispered, "Say, catch, your team *does* have another player who might like to catch, doesn't it?" The catcher didn't need telepathic powers to get the message. He maintained a low profile for the remainder of the contest.

Again, the official didn't want to embarrass anybody by going into a flying tirade. He opted to take a subtle approach, one that wouldn't upset the flow of action.

In each case, the official wisely let the athlete decide the next step. In this way, it would be the athlete who eliminated himself, not the official.

These two cases point up one thing. A coach should instruct athletes to cooperate with officials, not antagonize them. The coach, then, must follow this same advice by working with officials in a professional manner, one devoid of strong emotional outbursts.

MAJOR PROBLEMS BETWEEN COACHES AND OFFICIALS

Coaches and officials who enter the arena as competitors waste precious time tossing insults back and forth. Who suffers? Everyone connected with school athletics, especially the young athlete.

Why do some coaches and officials exchange barbs? In many cases, what starts out as a minor problem escalates into a major confrontation. Let's look at five areas likely to spawn major problems between coaches and officials.

1. After a contest the losing coach fills a reporter's ear with negative comments about the officials. The local paper plays up the "we was robbed" angle, and everyone in the community sympathizes with the coach.

   An official might be called incompetent or prejudiced. For example, in a high school basketball game School A held a two-point lead with three seconds left to play. A player from School B shot the ball as the final buzzer sounded. He missed the basket. The referee, however, signalled the shooter was fouled.

   After a lengthy discussion, officials decided the athlete was fouled after the buzzer. School B lost the game by two points. The coach from School B vented his anger by telling the press that the officials decision was "prejudicially motivated."

   A coach who ridicules officials through the press makes a big mistake. Officials immediately take a defensive stance, peg the coach as a cry baby, and refuse to work future contests for such a coach.

   Outside people, like reporters, sometimes pick away at a problem until it erupts and spews trouble for everyone. Therefore, an intelligent coach will be careful not to say anything that can be misconstrued by a reporter.

2. A coach spends most of the contest yelling and screaming at the official. The coach, acting as a cheerleader, stirs up athletes and gets them emotionally upset. This added pressure shakes an official's confidence and destroys concentration. Soon an official becomes agitated, loses composure, and heads for the nearest exit. When this happens, everybody loses.

Often the coach's behavior is a real test of sportsmanship, a moral lesson for young athletes. Take a baseball coach who rides an umpire over every close call. After a few innings a call or two goes in favor of the boisterous coach. The coach tells his athletes, "See. You've got to let umpires know who's boss." Message: Bully people, cheat a little, and you'll get your share of breaks.

Coaches and officials must work together and do everything possible to keep competition from getting out of hand. The key to establishing and maintaining a long-lasting relationship centers around three critical issues:

1. Demonstrating respect for one another.
2. Listening with interest to what others have to say.
3. Sharing ideas and continuing to seek the best ways to strengthen school athletics.

3. Two officials, X and Y, are working a contest together. Official X, a strong, aggressive person with several years of officiating experience has an excellent reputation. Official Y, however, is young, inexperienced, and has a tendency to rattle under pressure.

   Official X works extra hard to compensate for Official Y's inexperience. In doing so, a nervous coach may accuse Official X of overofficiating. This, of course, creates hard feelings between official and coach. Few officials smile when they are accused of being less than adequate.

4. Pressure builds during close contests. As tension increases, some officials turn into perfectionists. They try to thread the needle by coming up with perfect calls. Coaches complain that officials become more selective, but less effective.

5. A coach climbs all over an official with one thought in mind—to "jack up" athletes and get them fighting mad.

   A coach who attempts to gain an advantage by verbally abusing an official lacks sincerity, compassion, and intelligence. Perhaps a coach knows no other way to mentally gird athletes for action. Unfortunately, these negative examples leave a favorable impression on the minds of some athletes.

The only way coaches and officials can resolve their problems is to bring them out into the open, discuss them, and seek reasonable solutions. When both parties talk past each other the communication gap widens.

So whenever a problem occurs, coaches and officials should:

1. Pinpoint the problem.
2. Isolate the situation that created the problem.
3. Discuss the problem in a calm, sensible fashion.

4. Listen to the concerns of others.
5. Keep the problem within the confines of the school. Refrain from saying anything that might be misinterpreted by the press.
6. If a problem persists, seek the advice of others—athletic director, principal, district superintendent, commissioner of officials, and so on.
7. Come to a mutual agreement, one with positive overtones.
8. Remember, a final decision should benefit everyone, particularly the athlete.

HOW TO HANDLE PROTESTS

Webster says a protect is an objection lodged with an official. For instance, a coach may register a protest against a competing school for using an ineligible athlete. A protest, however, usually occurs when a coach feels an official misinterprets a rule.

In most areas throughout the country coaches file protests in accordance with rules and regulations governing interscholastic athletics.

As an example, coaches in the Sac-Joaquin Section, California Interscholastic Federation, who wish to file a protest are governed by these regulations:

1. A protest may be filed only for violation of the Sierra Foothill League Constitution or misinterpretation of rules by an official.
2. Protests shall be made in writing and mailed to the Commissioner of Officials within seventy-two hours following the game or contest, with copies to the league secretary, league president, and section commissioner.
3. Protests shall be handled by the principals within the league, meeting with the Commissioner of Officials who shall be chairman of the meeting, and who may vote in case of ties only.
4. Protests shall be sustained or lost by a simple majority of the principals present and voting.
5. Principals may appoint proxies to represent their school for voting purposes only.

WHY OFFICIALS DON'T LAST FOREVER

It's a sad day when a top-notch coach resigns. The local paper showers the departing coach with accolades and well-wishes. Most everyone who knew and respected the coach attends the farewell party. Yet when an outstanding official resigns, few people outside of the official association notice. That's really too bad. It might be different, though, if officials could build a win-loss record based on their confrontations with coaches.

In the next chapter we'll explore some of the reasons coaches hang up their clip boards, but for now let's consider five situations that occur often enough to convince some officials to retire their whistles.

1. People don't talk to officials about the weather, time of day, or coming trends in education. They bring up and pursue one subject: the bad call which caused all the furor in the last contest.

2. Coaches heavily dispute close calls even when their line of vision is more obstructed than those of the officials. To make matters worse, some coaches have to ask their athletes what happened before charging the official.

3. An athlete goofs, but tries to save face by shaking a fist at the official. Fans back up the athlete by hollering and stamping their feet. How loud the fans yell is directly proportional to the acting ability of the athlete.

4. Sometimes coaches, athletes, and fans forget that officials make mistakes and have off days too. If a coach has a bad day, there's always tomorrow. If an athlete slips, there's someone around to lend a helping hand. But if an official blows a call, the walls come tumbling down.

5. In most instances, officials stand alone. Once they make a decision, they must live with it. One official suggested the association should switch from striped shirts to jerseys with little targets all over the front and back. "Since we're out there alone," said the official, "we might as well make it easy for the fans to pick us off."

Officials, like coaches, need time to develop their skills. In doing so, they accumulate their share of bumps, bruises, and mental anguish.

A first-rate official never stops learning and never gives in to the pressures famous for driving marginal performers away. As coaches, we can't afford to lose people who have the potential for becoming exemplary officials. Therefore, a coach should strive to do the following:

1. Demand sportsmanlike behavior from athletes at all times. Stay in full control of athletes during contests.

2. Work with the school and community to keep crowds under control during contests. In many situations, the coach determines how a crowd reacts. If the coach throws a fit, athletes and fans will follow in kind.

3. When a problem occurs, discuss it without embarrassing the official, athletes, or school. A diplomatic approach reaps the highest reward.

4. Make sure athletes understand rules and regulations before a contest begins. Home court rules change from school to school. Familiarize athletes with problems likely to arise when competing on a strange facility. Needless questions asked by athletes during a contest slows down action and creates confusion. Uneasy fans strike back by yelling at the official to keep things moving.

5. Don't blame officials for coaching mistakes. Coaches should own up to their own miscues and let officials do the same.

COACHES AS OFFICIALS IN THE OFF SEASON

Coaches who decide to serve as officials during the off season gain in several ways.

First, they stay active in sports and learn what athletic departments in other schools are doing.

Second, they stay mentally alert by controlling the tempo of the contest.

Third, they experience another side of rule interpretation and how to make decisions on the spur of the moment.

Fourth, they experience a different kind of pressure by wearing the shoes of an official. They begin to see what kind of life an official lives.

POINTS TO REMEMBER

Officials add excitement to sporting contests. A close play, for instance, brings people to their feet. What happens next depends on what call the official makes. Life is seldom dull for an official.

Officials across the nation train hard for the coming season by attending clinics and workshops. Many officials donate their time by calling pre-season practice contests.

A Code of Ethics provides the framework necessary to keep officials going. A sincere official will uphold the educational aims and objectives of competitive sports.

Holding pre-season clinics helps sharpen an official's ability to call the right play at the right time. It also helps an official get into shape mentally and physically.

Officials may strain working relationships with coaches by being too rigid, too independent, or too quick on the trigger. Coaches, too, may be overly critical and abusive when it comes to questionable calls. In short, unless officials and coaches agree to coordinate their efforts, problems may continue for a long, long time.

A smart official sticks to the rules, remains unbiased, and limits conversations with athletes and coaches. The less said, the better.

Officials as well as coaches burn out when the negative outweighs the positive. As pressure mounts, survival becomes a challenge.

As coaches we must let officials know when they do a splendid job and encourage them to keep up the good work. Let's face it. Without an official to run the contest, chaos would soon replace order.

QUESTIONS

1. Why is it important for an official to receive adequate training before working a contest?
2. What type of training do many officials go through?
3. In your opinion, how effective is a rating system for officials? Explain.
4. Why should officials be guided by a Code of Ethics?
5. What should be included in a Code of Ethics?
6. How effective are pre-season official clinics? Explain.
7. What three things that can benefit an athletic program are covered in many pre-season official clinics?
8. Why do some officials experience more problems with coaches and athletes than others?
9. Why do some officials build prejudices against certain coaches and school districts?
10. How can "yellow light" officials create problems for the coach?
11. What can a coach do to eliminate consistently poor officiating?
12. Why do some coaches irritate officials? How can officials remedy the situation?
13. How does attitude play a big part in building rapport between coaches and officials?
14. What things can a coach do to make officiating more effective?
15. Why do some people become officials? List four reasons.
16. Which areas are likely to be trouble spots between coaches and officials?
17. How can coaches and officials resolve their problems? Give three examples.
18. What is the purpose of a protest?
19. Who should determine the guidelines for filing a protest?
20. Why do some officials give up officiating after a year or two?
21. Why should coaches do all they can to encourage competent officials to stay in the association?
22. How can officiating in the off season help a coach understand what an official goes through?

9

Coaching Burnout

The discontented man finds no easy chair.

Benjamin Franklin

There are different reasons why coaches give up their posts. It's understandable how a person who has coached for ten or fifteen years might choose to slow down, change direction, and try something new.

A person may decide to take a year off from coaching and teach night school, attend college, sell real estate, or go fishing. That's okay. The time off acts as a stimulant by pumping fresh energy into the coach's tired system.

What about the coach who waves a white flag and hollers "I've had it!"? The message comes through loud and clear—the coach wants out. Now.

Enter burnout. Exit coach.

COACHING BURNOUT: WHAT IS IT?

Burnout is a condition that results from the buildup of stress, tension, and anxiety. A coach weakens under the mounting pressure and becomes physically and emotionally drained.

Fatigued coaches who decide to "pack it in" say things like:

"I'm just totally drained."

"Hey, I'm wasting my time. The kids today aren't dedicated to sports."

"Nobody cares. Whenever I ask for something, I get the door slammmed in my face."

Why do some coaches burn out? Simply because they become emotionally exhausted from dealing with people. And, in many cases, these close encounters produce conditions of chronic tension and stress. Take, for example, a coach who turns out losing teams year after year. Negative feelings abound. Mental strain leads to physical exhaustion.

There seems to be a parallel between burnout and low morale, absenteeism, and mediocrity in coaching performance. A losing coach tends to blame failures on bad luck, poor officiating, and lack of support from others.

According to a recent survey given to active coaches across the country, these factors lead to coaching burnout:

1. Too much time spent in preparing for competition.
2. Athletes don't care if they win or lose.
3. Too much pressure from everyone.
4. Few positive strokes from parents or administrators.
5. Taking sports too seriously.
6. Overenthusiasm followed by too many disappointments.
7. Specialization in only one sport.
8. Parental conflicts.
9. Program develops too slowly. Losing seasons, tight money, and poor facilities hamper progress and dampen team spirit.
10. Coach dwells on the belief that athletes "aren't what they used to be" and feels compelled to leave coaching.
11. Coaching too many sports in a single year.
12. Problem athletes take the fun out of coaching.

RECOGNIZING BURNOUT SYMPTOMS

Nearly every coach, at one time or another, experiences early signs of burnout. A coach may ignore these signals and miss the hidden message they carry. An occasional headache, for instance, might hold little significance. But a series of pounding headaches brought on by losing streaks, unruly athletes, or complaining parents may wear down a coach faster than the incoming tide over a sand castle.

What are the telltale signs of burnout?

1. Disenchantment. In other words, the thrill is gone. A coach loses the pre-season urge to get under way. Here's what happens. A coach pours every drop of energy into building a competitive squad. However, for a hundred reasons the coach seldom builds a winner. The

coach's teams never seem to reach the superlative level of expectation. Disillusionment replaces hope. As each season grows longer and longer, the prospect of quitting looms bigger and bigger.

2. Fatigue. Excellent coaching demands a huge chunk of a person's time, energy, and patience. Such dedication saps the energy barrel and tests a coach's level of endurance. When a coach's output greatly exceeds the input, the coach is likely to try something less tiring and more rewarding.

3. Apathy. Apathy, a cousin of disenchantment, whispers, "You don't care any more. Leave coaching. Do something else." As the whisper grows louder, other things in the coach's life become more appealing.

   During this time a strange feeling comes over the coach. Many things suddenly become important and worth investigating. New interests spring up like fleas on a hot carpet. When the time is right the coach waves goodbye.

4. Anxiety. As pressure mounts, the coach pushes harder and expects more from each athlete. Others notice how little things irritate the coach. They begin to shy away. Stress and tension pave the way for early retirement.

5. Supersaturation. A coach agrees to handle two or three sports during the season. Everything seems fine until classroom paper work piles up on the coach's desk. The coach falls behind. Students grumble, parents complain, and counselors hammer away at the coach.

   As a classroom teacher, the coach resents student pressure to work faster and take more interest in academic affairs. As a coach, the classroom teacher might resort to cutting down on practice time, cancelling several practice sessions, and relying on scrimmages and intra-squad games to survive loosely organized sessions.

   The coach, like a ping pong ball, bounces back and forth between classroom and playing field. Frustration, tension, and anxiety gang up on the coach. This could well be the coach's last year.

6. Conflict. A coach grows weary battling other coaches over use of facilities and equipment. A sharing system only works when everyone cooperates. With few exceptions, two or three coaches manage to cause problems for others.

   Conflicts lead to emotional tantrums which promote hard feelings between coaches. A coach soon tires of stepping off ten paces with another coach just to get a fair share of the pie.

7. "Nomoneyitis." Everybody needs money. There never seems to be enough to go around. A coach may not have the time or desire to set up fund raising projects. Perhaps the coach feels it's the school's

duty to supply athletic teams with enough money to survive. At any rate, a non-supportive school district forces a coach to make a decision—either coach under adverse conditions or resign.

There are other symptoms that may eventually lead to burnout. They are:

- A feeling of being "used" by an underpaying school system.
- A feeling of being a servant to self-centered athletes.
- A sensing of disrespect for the monetary worth of what a coach does.
- Failing health partially due to overwork.
- Expecting more from self than capable of delivering.

The following questions will help active coaches learn if they have some of the symptoms of coaching burnout:

1. Do you get upset easily when your athletes make physical mistakes? YES NO
2. Do you feel there are no excuses for athletes to make mental mistakes? YES NO
3. When you lose a key athlete or two, are you ready to write off the season? YES NO
4. Are you easily intimidated by disgruntled parents? YES NO
5. Do you blame yourself most of the time when things go wrong? YES NO
6. Do you lose patience with athletes who show little or no improvement? YES NO
7. Do you find yourself "badmouthing" the school and community for showing a lack of support? YES NO
8. Do you often feel like you're "spinnning your wheels" and falling behind in your teaching responsibilities? YES NO
9. Do you often curse yourself for coaching when you could be doing something else? YES NO
10. Do you become more irritable and short-tempered while coaching than at any other time? YES NO
11. Are there certain occasions when you feel officials are favoring the other teams? YES NO
12. When pressure mounts during close contests, do you become overly excited? YES NO
13. Are you having trouble preparing yourself mentally for the coming season? YES NO
14. Do you feel today's athlete lacks dedication, desire, and determination? YES NO
15. Are you getting tired of maintaining your own playing facilities? YES NO

16. Do you feel the administration is supporting your program as it should? YES NO
17. Do you have a tendency to give up when things go wrong during a contest? YES NO
18. Do you find yourself holding grudges against certain athletes? YES NO
19. Are you more concerned with winning than with anything else? YES NO
20. Do you feel sports should be the most important event in an athlete's life? YES NO
21. Are you bothered by the low pay most coaches receive? YES NO
22. Are you finding it increasingly difficult to prepare yourself physically for coaching? YES NO
23. Do you feel that the local press "has it in" for you? YES NO
24. Are there several occasions when you cancel practice to do other things? YES NO
25. Do you have trouble sleeping at night during the coaching season? YES NO
26. Do you often feel depressed and threaten to quit coaching? YES NO

If you answered "yes" to any of these questions, you have symptoms that may indicate coaching burnout.

WHAT A COACH DOES TO BRING ABOUT BURNOUT

In this section we'll see how a coach contributes physically and mentally to the onset of burnout.

Physical Factors

- A coach, especially one new to the district, takes on too much work. This person wants to help out and finds it difficult to say no.
- A coach doesn't work out in the off-season and, as a result, nurses sore muscles for most of the year. The coach, being susceptible to injury, loses enthusiasm and limps through one practice session after another. The thought of doing something less strenuous becomes more attractive each day.
- A procrastinating coach waits until the last minute to organize practices, gather equipment, and inspect facilities. Usually the procrastinator wastes time running around looking for things. Confusion and frustration gnaw away on the coach's nerves like a termite in a rotting log.

- A coach from a poor school district spends considerable time preparing facilities for competition. Such a coach may line fields (soccer, football, and baseball), set up tables, mats, and bleachers (wrestling) or help clean playing courts (tennis and basketball). The same coach may volunteer to officiate contests for other coaches in order to save the school money.

  The school may have an understaffed maintenance department which only spends one day a week servicing athletic facilities. The coach becomes mentally and physically exhausted half-way through the season by trying to keep facilities in playing condition.
- An active coach tries to relive the past by vigorously working out with athletes. As the years pass, however, it grows harder for the coach to get into shape. Muscles stay sore longer and interest in competing dwindles. Under these conditions, a coach may bow out of athletics and seek other employment.

MENTAL FACTORS

- A coach takes on the characteristics of an acceptor by pleading guilty to most of the team's ills. As problems mount, the coach may lose confidence, become depressed, and decide to do something less strenuous.
- A coach allows outside forces to control the decision-making process. Let's take the hypothetical case of Anne Davis, girls' varsity basketball coach.

  Here's Coach Davis's problem: Should she start Louise or Rhonda at center in tomorrow's basketball game?

  The decision-making process lights up the electrical switchboard in Coach Davis's brain. Positive and negative thoughts bounce around like pebbles in the bed of a pickup truck. It works something like this:

Negative Alternatives	Positive Alternatives
1. If I start Louise, then Rhonda may quit the team.	1. If I start Rhonda, then her parents will be happy.
2. If I start Louise, then Rhonda's father will blow his stack.	2. If I start Rhonda, then she'll be happy.
3. If I start Louise, then Rhonda may think I favor Louise.	3. If I start Rhonda, then she'll feel I have confidence in her.

After weighing the alternatives, Coach Davis makes her decision: She'll start Rhonda. After all, Louise is more mature and less emotional than Rhonda. Louise will understand and accept the decision without becoming upset. Besides, both athletes will see plenty of action.

Does anyone lose? Maybe yes, maybe no. It depends on the attitude of athletes. For example, if team members suspect that Coach Davis is easily intimidated by moody athletes or aggressive parents, they'll turn thumbs down on practically any decision she makes. When this happens, a coach's days are numbered.

- A coach teeters back and forth in his or her treatment of athletes. The coach lacks consistency in handling discipline problems, makes impulsive decisions, and waits until the last minute to plan practice sessions. Athletes peg the coach as a flake and quit working to please the coach.
- A coach plays the role of dictator and runs the squad like an army drill instructor. Athletes bark, parents complain, and school officials reprimand the coach for overaggressive conduct.

    The coach retorts by accusing today's athlete of being soft, lackadaisical, and dull.

    The coach decides these young athletes aren't worth saving in a "soft touch" society. The coach resigns at the end of the season.
- A coach spends the pre-season building a powerful team on paper. Everything falls neatly into place. Unfortunately, three weeks after the season begins, injuries claim three athletes, one key player moves, and two more are declared ineligible. The coach's game plan melts like an ice cube in July. It only takes a few seasons like this to kill a person's desire to continue coaching.
- A coach allows negative impressions to smother positive thinking. One coach, for example, resigned after spending the last three years bickering with athletes. After turning in his resignation, he asked the principal, "Why should I continue to put my sanity in the hands of juveniles?"

ATHLETES AND COACHING BURNOUT

Some ex-coaches confess that crybaby athletes drove them out of coaching. Here are eight pressure situations brought about by athletes that push a coach near the breaking point.

One, moody athletes with sensitive feelings whine about anything that doesn't go their way. A coach makes a gallant effort to keep these athletes content without bypassing the needs of other team members. The coach, who is fighting a difficult battle, may crumble under the stress.

Two, certain athletes get down on themselves and give up in tight situations. A coach tries to instill confidence by pumping up these athletes with positive strokes. Nothing works. The coach feels responsible for not motivating these athletes.

Three, a coach builds a "buddy buddy" relationship with athletes. Athletes respond by developing a carefree attitude toward competition. After all, since the coach is their pal, nothing drastic will happen. The coach quickly realizes that a country club atmosphere suppresses competitive spirit. Now the coach faces the super challenge of tightening discipline and gaining control of the team again.

Four, a coach, acting as soul saver, keeps trouble makers on the team. These athletes miss practice, misbehave in class, and spend more time in the office than on the athletic field.

After several disappointing seasons the coach loses interest in trying to make chicken salad out of turkey liver. The coach fades into oblivion.

Five, a coach dedicates himself or herself to helping athletes reach their full potential. Some athletes, of course, develop into first-class performers; others fail because they either don't care, are too lazy, or have other interests.

The presence of apathetic athletes may suggest to others that the coach doesn't know how to develop talent. The coach may be thinking the same thing.

Six, a coach finds out that four veteran athletes aren't returning. It seems two found after-school jobs, and two plan on going out for another sport. The coach's dream of winning the league championship shatters into a million tiny pieces.

Seven, some athletes ridicule the athletic program and challenge the coach's ability to handle players. These athletes keep trouble brewing throughout the season.

Eight, a coach allows parental pressure to direct the thinking of certain athletes. For instance, an aggressive parent with miles of "athletic experience" offers to help the coach organize and guide the team. If the coach agrees, the coach may soon become the highest paid assistant around. Athletes fail to support a coach who allows others to take charge and run the show.

What can a coach do to limit problems created by athletes? Here are seven suggestions:

1. Make coaching philosophy crystal clear to athletes before the season begins. Leave no doubt in anybody's mind.
2. Be a tough, but fair, disciplinarian.
3. Be consistent, honest, and assertive when making a decision.

4. Direct parental complaints to the school principal or athletic director. Handle these problems in a calm, reasonable manner.
5. Weed out any athletes who attempt to downgrade fellow players or the athletic program.
6. When problems among athletes occur, find out why. Keep an open mind, but stay in control at all times.
7. Do the best job possible.

PARENTAL CONFLICTS
CONTRIBUTE TO BURNOUT

There are parents who relive their glory days in sports through their children. These parents see their sons and daughters as future college stars, albeit many struggle to make the high school squad.

These athletes are led to believe that they can play on nearly any college team in the country. But when these athletes fail, irate parents spill forward with comments like these:

"Mary's coach didn't understand her. She didn't know how to handle her."

"I wanted Bob to pitch, not play the outfield. Bob lost interest in athletics in his senior year."

"Frank practiced his heart out every day. What good did it do? He seldom got to start in a league game."

"Joan said the coach played everybody but her in league games. She felt the coach didn't like her."

"Mark told me the coach was unorganized, inconsistent in handling athletes, and didn't know the first thing about coaching."

Notice that in every case it's the coach who fumbles, not the athlete. Maybe a parent feels that the coach's unorthodox style of teaching techniques has retarded the progress of athletes.

A coach can be whittled down by two kinds of parental pressure —indirect and direct.

Indirect Parental Pressure

John B. won several athletic awards participating in youth programs prior to entering high school. However, John whines constantly during practice and finds fault in many things the coach does. Besides, John's not used to playing on the second team.

John's father believes the coach is making a mistake by not starting his son. He doesn't say anything to the coach, but tells John to keep playing "the way I taught you."

Direct Parental Pressure

Direct parental pressure enters with the force of a megaton bomb. A belligerent parent expresses anger by hollering out during a contest, collaring the coach before or after a contest, phoning the coach at home, complaining to the school principal or district superintendent, or by attending practice sessions and offering unsolicited advice.

These aggressive behaviors tax the staying power of a coach, and unfortunately, drive many outstanding people out of coaching each year.

How can a coach hold parental interference to a minimum? Many coaches find these five guidelines helpful:

1. Be sure each athlete returns a pre-season letter (outlining policies and procedures) signed by parents.
2. Hold a pre-season meeting with athletes and parents. Go over program goals and objectives. Give everyone a chance to speak on any issue relevant to improving the athletic program.
3. Stay within district and state guidelines.
4. Keep athletes and parents informed on present and future team plans. Whenever possible, find a way for parents to take part in building a strong athletic program.
5. Maintain an open door policy. Listen hard to what parents and athletes have to say, but weigh all factors before making any decisions. Encourage input but base decisions on what will be best for the total program.

A COACH SAYS GOODBYE

Coaches who resign their posts cite several major reasons for doing so. One of these is lack of administrative support.

Recently, for instance, a high school baseball coach resigned after ten years of dedicated service. His impressive record included six league championships. The local press ran a feature on the coach highlighting his successful coaching career.

According to the article, the coach resigned for personal reasons. He felt he could no longer work effectively under a non-supportive administration.

What did the coach mean by a non-supportive administration? He cited three specific areas:

1. The administration didn't share his interest in maintaining a highly competitive program.
2. He received little or no help in preparing and maintaining the playing fields during the year.

3. He found himself constantly arguing instead of discussing matters with the administration.

The administration accepted the coach's resignation without any offer of reconciliation. This led the coach to ask himself, "Just how important am I to the school district?"

Who suffers when a competent coach resigns under these circumstances? Everybody does.

The coach suffers because he's exchanging a ten-year investment for the twenty or thirty minutes it takes to prepare a resignation.

The athlete suffers because he is partly responsible for the coach's decision to leave. It's similar to the way a young child feels when his parents file for divorce. (Note: The coach stated in the newspaper article that his athletes had absolutely nothing to do with his decision to resign. In fact, he said the toughest part of resigning was leaving his athletes.)

The athletic program suffers because a new coach needs time to build a winning program. Both coach and athlete must learn to work well together. If may be several years before the team regains its championship form.

COMMUNITY PRESSURE AND BURNOUT

Some coaches feel the hot breath of local merchants blowing down their necks. If they hit a dry spell and lose too many contests, then pressure increases until the weather changes.

Major spectator sports like football and basketball attract attention in a community. A highly supportive community wants—and expects—a winning program. Simply stated, the coach either suits up a contender or looks for employment elsewhere.

In this situation a coach must go out into the community and talk to the merchants. The coach must keep merchants posted on team events and directly involve them in future plans.

Many local merchants are willing to support the athletic program by donating small awards (hamburgers, milk shakes, movie passes) to outstanding athletes. Also, they let the coach display photos of team players and team schedules in prominent places.

A coach who hides in the gym and criticizes community leaders doesn't last too long. If a community wants to get rid of a coach, certain merchants contact the district superintendent or school principal, register a complaint, and pour on the pressure until something happens.

A coach may not like the heat and head for the nearest exit. Whether or not a coach quits depends on how high the temperature rises. It also depends on the rapport between the superintendent, principal, and coach. For instance, if the superintendent refuses to fold under community pressure, the coach wins. Conversely, a wilting superintendent sends the coach down for the third time. In most cases, the principal supports the superintendent's decision.

Clearly, then, an aggressive community can convince a coach to try something less strenuous, something far away from coaching. A stubborn individual may choose to continue coaching despite the opposition. Most coaches, however, would gracefully bow out and let somebody else take over. These coaches are mentally and physically exhausted from battling with the community.

HOW THE LOCAL PRESS SHORTENED
A COACH'S CAREER

As a rule, the local press speaks favorably about athletes and coaches. Most newspaper make a sincere effort to print only those events that cast a positive light on an athletic program. After all, a reporter, in most instances, receives information directly from coaches.

Occasionally a feud erupts between the press and a coach. Maybe the paper misquoted the coach or criticized a decision that backfired. These are the exceptions rather than the rule.

A responsible reporter will not print any questionable or derogatory material about a coach or team without checking the sources firsthand. Several years ago a small town newspaper printed a letter written by an anonymous person. The letter accused the varsity basketball coach of being incompetent, stupid, and lacking in common sense. It also labelled the coach as prejudiced and "dangerous to the health and well-being of today's youth."

The outraged coach called the paper's editor, reprimanded him for printing such a damaging letter, and demanded that the editor print an apology. The district superintendent backed the coach by writing an editorial calling the person who wrote the letter a coward with questionable morals. The written apology appeared in the paper next to the superintendent's letter.

Unfortunately, the damage had been done. The letter's impact hit the coach hard; he resigned at the end of the season.

HOW TO PREVENT COACHING BURNOUT

Today there are specialists for practically every ill known to man. Yet a simple case of burnout can go undetected until a coach's energy pool dries up.

In educational literature, teacher burnout is commonly referred to as the big click; that is, the energy switch is stuck in the off position.

A coach, like a teacher, has a switch that can be turned off and on. Burnout does not have to be a final state, only an interim problem.

Dr. Dennis Sparks, director, Northwest Staff Development Center, Livonia, Michigan, offers these specific suggestions for avoiding burnout:

1. Good physical health helps immunize coach against stress and burnout. Practice what you preach with your team—get a good night's sleep; eat three meals a day, especially breakfast; use your "season" to get in shape, and maintain it throughout the year by regular, vigorous exercise; and quit smoking and consuming alcohol (or drink only in moderation).

2. Learn to pace yourself during the high pressure times of the school year. You can't do everything, so establish priorities and do only those things that are most important to you.

3. Involve yourself in activities that are intrinsically satisfying to you. Develop a hobby or avocation that presents a change of pace from your daily routine. The good feelings that come from this will help carry you through the unavoidable frustrations and disappointments of coaching.

4. Get together with others who understand your situation and talk about your feelings. Much of the internal tension you may experience will diminish and be put in its proper perspective as you discuss your concerns with colleagues.

5. Identify your strengths and successes. By focusing on the rewards that you get from coaching you can maintain a better sense of balance when things don't go well. Remember to attend and savor the moments and successes that can make working with young people so rewarding.

6. Most importantly, keep in mind that it is not the events of our lives that produce stress and burnout, but the interpretation or meaning that we give to these occurrences. Too often our expectations for self and others are unrealistically high, and consequently we cannot help but feel disappointment and failure. A "winning at all cost" philosophy on your part or at your school often leads to unnececessary (and unhealthy!) pressure and tension.

7. Recognize that a life-long coaching career may not be in your best interests. Don't sacrifice your health and happiness for an activity that is no longer satisfying.

POINTS TO REMEMBER

Coaching burnout—a condition that results from stress, tension, and anxiety in its victims—builds over the years and causes many coaches to quit.

What are the problems that lead to burnout? Apathetic athletes, deplorable playing conditions, lack of cooperation among fellow coaches and teachers, inadequate pay, interfering parents, community pressure, and non-supportive administrators are among those listed.

How can a coach prevent burnout? One way is by setting up a personal plan that includes the following:

1. Daily exercise.
2. Eating well and getting adequate rest.
3. Leaving your coaching headaches on the field.
4. Developing a hobby to take your mind off coaching.
5. Always having something to look forward to. This will keep your head up and your spirit happy.
6. Seeking to improve. Read. Talk to coaches in the field. Attend coaching clinics and seminars. Come up with fresh ideas to try in practice.
7. Setting realistic and flexible goals for yourself and athletes.
8. Doing your part, but knowing when to say no.

QUESTIONS

1. What is coaching burnout?
2. Why should a coach be on the lookout for early signs of burnout?
3. What are some of the early signs of burnout?
4. Why is it difficult to know when a coach might burn out?
5. Why might a coach develop the feeling of being "used?"
6. In your opinion, which factor—physical or mental—puts the most pressure on a coach? Explain.
7. What physical factors are most likely to lead to burnout? Why?
8. What mental factors are most likely to lead to burnout? Why?
9. Why is it a dangerous practice to "buddy up" to athletes?
10. Why does a coach who goes overboard trying to help an athlete sometimes run into trouble?
11. What can happen when a coach depends too much on certain athletes?
12. How can parents become a problem for the coach?
13. How should a coach handle interfering parents?
14. What is meant by indirect parental pressure? Give an example.
15. What is meant by direct parental pressure? Give an example.
16. What can a coach do to minimize parental pressure?
17. How does the athletic program lose when an experienced coach leaves?
18. How can a community help a coach build a strong athletic program?

19. What things can a community do to get rid of an incompetent coach?
20. How can the local press help a school's athletic program?
21. How can the local press be a detriment to a school's athletic program?
22. Can coaching burnout be prevented? If so, list four or five effective ways.

Reducing the Risk
of Athletic Injury

*It is a good thing to learn caution
from the misfortunes of others.*

Publilius Syrus

Athletes seldom anticipate injury when they practice or enter a contest. Yet many of them limp away wondering if they will see action in the near future.

All athletes must accept the possibility that they will get hurt, perhaps seriously. The potential for injury lies in any activity that requires an athlete to stop quickly, make sudden moves, or smash into another athlete.

In this chapter we'll stress those factors that lead to athletic injuries and what the coach, athlete, and school can do to minimize the risk of sports injury.

THE PRE-SEASON EXAMINATION

Some school districts hold group physical examinations during the summer. Athletes gather in the gymnasium or auditorium, form several lines, and are examined by attending physicians. Other school districts require athletes to make their own arrangements for physical examinations. These schools require athletes to file examination results before reporting to practice.

A summary of the examination results should be recorded on an Athletic Clearance Card (Figure 10-1). If an athlete has any special problem which might interfere with sports participation, it will appear on the section marked "Injuries."

Athletic Clearance Card

19___ -19___

Please Print

Name _____   Birth Date _____
     Last Name   First   Middle

Address _____   City _____

Telephone No. _____

Father's Name _____

Family Doctor _____   Telephone No. _____

Name of Health or Accident Insurance Co. _____

Consent Slip _____   Grade _____

Physical Exam. _____   Age _____

Tetanus _____   Weight _____

                                    Height _____

Signed _____
     Athletic Director or Dept. Head

INJURIES: _____

_____

_____

_____

_____

_____

_____

FIGURE 10-1 Athletic clearance card

James G. Garrick, M.D., the director of Center for Sports Medicine, San Francisco, California, has this to say about the pre-season examination:

The pre-participation examination is much like the elephant being examined by blind men—it appears differently depending upon how it is approached. To the school administrator it fulfills the school's legal and insurance requirements. To the coach it is theoretically a means of starting the season with athletes who have some common level of health and fitness. To the idealist it may be a means of attempting to prevent injuries. To the physician it should be an opportunity to discover "treatable" conditions that will interfere with or be worsened by athletic participation. In reality, it is probably an annual period of frustration, unkept office appointments, and frantic phone calls the day before the first turnout.

A child athlete offers the most potential for accomplishing something meaningful in the pre-participation examination. As athletes become more experienced, one is less likely to discover significant medical problems during the course of an examination. Thus the first few pre-participation examinations uncover conditions that will preclude specific athletic activities. Later in the athlete's career one usually looks for (and finds) only the residuals of previous injuries. For the experienced athlete, the examination serves primarily as a quality control of treatment and rehabilitation of previous injuries.

Realistically, save for requiring complete rehabilitation from prior injuries, the pre-season examination offers little opportunity for preventing injuries. Generally, we know little about the factors predisposing to injury. Commonly advocated conditioning programs that stress stretching and strengthening are better justified in enhancing performance than in preventing injury due to the absence of any evidence of injury reduction associated with their use. Most conditions generally regarded as disqualifying—apparently so considered because they would appreciably increase the risk of injury or the consequences of injury were one to occur or worsen health—are so obvious that there would be little question of participation because the athlete would be under active medical care.

The keys to a successful pre-participation examination program are planning and adequate assistance. The physician is required for a small portion of the process. Those responsible for the conduct of the sport (coaches, school administrators, etc.) must assume the responsibility for organizing and providing personnel for the examination.

Regardless of how physical examinations are planned, no school district should allow an athlete to compete without completing an examination and filing the results with the school district.

In order to avoid legal problems, a coach should:

- Have in possession at all times an Athletic Clearance Card for each athlete.
- Make sure each card is properly filled out and signed by the Athletic Director or Department Head.
- Under no circumstances allow an athlete to practice or play in a contest until the coach receives an Athletic Clearance Card.

Athletes use various excuses for not having their clearance cards. Here are some favorites:

"The track coach has my card."

"It's in my locker. I'll bring it tomorrow."

"It's in my dad's glove compartment."

"I gave it to you yesterday, remember?"

Simply stated, no card, no play. This basic rule will keep everyone out of trouble.

AVOIDING EARLY-SEASON INJURIES

An early season injury can occur to any athlete at any time. But many injuries could be avoided if the coach adequately prepared athletes beforehand.

Coaches who neglect to prepare athletes before the season begins make a big mistake. Often these athletes arrive on the first day of practice at different levels of fitness. Some athletes have been working out on their own; others have done next to nothing. Yet, in many cases, the coach starts everyone at the same pace.

Let's examine several things a coach can do to prepare athletes for early season conditioning drills.

1. During the pre-season meeting, discuss the importance of pre-season conditioning. Demonstrate the proper way to exercise and stretch out tight muscles.
2. Give athletes a list of exercises and activities necessary to condition those muscles needed for active competition.
3. Give athletes a weekly exercise schedule to follow. Include such things as diet (nutritional requirements), health tips (weight control, energy requirements, etc.), how to dress during inclement weather.
4. Provide athletes with a list of common injuries that occur during pre-season conditioning. Include the recommended first aid procedures for those injuries.

    For example, under "Muscular Soreness," a coach might offer these suggestions which the American Medical Association lists in its book, *Comments in Sports Medicine.*

   • Warm up before beginning an exercise program or engaging in an athletic event.

- Include stretching exercises in the warm-up.
- Incorporate progression in a training program to gradually increase the load and duration of the exercise program.
- Avoid bouncing exercise and jerky muscle contractions that exert excessive tension on muscle fibers and connective tissue.
- Warm down after vigorous activity to allow the muscles to dissipate the waste products (lactic acid).

For relief of sore muscles, use ice, cold packs, or cold water for about fifteen minutes to help ease the pain. Cold will also help reduce the possible swelling.

Light exercise should also help, as will a quick rub-down with soothing massage lotion. Many trainers advocate putting the sore muscles on stretch.

5. Encourage athletes to begin working slowly at first. Then, as the season nears, have them step up the pace.

When the season begins, a coach should be able to start practice sessions at a steady clip. Theoretically, every athlete will report in top shape. Realistically, few of them do. For one reason or another, many athletes fail to follow their pre-season conditioning schedule. So a wise coach, rather than risk injury, will do the following.

1. Adjust activities to match the conditioning level of most athletes.
2. Gradually bring athletes into shape. Provide sufficient rest periods during heavy workouts.
3. Stress those activities that condition muscles needed for sport.
4. Caution athletes about warning signs of pre-injury symptoms. For example, chest pain, nausea, headache, and dizziness.
5. Insist that athletes dress appropriately during workouts. This seems obvious but some athletes think that wearing tee shirts and shorts during cold, windy days is a sign of strength.
6. Regulate practice sessions to coincide with weather conditions, available facilities, and time of year. It makes little sense to hold long, tiring workouts in a crowded gym or on a wet playing field.
7. Be aware of player attitude. If athletes grow restless and begin complaining, re-examine practice sessions. They may be too long or devoid of challenging activities.
8. Keep athletes moving from one activity to the next. Lingering athletes tend to bunch together and waste time.

HOW ATHLETES CONTRIBUTE
TO THEIR OWN INJURIES

The most conscientious coach in the world can't prevent careless athletes from getting hurt. The coach, of course, can supply athletes with safe equipment and facilities. However, athletes must be willing to do their part in preventing injuries.

Some athletes get into trouble when they do the following:

1. Neglect to report hazardous playing conditions to the coach.
2. Wait until a slight injury turns serious before reporting to the coach.
3. Attempt to go beyond their physical ability.
4. Accept dares from fellow athletes to perform feats of strength.
5. Attend practice sessions while running a high temperature or feeling nauseated.
6. Fail to wear protective equipment. Some baseball players detest wearing sliding pads until they develop sliding burns (strawberries).
7. Fail to dress appropriately for existing weather conditions.
8. Engage in high-risk weekend activities such as skiing or motorcycle racing.
9. Fail to get enough sleep or eat a well-balanced diet.
10. Rely on drugs to give them extra strength and endurance.
11. Give a half-hearted effort in practices and contests. These athletes waste time horsing around and someone may get hurt.
12. Disobey rules and regulations.
13. Fail to follow prescribed treatment for minor injury. Athlete returns to action too soon and risks further injury.

How can a coach convince athletes to stay healthy? Here is a six-point plan:

- Be a trouble-shooter. Keep on the lookout for warning signs of impending danger. Point out potentially dangerous situations.
- Make a list of the previous year's injuries that restricted athletes from action. Look for a common denominator; that is, find out why most of these injuries occurred. Then seek specific ways to keep them from recurring. Seek the advice of others.
- Identify and isolate trouble spots. Restrict athletes from taking part in any unnecessary high-risk activity.
- Insist that athletes follow rules and safety regulations at all times.
- Remove from the squad those athletes who refuse to cooperate and are a threat to others.

- Emphasize that excellent health is the key to any successful athletic program.

COACHING ERRORS THAT LEAD TO ATHLETIC INJURY

Coaches don't purposely set out to maim their athletes. Yet some coaches unintentionally create conditions that lead to athletic injury. In some cases, athletes are reluctant to report injuries to the coach. Why do they hold back? What problems do coaches create for themselves and their athletes? Let's examine eleven situations that answer these two questions.

One, a coach pressures an injured athlete to be tough and fight off pain. The coach's fervor spreads to other athletes. Peer pressure mounts and "forces" the injured athlete to continue play.

Two, athletes may balk at reporting injuries to a tough, aggressive coach. They may feel the coach will embarrass them by playing down their injuries. Therefore, by not reporting, a simple injury might balloon into a serious problem.

Three, a coach asks an injured athlete to see a doctor. The athlete, not wanting to miss action, doesn't go. The athlete, however, tells the coach that everything checked out fine. The coach accepts the athlete's word and allows the athlete to continue play. Without a doctor's clearance, the coach leaves the door wide open for a possible law suit.

Four, a coach overstrains athletes. Jay Dirksen, assistant men's track and field coach, University of Illinois, believes that a system can be changed or modified by adapting to the training load or stress. It can fail to adapt to the training load if the stress is too great—the result is overtraining.

Coach Dirksen relates how symptoms of overtraining can be categorized as chronic and acute, depending on the severity of the failure. Chronic symptoms include such things as persistent soreness of joints, aching muscles (for more than two to three days), lingering colds or running noses, cold or fever sores, irritability, restlessness, inability to sleep throughout the entire night (even when very tired), inability to concentrate, or just a plain run-down feeling. These symptoms can be relieved in most cases with several days of rest or a significantly reduced training load.

Coach Dirksen feels that if chronic symptoms occur and the coach or athlete does not recognize them, or if a rest period enabling the system to recover is not taken, acute symptoms may eventually show up. These symptoms include stress fractures, emotional disturbances, mental breakdowns, mononucleosis, and other serious medical problems. Both coach and athlete must work together to recognize and eliminate any chronic symptoms of overtraining before they become acute. Acute symptoms can cause physical or mental damage and necessitate an extended period of rest and inactivity in order for the body to recover to a normal level.

Coach Dirksen adds that it is equally important to realize that the stresses from outside the athletic environment of the athlete can also affect the recovery from training loads or stresses.

Five, poor conditioning programs. According to Thomas E. Abdenour, head athletic trainer, Weber State College, Ogden, Utah, some coaches run into trouble because they:

- Improperly prepare athletes for a sport by: 1) Excluding flexibility and conditioning programs during practice; 2) Not offering activities to build muscular strength; 3) Allowing an injured athlete to return to activity without complete rehabilitation.
- Rely on obsolete information relative to care and prevention of injury.
- Permit an injured athlete to return to activity too soon and without proper rehabilitation.

    Dan Riley, strength coach, Penn State University, says this about rehabilitation: "We see many athletes who were injured at the high school level. During their freshmen year in college we observe a significant imbalance in strength or atrophy of one side of the body. This can be attributed to a lack of properly restrengthening the affected muscles."
- Provide improper and incomplete weight training programs during the season.

Six, a coach tries to get by on a tight budget by using old, worn-out equipment.

Seven, several coaches hold practice sessions during inclement weather in a crowded gymnasium.

Eight, a coach holds loosely organized practices. Athletes become bored, goof around, and risk hurting themselves.

Nine, a coach fails to properly supervise the practice area.

Ten, a coach fails to give adequate instruction on how athletes should perform certain activities.

Eleven, a coach fails to give adequate instruction on how to use athletic equipment.

How can a coach avoid making these costly errors? Here are seven ways:

1. Encourage athletes to consider all injuries as potential threats to their well-being.
2. Insist that all injuries be reported to the coach immediately.

3. Keep a log or record of reported injuries. The log should include name of athlete, date of accident, time of accident, where accident occurred, how accident occurred, and any special circumstances leading to the accident (Figure 10-2). A designated person—assistant coach, team manager, or team trainer—should be in charge of filing these reports. Also, the coach should have a definite plan for following up on all reports.

4. Post specific guidelines for athletes to follow in case of injury. These guidelines should answer such questions as:

- Under what circumstances should an athlete see a doctor?
- What should athletes do to ready themselves for competition again?
- What must athletes do to secure a release from the doctor?
- How can parents help their youngsters recover?
- What can athletes do during recovery period to help the team?

Name of athlete	Date of accident	Time of accident	Where accident occurred	How accident occurred	Special circumstances

FIGURE 10-2 Athletic injury report

5. Properly supervise athletes during practice sessions and contests.
6. Hold fast-moving, well-organized practice sessions.
7. Give crystal clear instructions to athletes. After demonstrating the proper use of athletic equipment or explaining how to perform a specific task, ask questions. Make sure everyone understands what to do and how to do it. Leave no doubt as to what should be done.

Several athletic trainers throughout the country offered these suggestions to coaches for cutting down on athletic injury.

One, incorporate a Certified Athletic Trainer into the coaching staff.

Two, stress to administrators, faculty members, and booster clubs the need for a Staff Certified Athletic Trainer.

Three, encourage each head coach to attend an annual in-service seminar in the field of athletic training.

Four, each head coach should have a course in basic care and prevention of athletic injury.

Five, follow the recommendations of the experts in weight training, flexibility, water availability, and others.

Six, purchase the best equipment.

Seven, teach and coach the safest techniques.

Eight, strengthen the muscles used to play the game.

Nine, stress in-season training. In-season training, according to Dan Riley, is more important than strength training in the off-season. Most athletes stop lifting once the season begins and continue losing strength as the season progresses. This loss in strength leaves them more vulnerable to injury as the season wears on.

EXAMINING THE PROBLEM
OF OVERUSE SYNDROME

We mentioned how overtraining often leads to athletic injury. Dr. James G. Garrick in his article "Sports Medicine" gives excellent advice concerning overuse syndrome. Dr. Garrick offers the following information:

> Overuse syndromes in athletes are among the most difficult medical problems with which to deal. Their insidious onset and initially benign character, as opposed to the dramatic onset of the usual athletic injury, do not seem to demand prompt medical attention. Thus generally the athlete with an overuse syndrome presents for treatment only when his performance is suffering badly and there is no other choice.
>
> Early in their course, overuse syndromes are related to specific athletic activities (such as excessive running, pitching, or swimming), and stopping the

particular activity alleviates the problem. Often the athlete has already discovered this: "The only time it hurts is when I run." However it is for this very reason that he has sought medical help; only stopping the activity gives him relief and he is unwilling to do this. Treatment of overuse syndromes follows one of two courses: convincing the athlete that he must stop the activity (temporarily) and then resume it gradually or attempting to balance the symptoms and the activity in order to allow continued participation.

If dealt with early, overuse syndromes rarely progress to significant medical problems or permanent disability. The intraarticular changes of "little league elbow" do not occur overnight nor do the lesions resulting in activity-related spondylolysis in gymnasts. Treatment by the athlete or parent and coach, however, is the rule and by the time the physician is consulted, permanent changes may have resulted.

Most overuse syndromes have names related to specific sports. Although the two examples mentioned involve bone, the syndromes usually originate in soft tissue, most often the musculotendinous units. Examples can be found in any sport that involves repetitive activity and includes involvement of the rotator cuff in pitcher's, gymnast's or swimmer's shoulder, the common extensor origin in tennis elbow, the patellar or quadriceps tendon in jumper's knee, and the Achilles tendon in jogger's heel.

A few general rules apply to overuse syndromes: 1) precipitating activity must be discontinued to allow for an interval free from disability and pain; 2) resumption of athletic activity must be gradual and the fervor of the activity determined by the presence (or absence) of symptoms; 3) appropriate rehabilitation must precede resumption of activity; and 4) the athlete must be watched carefully (and given definite guidelines) for recurrence.

DIAGNOSING ATHLETIC INJURY:
A PHYSICIAN'S VIEWPOINT

Dr. James Garrick, director, Center for Sports Medicine, San Francisco, California, holds workshops for coaches on how to evaluate injuries. He stresses the tough job a physician has in diagnosing athletic injury. Here, in part, is what Dr. Garrick tells coaches regarding making sideline decisions.

One of the most disquieting thoughts of most team physicians is that of having to decide whether an athlete can continue playing after sustaining an injury. Although making such a decision in a championship game in front of 10,000 people may indeed be difficult, such a situation rarely occurs. About sixty-five to seventy-five percent of injuries occur during practice. Thus it is probably more appropriate to teach the coach how to deal with an injury decision (during practices) and then to "teach by example" during games using the same decision model.

Athletes should not be allowed to return to participation until the following conditions have been satisfied: 1) the injury has been diagnosed. A definitive diagnosis must be made. It is not enough to say "swollen ankle"; one must state "ankle sprain" and by doing so rule out other possibilities such as a fracture or contusion; 2) the examiner is sure the injury will not worsen with continued play; 3) the examiner is sure continued participation (with the injury) will not result in another injury (for example, the post-concussion wrestler sustaining additional injury due to inability to protect himself). This decision requires a fair degree of sophisticated knowledge of both the injury and the sport in question.

About which conditions should these questions be asked? In other words, what constitutes an injury? The following is a list of signs or symptoms which generally preclude further participation unless the three preceding questions can be answered completely or until they have been completely evaluated.

1. Unconsciousness, however brief.
2. "Dazed" or inappropriate responses for greater than ten seconds as a result of being struck on the head.
3. Any complaint of neurologic abnormalities such as numbness or tingling.
4. Obvious swelling—except occasionally that involving the fingers. Swelling obvious to the coach or lay person generally merits attention regardless of its location.
5. Limited range of motion (compared with the opposite side).
6. Pain within the normal range of motion.
7. Decreased strength through the normal range of motion.
8. Obvious bleeding.
9. An injury the examiner does not know how to handle.
10. Obvious loss of some normal function.
11. Requirement of the athlete to have assistance to get off the mat, field, or court at some time earlier in the practice or the game.
12. Any time an athlete says he or she is injured and cannot participate— regardless of what the examiner thinks of the injury.

At first glance this seems too extensive, resulting in excessively conservative decisions. In the context of common athletic injuries, however, it becomes apparent to a physician that these decisions would be obvious and the list is merely a means of practically applying an appreciable body of medical knowledge. The treatment of the lateral ankle sprain, the commonest of athletic injuries, might serve as an example of this system.

In nearly half of the instances the athlete will be unable to get off the court or field without assistance or obvious disability. The ankle will be obviously swollen. The extremes of dorsiflexion, plantar flexion, and any inversion will be painful and thus normal motion will be lost. This picture would result in the cessation of participation for the child athlete.

Three weeks later after: 1) the x-rays have revealed no fracture or epiphyseal injury; 2) examination reveals intact ligaments and normal strength, and 3) normal motion has been reestablished, there still may be some residual swelling, but now the three initial questions can be answered: 1) the diagnosis is a "grade one sprain of the anterior talofibular ligament"; 2) the injury will not worsen with participation, as the athlete can now run, start, cut, and stop normally without pain and will be supported by taping; and 3) because he or she can function normally there is no increased risk of another injury. Hence participation is permitted.

Thus we find that the initial scheme of evaluating initial injuries is also appropriate for determining whether or not patients can return to athletic participation.

Dr. Garrick states that although few athletic injuries are truly emergencies, frequently they are accompanied by a sense of urgency by the athlete, parent, and coach. None of these individuals is the least bit reluctant to inform the physician that the decisions regarding the particular injury will probably influence the child's well-being, the team's success, the likelihood of someone receiving a college scholarship, and so on. Often this places the physician in an anxiety-surrounded situation to which he is unaccustomed.

Too often the physician overreacts to the plight of the injured athlete. If the physician is unsure of the diagnosis or the demands of the sport, overtreatment may result and the athlete needlessly may miss a season of play. On the other hand, expedient treatment may be given by a physician who is unaware of the long-term problems resulting from the injury or one who is too willing to accede to the demands of the youthful competitor wishing to return to play. More familiarity with the demands of various sports and the resulting injuries will enable the physician to make decisions in the long-term best interests of the patient.

HIRING AN ATHLETIC TRAINER

Athletic trainers Glen Snow, Floyd Central High School, New Albany, Indiana, and Ron Sendre, Central Michigan University, Mt. Pleasant, Michigan, see an increasing need for qualified personnel on the high school level as injury rates increase, as sports programs expand, and as today's high school sports grow in sophistication.

What are the points in favor of hiring an athletic trainer? Here are four:

1. They can prevent potentially dangerous situations from developing into law suits.
2. They are knowledgeable people trained in establishing and maintaining a sound athletic training program.
3. They provide emergency first aid, treatment, preventive techniques, and a rehabilitation program for all athletes.
4. They help prevent injuries and keep many injuries from becoming serious.

Why, then, do few high school districts hire athletic trainers? These are the major reasons:

1. School districts may feel there isn't a sufficient need to hire athletic trainers. They may cite such evidence as declining enrollment, inadequate space, small student body.
2. No money available.
3. Unable to find a certified trainer.
4. School personnel, including many coaches, may feel an athletic trainer would be used primarily for football.

5. If there's enough interest, a school's athletic department could send selected students to training seminars, clinics, and workshops. After successful completion of a Student Trainer Course, these students would be available to act as trainers.

Trainers Snow and Sendre suggest that if a school district is unable to hire a certified trainer, a coach can find an interested faculty member and send him or her to a National Athletic Trainers Association (N.A.T.A.) approved educational program. If this is impossible, utilize physical therapists in the community who have an athletic background and are interested.

Many schools and booster clubs have helped with the expenses of those coaches who give up part of their summers to attend training workshops.

Suppose everything turns sour; that is, there isn't anybody who wants to be an athletic trainer. What recourse does a coach have? To begin with, no athletic team should be allowed to play or practice without someone present who has a basic knowledge of first aid. In most cases, this person would be the coach.

A coach should at least be familiar with first aid procedures for taking care of the most common injuries sustained by athletes. According to Thomas E. Abdenour, trainer, Weber State College, the five most common injuries are knee injuries, ankle injuries, foot problem, muscle strain and contusion, and shin splints.

Without a doubt, every coach should know how to treat these injuries and have a first aid kit on hand during all practices and contests.

POINTS TO REMEMBER

Pre-season physical examinations can be a real headache for coaches, parents, and school officials. Some athletes report late for practice because they wait until the last minute to take their physicals. With few exceptions, a school won't allow an athlete to participate without an Athletic Clearance Card.

The pre-season examination does little to prevent injury, but it does satisfy a school's legal and insurance requirements.

It's extremely important that every coach evaluate the physical readiness of athletes early in the season. Athletes report in different stages of conditioning.

If a coach starts off too fast, some athletes may lag behind, complain of injury, and quit after the first few days.

A coach can prepare athletes for practice sessions by holding a pre-season meeting and explaining proper conditioning procedures. Topics such as diet, weight control, and care and prevention should be included.

A wise coach will give athletes a pre-season conditioning schedule. A determined athlete will follow these guidelines, get into shape, and make an effort to stay healthy.

Careless athletes risk injury. They fail to use common sense during practice sessions and contests. A coach must stress the importance of safety by constantly reminding athletes to stay sharp by watching out for hazardous conditions.

Coaches, too, must be alert for possible danger spots. Some coaching errors that lead to athlete injury are overtraining, operating poor conditioning programs (excluding flexibility and muscular strength activities), allowing athletes to return to action before they are completely rehabilitated, using worn-out equipment, and holding practices in a crowded area.

Coaches can reduce the number of athletic injuries by hiring a certified athletic trainer, learning up-to-date methods for care and prevention of athletic injury, following the recommendations of experts in weight training and conditioning programs, purchasing the best equipment, teaching and coaching the safest techniques, strengthening the muscles used to play the sport, and stressing in-season training.

Dr. Garrick points out that about sixty-five to seventy-five percent of injuries occur during practice. Therefore, it behooves a coach to take extra care in setting up safe practices.

Dr. Garrick's procedure for checking injured athletes before allowing them to continue play is: 1) Make a definite diagnosis; 2) Make sure injury will not worsen; 3) Make sure participation will not lead to another injury.

Few high school districts hire a certified athletic trainer. However, if there is sufficient need for an athletic trainer, a school can select certain students or an interested teacher to go through a training program. In many instances, schools and booster clubs will help with training expenses.

Trainer or not, a coach should know how to treat common athletic injuries and have a first aid kit on hand at all times. Perhaps the best piece of advice a coach can follow is: If in doubt, don't.

QUESTIONS

1. Why do you think some districts prefer to hold group pre-season physical examinations?
2. What is the main objective of requiring physical examinations for athletes?
3. Why should a coach have an Athletic Clearance Card for each athlete?

4. Should a coach allow an athlete to participate without an Athletic Clearance Card? Explain.
5. In what ways can a coach reduce the possibility of early-season injury?
6. How should a coach prepare athletes for early season conditioning drills?
7. What precautions should a coach take during the first few days of practice?
8. In what ways do athletes bring injuries upon themselves?
9. What things can a coach do to help athletes stay healthy?
10. What problem areas often lead to athletic injury? What can a coach do to minimize the risk of injury?
11. According to some athletic trainers, what can coaches do to cut down on athletic injury?
12. What is overuse syndrome? Why is it difficult to deal with?
13. What general rules should a coach apply to treating overuse syndrome?
14. Why does a physician often have trouble deciding whether or not to allow an injured athlete back on the field?
15. What conditions must be met before a physician or coach allows an athlete to play?
16. What conditions or pressures cause some physicians to allow injured athletes to compete?
17. Why do some school districts fail to hire athletic trainers?
18. In what ways are athletic trainers an asset to athletics?
19. How much should a coach know about care and prevention of injuries? Explain.

The Coach and the Law

*You can't legislate intelligence and
common sense into people.*

Will Rogers

The legal aspects of coaching are more vital to the coaching profession today than ever before. Why? In recent years large judgments have been awarded to injured athletes.

A good example of this is the football helmet manufacturing industry. In 1977, a Florida youth won a judgment of $5.3 million against Ridell. By the end of 1978, helmet manufacturers nationwide were facing between $116 million and $150 million in negligence suits.

Richard Ball, one of the country's most prominent athletic litigation attorneys, warns coaches of the seriousness of the involvement of the law in athletics. Without question, legal involvement remains a critical issue in athletics.

In this chapter we'll see how school districts and coaches can avoid lawsuits, how to handle lawsuits should they occur, and how coaches can become more liability-conscious.

LAW TERMS THE COACH SHOULD KNOW

Let's look at thirteen law terms (with examples) which enter the sports injury scene.

Assumption of risk—The athlete assumes that there is some inherent danger in sports participation. A football player, for example, realizes a hard tackle could possibly lead to injury.

Contributory negligence—The injured athlete, by own negligence, contributed to the injury. For example, a batter who refuses to get out of the way of a wild pitch.

Forseeability—A coach should have known or foreseen that a particular act or omission would or might result in the injury sustained. A tennis coach, for instance, allows athletes to practice on a wet, slippery court.

High degree of care—The degree of care that would be exercised by ordinarily prudent, trained, and experienced coaches under the same or similar circumstances. A coach who stresses safe play during practices and contests exercises a high degree of care.

Liability—The responsibility to answer for another's damages. A coach must provide a safe and secure atmosphere for every athlete.

Litigation—The act or process of bringing about a lawsuit. For example, an athlete breaks an ankle after stepping on an exposed sprinkler head. The athlete brings suit against the school district for negligence.

Malfeasance—A coach performs an act that is definitely illegal and one that should not have been performed. As an example, a coach gives an injured athlete a pain-killer drug.

Misfeasance—A coach has the right to perform the function but performs it incorrectly. For instance, a football coach who teaches players to make contact by using their helmets to spear opposing players.

Nonfeasance—A coach fails to perform an act that should have been performed. For example, a coach makes no attempt to remove an injured athlete from action.

Negligence—A coach fails to exercise the due care that an ordinary, reasonable person would exercise in similar circumstances. For example, a wrestling coach allows a 200-pound wrestler to practice takedowns on a 130-pound wrestler.

Prudence—Cautious and wise conduct. A prudent coach is one who properly supervises and guides all activities performed by athletes.

Tort—A wrongful act or omission to act that causes damage to another. A basketball coach might begin practice with fast-moving drills before allowing athletes sufficient time to warm up properly.

Unavoidable accident—A coach does everything possible to avoid athletic injury. An injury, however, occurs without negligence on the part of either party. For example, an outfielder who breaks a collar bone while diving for a sinking line drive.

A basic knowledge of law terms serves to arouse an awareness of the potential personal liability inherent in coaching.

COACHING DANGER ZONES

Some coaches make serious mistakes that open the door for litigation. Let's examine seven areas that are particularly dangerous for the coach.

1. Failure to adequately warn. Several recent athletic litigation cases have been based upon "failure to warn." Courts and juries today consider this duty to be one of the more important or essential responsibilities of coaches and athletic administrators.

   To be effective practically and legally, a warning must be so disseminated, explained and enforced as to provide a realistic basis for the expectation that it will prevent the conduct against which it is directed. A warning has to be repeated frequently with clear explanation of the harm that might result from failure to comply. Coaches must take elaborate care to assure that their athletes understand the severe consequences of their actions.

   Manufacturers, too, have a responsibility to warn athletes that improper use of their product may lead to sports injury. This has been particularly critical for football helmet manufacturers.

   In Richard Kazmaier's article, "The Naked Truth About Sports," *Scholastic Coach*, October 1977, he relates that as more manufacturers are being sued, insurance companies are increasing their rates. The insurance companies, in many cases, settle out of court and pass along the costs to the insured in the form of future premiums.

   Manufacturers pass their increased premium costs along to their customers in the form of higher helmet prices. Kazmaier points out that a few school districts have already refused liability insurance coverage for their sports programs, and trial attorneys have identified coaches as probable targets for future action.

2. Failure to strictly adhere to the rules of the game. Many of the rules are made for the safety of the athlete. This is particularly true in football. The rules related to hitting with the head are good examples. Yet coaches still teach blocking and tackling techniques that use the helmet as the initial point of contact. These coaches justify teaching these dangerous techniques on the basis that other coaches do it or that they've been doing it for years and no one has gotten hurt.

3. Failure to keep informed on matters dealing with sports injury and litigation. Many coaches display a lack of interest in athletic litigation and act as though such problems don't exist.

   Some coaches become complacent; that is, they are perfectly satisfied with the way things are going. Since they've never been involved in a lawsuit, there's no reason to become overly concerned. Complacency leads to carelessness; carelessness invites trouble.

4. Failure to stress safety regulations throughout the season. Some coaches feel safety warnings at the start of the season are sufficient to keep athletes out of trouble.

5. Failure to monitor athletic program with the intention of spotting and correcting hazardous situations. The following suggestions will help coaches avoid sports litigation:

   - Look at the rules of the game. Follow them religiously.
   - Instill a positive attitude among athletes to place individual safety as a top priority.
   - Provide a safe physical environment at all times.
   - Do everything possible to assure maximum safety for athletes.

6. Failure to transport athletes properly. For example, if athletes travel by bus under a coach's supervision, they should return to school in the same manner.

   Some districts allow parents to take their athletes home in the family car. Those doing so usually provide a Release of Liability Form (Figure 11-1) which requires the parent or guardian to sign in the presence of the coach and witnesses. This paper releases the coach and district from any liability should an injury occur to the athlete while returning home.

   Let's suppose an athlete goes home with a friend. Is the coach responsible for the athlete's safe return? Yes, it's the coach's responsibility to make sure every athlete boards the bus after a contest. What should a coach do if an athlete rides home with another person? Here are four suggestions:

Release Of Liability

We, the undersigned, hereby request that the Roseville Joint Union High

School District of Placer and Sacramento Counties allow _____
                                                                 (Student)

to make the trip from _____ to _____

in the care of _____ (Parent or Guardian only.)

In consideration thereof, we do hereby release and discharge for ourselves,

our heirs, executors, administrators, and assigns, release and forever discharging the

Roseville Joint Union High School District and its officers, agents, and employees

of and from any and all claims, whatsoever kind or nature, for or because of injury

of any kind or nature which may occur to the same _____
                                                              (Student)

during the said trip.

_____
(Parent or Guardian)

_____
(Student)

_____
(Witness)

_____
(Witness)

Date: _____

Time: _____

Return to District Superintendent

FIGURE 11-1 Release of liability

1. Report the incident in writing. Have several witnesses, including the bus driver, sign the report.
2. File the report with the principal as soon as possible.
3. Upon arriving at the school, call the athlete's parents and report the incident. Make sure the parents understand the seriousness of the matter.
4. Take the necessary disciplinary action.

A coach can help prevent this situation by:

- Discussing the rules governing transportation with athletes early in the season.
- Citing specific reasons—safety of athletes, district liability, etc.— for establishing these rules.
- Citing the penalty for breaking these rules.

7. Failure to diagnose an injury properly, thus allowing an athlete to continue play.

Joe Gieck, head athletic trainer, University of Virginia, Charlottesville, recommends three things a coach can do to reduce the chances of being sued. They are: 1) treat only those injuries you're qualified to handle; 2) Take courses in first aid, cardiopulmonary resuscitation, and emergency medical treatment; 3) create a favorable rapport with parents.

SELF-PROTECTION FOR THE COACH

A smart coach learns early to "cover his tail" regarding the safety of athletes. A coach can't afford to relax, get careless, and take a chance when another person's well-being is at stake. Coaches must continually ask themselves these questions:

1. Is what I'm doing safe for all athletes?
2. Am I doing what another coach with ordinary prudence would do under the same or similar circumstances?
3. Am I providing adequate supervision?
4. Did I give proper instruction?
5. Did I warn athletes of potential danger spots?
6. Am I providing safe equipment and facilities for athletes?
7. Am I teaching safe, acceptable techniques?
8. Am I doing everything possible to minimize the risk of athletic injury?

A "no" answer to any of these questions puts the coach in a vulnerable position. For instance, take Question 6: Am I providing safe equipment and facilities for athletes? The key word is I.

A coach might answer this way: "No. Some of the equipment needs to be replaced, but we don't have any available money in the budget right now." Who can get sued if the damaged or worn-out equipment leads to athletic injury? Both the coach and the school district. Therefore, self-protection becomes a critical issue in giving the coach ammunition to present in case of personal litigation.

How can coaches protect themselves and provide safe conditions for their athletes? Here are twelve suggestions:

1. Use only the best available equipment.
2. Constantly be on the lookout for worn-out or damaged equipment and facilities.
3. Properly fit all uniforms and protective equipment. Establish and enforce rules concerning safe use of equipment.
4. Ask athletes to report unsafe conditions immediately.
5. Select opponents with care to avoid potentially dangerous mismatching.
6. In teaching progression of skills have adequate review procedures to assure that participants will not move too rapidly into areas beyond their ability.
7. Notify the athletic director and principal, in writing, of hazardous conditions. Keep a copy of the report.
8. Follow up written report. Refuse to use facility or equipment until repaired or replaced.
9. If nothing gets done, notify district superintendent. If the superintendent fails to act, send a letter to the school board pinpointing hazardous conditions. Keep a copy of the letter.
10. Make a careful inspection of equipment and facilities at the end of the season. Replace worn-out equipment and file a maintenance request to repair damaged facilities.
11. Establish and enforce rules regarding reporting of illness or injury. Show a concern for all injuries. Establish a check-up procedure for those who have been ill or injured to assure that illness or injury is no longer an impairing factor.
12. Cautiously exercise best discretion in directing athletes. Also, it's a good idea to carry liability insurance.

HOW A SCHOOL DISTRICT CAN REDUCE
THE CHANCES OF BEING SUED

A school district owes a duty to its athletes to exercise ordinary or even extraordinary care in selecting, employing, and training its coaches. It also has a responsibility to manage and conduct the athletic program with ordinary prudent skill so that the rights, safety, and lives of its athletes will be protected. This duty is basic to the willingness of parents to entrust their children to a coach's care.

In the *Rudy Tomjanovich* vs *Los Angeles Lakers Basketball Team*, Tomjanovich, who received serious injuries when punched in the face by a Laker player, won a $3,246,000.00 judgment from the Lakers, primarily because they inadequately trained or instructed their coaches and players (employees) that physical violence could reasonably be expected to result in serious injury to other players.

In a Franklin, Texas, athletic suit (May, 1980) a young Franklin High School football player received serious head injuries when his helmet caved in making a tackle. He won a $1.5 million judgment from the Rawlings Sporting Goods Company because they "failed to warn" him that the helmet might cave in if he received a hard blow on it.

These same principles of law apply to school districts. A district is responsible for adequately training, instructing, and educating its coaches concerning safety standards and practices of the sports they coach. Coaches are then responsible for instructing their athletes.

A school district also has a duty to warn athletes of the risk involved in athletics. In the fall of 1980 the National Federation of State High School Associations helped fulfill their "duty to warn" football players by sending out posters to all member schools. The poster in part states, "Participation in all sports requires an acceptance of risk of possible injury. You as a player can help make the game safer by not intentionally using techniques which are illegal and which can cause serious injury. . . . DO NOT USE the helmet to butt, ram or spear an opposing player. This is in violation of the football rules and such use can result in severe injury . . . ."

All administrators of athletic programs have this same duty to warn athletes of all foreseeable risk involved in athletic participation.

Let's examine eight more ways a school district can reduce the number of lawsuits in its athletic department.

1. Set up a program of education and instruction in the legal aspects of coaching for all district coaches. It is not necessary that the instruction be in technical legal jargon. Simple laypersons' terms will suffice. Coaches should be aware of certain elementary principles of law. Coaches must realize that they and their schools might be subject to liability for injuries suffered by athletes under their supervision. They should have an extensive knowledge of negligence since many lawsuits brought against a school district are for negligence.

2. Document the legal education program. Put the program in writing and distribute it to every coach.

3. Monitor the program to see if it is being followed. Having a program is not enough. School administrators must constantly supervise their coaches to be sure they are not teaching or allowing techniques or practices that are illegal or dangerous and which can cause serious injury. They must also make sure coaches are not violating any of an athlete's individual or fundamental constitutional rights.

4. Employ competent coaches. As the public has become more aware of the legal responsibilities of the school district and personnel, the school's administrators have become more selective in their hiring practices.

5. Provide safe facilities and maintain all equipment in a state of reasonable repair. Athletic equipment should be checked periodically to see that it is in good working condition.

6. If a serious injury occurs, the school district should instruct coaches not to make any speculative statements to parents, athletes, students, spectators, or press about how the injury occurred. If game or practice films that show how the injury occurred are available, store them away as well as the equipment involved. Immediately notify the manufacturer.

7. Select an attorney knowledgeable in athletic litigation.

8. If possible, hire a certified athletic trainer.

The school district and coach must work together in establishing good public relations and communications with parents early in the season. Parents should know the goals and objectives of the athletic program and all the risks involved in the sport their child is participating in. As a rule, more parents can be reached by the written word.

Open the program to parents. Encourage questions and comments. Make a special effort to invite parents to practices and contests. It seems smaller school districts are less threatened by litigation than larger districts. Perhaps a closer personal contact between the parents and coaches results in better public relations. Therefore, it follows that a strong public relations program is an essential step in avoiding and reducing litigation.

THE VALUE OF COACHING CERTIFICATION

According to Samuel Adams, Ed.D, in his article "Coaching Certification: The Time Is Now" (*USSA News*, September-October, 1979), many different factors have arisen since the late 1960s that point to a need for certification of coaches. These factors are as follows:

One, the effect of Title IX is being felt by all school districts in their sports program. This has placed a heavy demand on school districts to hire more coaches for girls' sports.

Many of the women teachers have little or no background in competitive athletics and perhaps are only able to perform skills at an acceptable level. Additional help is needed if a successful program is to be realized.

The need for more qualified coaches, accentuated by increased participation by boys and girls in secondary school sports since the late 1960s, became acute with Title IX.

Administration of secondary schools have relied, historically, upon physical educators to handle the coaching responsibilities. The problem inherent in the increase in participation in sports is the lack of teaching positions related to coaching positions. For example, in a typical high school of 1,000 students there are approximately twenty to twenty-five coaching jobs for ten boys' sports. In this same school there are usually two or three full-time male physical education and health education teachers. Even with each man coaching three sports, only nine of the twenty positions are filled. Personnel from other teaching and district positions have had to be utilized, many of them without any form of professional training. The same staffing problem is now facing girls' sports. Therefore, there is a dire need for professional training for coaching personnel from the other areas of education.

Two, severe legal implications face a nonqualified athletic coach. If an administrator assigns unqualified personnel to conduct an activity, the administrator may be held liable.

A coach must meet the standard of care for coaching a sport. Standard of care refers to duty to conform to a standard of behavior that will not subject others to an unreasonable risk of injury.

Other factors such as district accountability (assessment of educational practices) and use of para-professionals and lay personnel in coaching suggest a great need for coaching certification.

Samuel Adams points out in his article that being a good physical educator doesn't assure one of being a good coach. There are specialized knowledges needed for coaching expertise; in sports medicine, sports psychology, sports technique, sports administration, sports physiology, public relations, sports facilities and equipment, and sports problems that include law and liability and assessment of personnel and programs.

Any plan must include these areas and include a means of certifying the coaches that are presently coaching in the public schools. Thus, coaching certification is a giant step toward reducing sports injury and litigation.

WHY ARE THERE SO MANY LAWSUITS TODAY?

Coach Charles S. Frazier, Houston, Texas, has been writing and publishing articles on sports litigation since 1973. He lists six specific reasons lawsuits are on the rise. They are:

1. Some schools are better targets for suits than others. A school that carries a large amount of liability insurance or is wealthy is more likely to be sued than the school district that carries little or none. Some medical doctors who have dropped or significantly reduced their liability insurance have found that they are less likely to be sued. A one-million dollar judgment against a defendant is worthless

if the defendant has nothing. (This is not to say or suggest that a school district not carry liability insurance.)

2. Publicity about large awards in lawsuits tends to generate more suits. A judgment against a school district may encourage others to sue.

3. Athletes and parents are more aware of their legal rights than they used to be. They expect more from coaches and are less willing to accept incompetence.

4. There is a new spirit of advocacy in the law today that was not apparent twenty years ago, and this spirit—defending the rights of the little man—may well play a part in the demands of professional competence (i.e., coaching certification).

5. People assume that insurance companies have an unending capacity to pay claims, not drawing any connection between claims paid, rates of insurance, costs, and availability of service.

6. The public has less hesitation about taking complaints to court.

THE CASE OF THE "ALMOST" LAWSUIT

Several years ago a baseball coach held an early season drill on the field without using the bases. The drill required athletes to hit, field, and throw. Since the drill didn't include base running the coach felt no need to use bases. Besides, the steel pegs needed for holding the bases were buried under several inches of dirt.

About halfway through the drill a player limped over to the coach. He told the coach that he had stepped on an exposed peg and twisted his ankle.

On the following day the athlete's mother called the school superintendent and told him that her son had broken a small bone in his right foot. She threatened to sue the coach and school.

Two weeks later the mother informed the superintendent that she decided against filing a lawsuit for these reasons: 1) the bone break was relatively minor; 2) the boy wanted to go out for football and felt a pending lawsuit might turn coaches against him; 3) the parents didn't want to go through litigation.

The district superintendent, principal, and coach met to discuss the problem. The superintendent castigated the coach for negligence (not covering the pegs with bases) and placed a letter of reprimand in the coach's personal file. Immediately following the incident, the superintendent had the steel pegs removed and purchased bases that didn't require protruding steel pegs for attachment.

In this case, the coach was lucky. He escaped the agony and embarrassment of courtroom litigation.

What lessons can a coach learn from this incident? First, a coach must always provide maximum safety for athletes. Second, a coach must remember that litigation problems in athletics exist. Third, a coach must correct any situation that could possibly lead to athletic injury.

ANATOMY OF A LAWSUIT

Not all coaches receive a second chance like the baseball coach in the preceding case. For instance, three track coaches and two school districts became involved in an athletic lawsuit. Here's what happened:

School A's track team traveled to School B for a dual meet. A light rain fell earlier in the day. The rain muddied the broad jump pit runway and contestants were allowed to approach the pit by sprinting alongside of the runway.

During the broad jump event an athlete from School A broke his foot. He landed on a raised wooden siding which separated the pit from the infield grass.

The athlete's parents brought suit against coaches from both schools and their districts. The boy's parents registered these complaints:

1. The coach from School A allowed the athlete to participate before a prior leg injury healed properly.
2. A slippery runway forced the athlete to make his approach and takeoff from a dangerous angle, thus throwing off his rhythm and balance.
3. The raised wooden siding presented a definite hazard to athletes. (School B used the siding to keep Bermuda Grass out of the pit.)
4. The broad jump pit was too narrow.

The boy's parents refused to settle out of court. They went to trial two years later and won a $25,000 judgment.

One coach from School B related how the trial was an "eye-opening experience which resulted in several sleepless nights." He described how the plaintiff's attorney smothered him in a barrage of anxiety-producing questions such as:

How many coaching technique and safety courses had you taken prior to the accident?

How many athletes had jumped in the broad jump pit prior to the accident?

How many athletes have jumped in the broad jump pit since the accident?

Is it a common practice for you to allow athletes to run alongside the runway during adverse conditions?

If a slippery runway presented a danger, then why didn't you cancel the event?

Didn't you realize an athlete could injure himself by leaving the runway at an angle?

In short, a coach must realize accidents do happen, litigation does exist, and the horrors of a courtroom trial should be avoided at all costs. Again, the key to avoiding litigation is doing everything humanly possible to eliminate hazardous conditions.

WHAT TO DO IN CASE OF A LAWSUIT

Most coaches run their athletic programs in a reasonable, prudent manner. However, just in case the threat of litigation turns into reality, a coach should do the following:

1. Seek the services of an attorney knowledgeable in athletic litigation.
2. Discuss the matter only with the attorney representing you.
3. Discuss litigation issues with the plaintiff's attorney only under court order or with your attorney present.
4. Do not discuss the situation with any lay people—ever!
5. Write a summary and make a list of witnesses to use to refresh your memory later on.
6. Never admit liability to any one—ever!
7. Avoid any "self-incriminating" statements at the time of the accident.
8. Be sure that the Incident Report is completed and carries accurate statements.
9. Obtain witnesses at the time of the incident. Witnesses are very hard to locate later, especially if they think something may go to court.
10. Follow district policies regarding litigation.

Looking at sports litigation from another objective view, the emergence of athletes into the legal arena is a positive recognition of the importance of sports in our society today.

POINTS TO REMEMBER

Litigation can be the most destructive force in a coach's career. However, a liability-conscious coach who strives to provide maximum safety for athletes shows wisdom, intelligence, and concern.

Coaches can significantly reduce litigation problems if they:

1. Know and scrupulously follow district policies and regulations.
2. Develop good public relations with parents.
3. Strictly teach and follow the rules guiding their sports.
4. Adequately instruct and teach progression of skills.
5. Emphasize and enforce safety standards and procedures.
6. Fulfill their "duty to warn" athletes of the risk involved in participation.
7. Honor athletes' individual and constitutional rights.
8. Diligently fulfill their "duty to supervise" at all times.
9. Keep informed on litigation matters in athletics.
10. Establish and enforce rules regarding reporting of illness or injury.
11. Select opponents with care to avoid potentially dangerous situations.
12. Properly fit all uniforms, particularly protective equipment. Establish and enforce rules concerning the safe use of equipment.
13. Provide safe facilities and maintain all equipment in a state of reasonable repair.
14. Transport athletes to contests in accordance with school district policies.
15. Keep abreast on the latest acceptable methods for applying first aid.
16. Treat only those injuries that they're qualified to handle.
17. Use only the best available equipment.
18. Ask the question: Am I doing what another coach with ordinary prudence would do under the same or similar circumstances?

Coaches must protect themselves as well as their athletes. They should make periodic safety checks on all equipment and facilities. They should report any hazardous conditions to the administration and retain a copy of the report. Coaches should prevent athletes from participating until the problem has been corrected. Coaches need to exercise discretion in directing athletes and they need to carry liability insurance.

A school district can help avoid athletic litigation by:

1. Exercising extraordinary care in selecting, employing, and training its coaches.
2. Protecting the rights, safety, and lives of its athletes.
3. Adequately warning athletes of potentially dangerous situations.
4. Adequately training, instructing, and educating its coaches concerning safety standards and practices of the sports they coach.

5. Documenting the legal education program and distributing it to every coach.
6. Carefully monitoring the program to see that it's being carried out.
7. Employing competent coaches.
8. Providing safe facilities and maintaining all equipment in a state of reasonable repair.
9. Working with coaches in establishing good public relations and communications with parents.

If a lawsuit occurs, a coach should consult an attorney familiar with athletic litigation.

QUESTIONS

1. Why are the legal aspects of coaching so important today?
2. Why should coaches have a basic knowledge of law terms?
3. What effect does the rise of lawsuits have on athletics in the schools today?
4. What are football helmet manufacturers doing to offset the expense of lawsuits? How is this effecting school athletic programs?
5. How can complacency lead to problems for the coach?
6. What are four mistakes some coaches make that lead to athletic litigation?
7. Why must coaches continually quiz themselves regarding the safety of athletes?
8. In what ways can coaches protect themselves from litigation?
9. Why should a coach carry liability insurance?
10. What are some things a school district can do to protect itself from athletic litigation?
11. In your opinion, do you feel coaches should be certified? Explain.
12. How can a school district and coach work together in establishing sound public relations with parents?
13. As a rule, why are small school districts less likely to suffer athletic litigation than large school districts?
14. What subjects should be included in a coaching certification course?
15. What are three reasons athletic litigation is on the rise?
16. What emotional effect might athletic litigation have on a coach?
17. What physical effect might athletic litigation have on a coach?
18. Why should athletic litigation be avoided at all costs?
19. What should a coach do in case of a lawsuit?
20. Why should coaches stay informed concerning the legal ramifications of athletic litigation?

Working Effectively
with the Community

*Life affords no higher pleasure than
that of surmounting difficulties,
passing from one step of success to
another, forming new wishes and
seeing them gratified.*

Samuel Johnson

Many schools today report serious problems finding funds to continue their athletic programs. Some drop from one sport to, in many
cases, the entire sport program; others have dropped their junior high
sport program. It follows, then, that as the money pinch tightens, many
more athletic programs are going to find it extremely difficult to survive.

Athletic programs around the country are searching for answers to
their money problems. Many reach out into the community for help
with fund raising projects.

We'll review some hard-hitting facts regarding sports survival, see
what some school districts are doing to stay alive, and investigate how
the community can help athletic programs survive through fund raising
projects.

A LOOK AT SPORTS SURVIVAL FACTS

Major issues causing the crises in school athletic budgets, according
to a recent national survey conducted by the American Sports Education
Institute, are:

1. Lack of gate receipts due to forced busing and crowd control.
2. Title IX eating heavily into already limited budgets.
3. Product liability causing a dramatic rise in equipment costs.
4. Failure to pass bond issue for schools.
5. General inflation resulting in a significant increase in transportation costs, officials' fees, and maintenance.

The survey also revealed these startling conditions:

- Carrollton High School in Saginaw, Michigan, had to drop all but varsity sports.
- Belleville High School in Michigan has very serious problems; they have had to drop sixteen coaches and six individual teams.
- Muskegon High School in Michigan has dropped all non-revenue producing sports.
- A Board of Education in New York has made a forty percent cut in senior high athletic programs and a one-hundred percent cut in junior high programs.
- In Cleveland, Ohio, Alexander Hamilton High School is dropping their entire program.
- McGuffey High School in Claysville, Pennsylvania, has dropped all non-revenue sports.
- In Lacey, Washington, Timberline High School will drop their programs due to lack of funds.

The Boosters Clubs of America report that the State of Washington has been hit with an extraordinary increase in insurance. Recently the state's High School Association paid $5,000 for liability insurance to cover its statewide tournaments. And because of one lawsuit, the insurance went up to $50,000.

Some California schools, hard hit by the passage of Proposition 13, have either dropped sports from their athletic programs or charged athletes a fee to participate.

The survival of certain high school sports may well depend on the efforts of everyone—parents, students, coaches, teachers, athletes, and administrators—to go out into the community and solicit help in raising funds.

Before going out into the community, however, let's see how a coach might raise money within the school itself.

HOW TO SET UP AN IN-SCHOOL
FUND RAISING PROJECT

A coach needs a particular piece of equipment, say a pitching machine or tennis serving machine. Unfortunately, there isn't enough money to purchase the equipment. Rather than do without, an energetic coach can organize an in-school fund raising event. The following guidelines will help a coach succeed:

1. Determine exactly how much money will be needed to purchase equipment, including sales tax and freight (if applicable). Then plan to raise a few dollars extra. For instance, if the apparatus cost $850.00, shoot for $1,000.00. Extra money in the fund will buy those accessories a coach invariably forgets.

2. Select only the best available equipment. Check around. Ask other coaches for advice. Then decide which product will be the most beneficial for the squad.

3. Have a definite plan in mind. Establish a step-by-step approach toward a realistic goal.

4. Discuss the plan with the administration. Receive, in writing, administrative approval before moving ahead with the campaign. Ask an administrator, experienced in raising funds, for advice concerning such things as what projects produce the best results, what products consistently sell well, and what specific problems to watch for during the campaign. *Note:* Figure 12-1, Fund Raising Request and Figure 12-2, Fund Raising Request Response, help pave the way for a coach to work directly with the administration.

5. Carefully select the proper time to hold the campaign. Too many money raising projects going on at the same time limits the chance of success.

6. Hold a team meeting. Outline fund raising plans with athletes and interested students. Keep in mind that the formula for a successful fund raising campaign is: 1) excellent organization; 2) enthusiasm; and 3) maintaining a positive attitude.

7. Insist on total team commitment before beginning activity.

8. Check on the possibility of receiving help from others within the school. For example, the student council may provide assistance, taking a small percentage (e.g., ten percent) of the profits for services rendered.

9. Carry out fund raising activity in accordance with the district policies. Problems often arise regarding the handling of money. Again, check with the administration before going ahead with plans.

10. Keep students and teachers informed. Run daily notices in the school bulletin. Write a short article in the school paper describing the project.

11. Keep the student body posted on how well the project is going. Keep the activity fresh in everyone's mind.

Fund Raising Request

To: Dean of Student Activities

From: _____

Fund raising event requested: _____

Date of request: _____

Date of the fund raising event: _____

Alternate date: _____

Purpose of the event: _____

_____

Description of the event: _____

_____

Assistance requested from Student Council: _____

_____

Assistance requested from Dean of Student Activities: _____

_____

Is a fund raising company involved? _____

If so, what company? _____

What advisors will supervise the event? _____

Who will benefit from this fund raising? _____

Is any special scheduling of the school day required? _____

What facilities are needed? _____

What equipment is needed? _____

Who will provide the equipment? _____

FIGURE 12-1 Fund raising request

12. Set a reasonable time limit for holding the project. A lengthy campaign leads to tension, loss of interest, and lethargy.

13. After completing the campaign thank everyone for their effort and support.

From: Dean of Student Activities

To:

Your request for a fund raiser is _____

_____

_____

Your event is scheduled for: _____

Please notify me if you have any needs in addition to those listed on your request. A financial statement sheet is attached.

FIGURE 12-2 Fund raising request response

A project will reap a respectable harvest if a coach:

- Plans ahead.
- Employs sound organizational skills.
- Involves others.
- Keeps the activity on a professional level.
- Shows appreciation.

FUND RAISING WITHIN THE COMMUNITY

Coaches who include the community in money raising projects have the battle half-won. For example, according to the Sacramento Bee Newspaper, Sacramento, California, students, parents, and volunteers from Woodland, California, transformed 800 tons of crushed Auburn granite into a "rain-proof" running oval worth an estimated $40,000—for $1,800.

The track coach and principal from Douglass Junior High School combined efforts with a track committee to haul in granite. It took two hundred adults and children five weekends to spread, level, compact, and survey the granite. They also installed drainage and curbing.

Materials (concrete and pipes), equipment, and machinery operators came from various local construction companies. The project required over twenty different drivers (fourteen were independent truckers) to cover over 4,000 miles, and the city helped with drainage hookups.

In all, the track cost the school district nothing. The school's student council reached into its funds to pick up the tab.

Half the money came from the jogathon, which the Athletic Director started the previous year after reading an advertisement about a nationwide fund raising program.

Here, then, is an excellent example of what community spirited and self-proficient students, parents, and volunteers can do to help an athletic program.

Such a program, of course, requires intelligent, advance planning, and a super selling job by the coach and administration. Clearly, in this case, the project succeeded because a supportive administration, student body, and community worked together toward a common goal.

Big selling projects which depend upon community support for success require big thinking and, in many cases, the help of fund raising specialists.

ASCO, Inc., Winona, Minnesota, has specialized in fund raising projects since 1928. They offer the following basic procedure for setting up a fund raising campaign:

1. Set realistic goals. Determine your dollar objective and how you will attain it. Don't be too conservative. You may be surprised at results when you've got a good program going for you. There are plenty of ideas to consider. Don't try them all at once. Select a few that you believe will work for you.

2. Outline a master plan. Work out a schedule and establish deadlines. This avoids unnecessary panic and prevents duplication of effort. A plan assures coordination and promotes teamwork.

3. Choose committee members. Try to enlist campus leaders such as club presidents, cheerleaders, and drill captains. Other students look up to school leaders. If students know that the school's leaders are participating, they'll know it's a great project and will want to become part of the group, also.

4. Set a campaign theme. Coordinate your total promotional efforts like those in advertisements on TV or in magazines. Themes or slogans like, "It's Better in the Bahamas," or "Reach Out and Touch Someone," are recent examples. All of your buttons, posters, banners, and advertisements should carry the theme or slogan in the copy and art. Some theme ideas to get the whole school involved might be: "(Your School's) BETTER . . . 'cause we want to be." If you're having a car wash, you might have a theme like: "Saturday's washday at (Your School)." Or, if you're promoting a prom, use the name of the prom as the theme. Develop your theme and a slogan around a positive statement—then use it everywhere—it can serve you well.

5. Establish incentives. These would include publicity, prizes, and ribbon awards. Winners would include the person who brought in the

most money, those who brought the most pledges, those who collected cash payments the fastest, and so on. Awards should be planned to keep enthusiasm high. As a campaign incentive, consider using thermometer banners, class competitions, etc.

6. Publicize for maximum impact. Make your announcement at school. Call an assembly or pep rally. Plan a program that will inform and excite your audience. Be sure they catch the spirit! This first announcement sets the pace for the entire project. Simultaneously with your school announcement, community publicity for your projects should break. Work with your local newspaper to furnish advance photographs and written copy. Give the paper complete and accurate information on who, what, where, and when. Remember that people make news. Be sure to include the names of committee members and other participants. Do the same with your local radio and TV stations. Furnish the announcer with written scripts. (Ask for help from aspiring student writers.) Stations provide public service announcements free of charge.

7. Keep careful records. Whenever money is involved, accurate bookkeeping is essential. Donations must be recorded immediately. Expenses must be itemized and controlled. Keep in mind that poor money management can undercut your profits and undo your overall efforts.

8. Announce the results and thank your workers. Give recognition to all workers who deserve it, publicize special awards, and send the information to the newspapers and radio and television stations. People should know about a job well done.

SELECTING A MONEY MAKING PROJECT

How should a coach go about selecting a project? First, choose the project that has the best chance of succeeding. Get together with the student activities coordinator (or person designated to handle fund raising events). Professional fund raising organizations inundate school personnel with catalogs, guides, suggestions, and ideas for fund raising activities.

Carefully go over these activities. Study the familiar ones as well as the new ones. Single out those that show the best potential for high sales.

Here is a partial list of popular project ideas:

1. Jogathons
2. Alumni athletic contests
3. Sports night
4. Car washes
5. Candy sales

6. Selling coupon advertising books
7. Talent shows
8. Selling seat cushions, pennants, or decals
9. School carnivals
10. Selling tickets to drawings
11. Potluck dinners, spaghetti feeds, and so on.

Second, contact a professional fund raising organization if the project requires extensive planning. Seek the advice of experts. It's extremely important to start off right.

A HIGHLY SUCCESSFUL GOLF MARATHON

Hard hit by Proposition 13, the Junior Golf Program of Roseville, California, needed money to continue offering scholarships, equipment, and tournament fees for promising youth golfers in the community. Junior Golfers are from six to eighteen years of age.

Ed Vasconcellos, head golf pro at Diamond Oaks Golf Course, Roseville, and Carl Foote, golf coach, came up with an excellent idea for raising money—a one day golf marathon.

On May 25, 1979, Ed played seven rounds of golf (126 holes) from 5:35 am to 2:30 pm. Here were the results: Pars—74; Birdies—20; Green in regulation—81; Putts—219; Average score—75.

The local press played up the marathon weeks in advance by urging people to sign pledge forms. For example, a person might pledge 1¢ per par, 2¢ per birdie, 3¢ per eagle, or donate a set amount, say $1.00, $2.00, or $5.00 for the entire event.

The marathon netted $1,350.00. Ninety percent of the pledges came from the Diamond Oaks Mens' Club, Service Organizations, and local business merchants.

Why did the marathon succeed? First, everyone pooled their efforts—coach, golf team members, golf pro, and the community. For instance, golf team members took turns caddying, spotting balls, and keeping score. Second, the golf pro readied himself by dieting and playing racquetball to reach the level of fitness necessary to keep up a strong pace. Third, the golf pro generated interest by attempting to improve his playing performance from the previous year. He played out of a cart in an attempt to break his previous record of total holes played.

The fund raising event succeeded for these reasons:

1. Many people pledged their support to a worthy cause.

2. The professional golfer attracted considerable interest in the community. He let everyone know thirty days in advance when the marathon would take place. He sold pledges to club members and emphasized that the money would go directly into the Junior Golf

Fund. Note: It takes an outstanding golfer to generate substantial revenue. People tend to lean toward the efforts of a professional.

3. The marathon took place during ideal weather conditions.
4. The community showed its appreciation for the time donated by the golf pro and his personal sacrifice to insure the success of the campaign. Few golfers, pro or amateur, can play golf for nine straight hours without mental and physical preparation.

The coach spent many hours designing and posting signs advertising the marathon. He also designed pledge forms (Figure 12-3), distributed them throughout the community, and contacted service clubs for group pledges.

Support Junior Golf
May 25, 1979

Ed Vasconcellos, head pro at Diamond Oaks, will play a golf marathon on May 25, 1979 in support of the Rosevillle High School District golf teams and Junior Golf Projects. Ed will play all day for a small pledge based on pars, birdies, and eagles. All money will be for support of Junior Golf in the Roseville Area.

A pledge of 1¢ per par, 2¢ per birdie, and 3¢ per eagle can be a tremendous help. Higher pledges will be greatly appreciated.

Eddie will be playing from dawn to dusk with an objective of at least 108 holes.

Roseville High School District Golf Pledge
For Junior Golf

_____ cents per par   _____ cents per eagle

_____ cents per birdie   _____ cents for reaching
                                                          greens in regulation

Send Pledges to: Diamond Oaks Golf Course, or Carl Foote, Roseville High School.

Jerry Williams, Oakmont High School

Bill Barker, Del Oro High School

Name _____

Address _____

City _____

Phone Number _____

FIGURE 12-3 Support junior golf

All the money earned went directly into the Junior Golf Program bank account. Part of the money will support three two-hundred-dollar scholarships for Junior Golfers representing three different high schools in the area.

The golf marathon holds a bright future. In Spring, 1980, the marathon earned approximately $1,500.00.

THE MAKINGS OF A BOOSTER CLUB

Several years ago an assistant football coach and a local businessman from Roseville, California, decided to form a Booster Club to raise money for the football program. The football field needed renovation and there wasn't enough money available to cover the expense. The football field required new bleachers and stadium lights. Because of the conditions, football teams had to play their games elsewhere. Thanks to strong community support, the Booster Club provided enough money to install new lights and bleachers.

Eighty families within the community make up the bulk of the membership. Only six to twelve families, however, take an active part in club events.

The club's first vice-president, a school administrator, regularly attends meetings and directs activities between the club and school. Club fund raising projects include such things as selling jackets, seat cushions, buttons, and tee shirts. The club also sponsors dances, jogathons, and athletic tournaments.

The Booster Club raises an average of $13,000 a year. The money, however, doesn't come easily. Many people, including coaches, athletes, and teachers, downgrade the efforts of the Booster Club. Why? They feel the club works only for football. "We help other athletic teams too," says Beverly Nelson, club president. "In fact, we've given money to the girls' gymnastic team, varsity baseball team, and helped pay for the new basketball scoreboard."

The local press and school newspaper helped out by printing articles that outlined the goals and objectives of the club. Communication is the bread and butter of any successful fund raising organization. The Roseville Booster Club distributes a single page information sheet to stimulate interest, gather community support, and encourage people to join. (Figure 12-4).

How might a coach go about starting a Booster Club? Here are seven suggestions:

One, find out if the community will actively support a Booster Club. Talk with local merchants and business people. Volunteer to speak at service club luncheons. Spend time selling the idea around town. And above all, use an enthusiastic approach when selling the program.

Roseville High School Boosters Club
P.O. Box 457
Roseville, CA 95678

Dear Faculty:

Roseville High School Boosters Club is organized to provide support for the athletic teams at Roseville High School.

The primary goal for the last several years has been returning the Tigers to Hanson Field. This major project is in the final stages. New lights were installed in 1979-80. A portion of the new bleachers will be completed in 1980. Additional improvements will be made in the next several years.

Donations were also made to the gymnastic, basketball, track, wrestling, football, soccer, and girls' basketball teams.

Meetings are open to the public on the first Wednesday of each month at 7:30 p.m. in Room 708 behind Moeller Gym. Dues are $3.00 per family per year.

Please join us.

Duane and Beverly Nelson
President
624-3798

– –

Please add our names to the membership list of the Roseville High School Boosters Club. Enclosed you will find our $3.00.

Name _____ Telephone _____

Address _____
Street   City   Zip

We would be happy to help with one or more of the following projects.

_____ Country Western Dance September 27, 1980	_____ Tiger Run Spring, 1981
_____ Girls' Basketball Tournament January, 1981	_____ Football Programs Summer, 1981
_____ Dinner Dance February 28, 1981	_____ Raffles and Cushion Sales
_____ Recycling	_____ Baking
_____ Other _____	

FIGURE 12-4 Roseville High School Boosters Club

Two, prepare a tentative plan of action. Establish realistic goals and objectives. Contact other Booster Clubs for helpful advice.

Three, seek administrative assistance. Receive clearance for future plans and activities. A local Booster Club needs the support of the school district.

Four, find key people in the community to hold offices in the club.

Five, make a personal commitment to work hard and not to be easily discouraged when things go awry.

Six, keep the community informed concerning club meetings, activities, and fund raising projects. Encourage the local press and school newspaper to run news bulletins about club functions.

Seven, solicit the support of athletes, parents, teachers, and students.

BOOSTERS CLUBS OF AMERICA

Boosters Clubs of America is a program of the American Sports Education Institute (A.S.E.I.), a nonprofit service organization whose program plans to help schools throughout the United States raise the necessary funds for conducting sports activity and physical education. All the money raised by local booster clubs remains within the community from which it was raised.

A yearly membership fee of $35.00 per booster club provides many free services. These services include some twenty-five free publications written to develop club operations and fund raising ideas and procedures. A professional staff is available to research and develop specialized programs to meet the specific needs of booster clubs.

Why is the Boosters Clubs of America necessary?

The higher costs of officials, transportation, the rising costs of uniforms and equipment are placing enormous strains on athletic budgets, particularly at the school level. An additional problem is Title IX's mandate requiring that the number of girls' sports equal the number of sports for boys. The increased costs and product liability have forced insurance costs sky high. To offset the increased financial demands, school and community youth groups must lean more heavily on supportive groups such as booster organizations. It is the purpose of the Boosters Clubs of America to help start new boosters clubs where needed and to help existing groups become more efficient in their over-all operation.

How is the Boosters Clubs of America funded?

Initially, seed money came from sporting goods manufacturers, the Sporting Goods Agents Association, the Sporting Goods Manufacturers Association, and individuals concerned with the serious funding problems facing school sports. Significant progress was being made, and the Sporting Goods Manufacturers Association decided to contribute additional funds to the program to see it through its second year of operation. The Boosters Clubs of America seeks to become self-supportive within the next three years through membership, individual sponsorship, grants from foundations and national and state-wide conventions.

What are the goals of the Boosters Clubs of America?

The goal of the Boosters Clubs of America is to help thousands of volunteer members of booster clubs raise one billion dollars for sports and physical education programs in the United States. They hope to accomplish this through educational and leadership training programs and by providing forums for learning and sharing ideas in successful activities. A nationwide program is directed at creating new boosters clubs and teaching others how to conduct fund raising.

In the future, booster club members will be instrumental in the enactment of legislation that is concerned with the support of school and community sports programs.

For more information contact:
Boosters Clubs of America
200 Castlewood Drive
North Palm Beach, Florida 33408

POINTS TO REMEMBER

It's costing school districts more money each year to operate their athletic programs. Coaches needing new equipment and facilities are busy organizing fund raising projects. They employ the services of athletes, students, parents, administrators, and community leaders.

Many coaches spend long, hard hours soliciting funds within the school and community. A coach should seek advice from those experienced in raising funds—the dean of student activities, president of local booster club, school principal, and fund raising organizations.

A one-time fund raising event earns a limited amount of money. In order to keep funds flowing into the athletic program, a coach should work with key people in the community to form a local boosters club.

Fortunately, the Boosters Clubs of America offers help to schools throughout the United States. The organization distributes free information designed to develop club operations and fund raising ideas and procedures.

QUESTIONS

1. According to a survey by the American Sports Education Institute, what factors are causing shortages in school athletic budgets?

2. What are the advantages of charging athletes a fee to participate?
3. What are the disadvantages of charging athletes a   fee to participate?
4. What guidelines should a coach follow in organizing an in-school fund raising campaign?
5. Why should coaches seek help before organizing community fund raising events?
6. What factors should a coach consider before setting fund raising goals?
7. How will a fund raising master plan aid the coach?
8. Why are campus leaders important to the success of a fund raiser?
9. Why should a fund raising campaign use a positive theme?
10. How do incentives help volunteer workers try harder?
11. How should a coach publicize a fund raising project?
12. Why is keeping accurate records important in fund raising?
13. In what ways can a coach give recognition to volunteer workers?
14. What things should a coach consider in selecting a project?
15. How can a local booster club help an athletic program?
16. What problems do some booster clubs face?
17. What things should a coach consider before starting a booster club?
18. How does the Boosters Clubs of America help schools throughout the country?

Putting Together an Athletic Handbook and Yearbook

> *All that is valuable in human society depends upon the opportunity for development accorded the individual.*
>
> Albert Einstein

Coaches need to drive nails of wisdom into the cerebrums of their athletes. Occasionally a nail strikes something hard causing it to bend or fall out, thus failing to penetrate. Bent nails give way to shaky memories, which, in turn, produce athletes who fail to respond in an acceptable manner. Yet a coach shouldn't expect athletes to remember everything that has been thrown at them at one time. After all, coaches rely on experience and knowledge to get them by. Most athletes, however, aren't as fortunate. They need specific directions to guide them through the season. Therefore, an athletic handbook saves time and energy by listing policies, procedures, and guidelines which direct the behavior of athletes.

A yearbook, on the other hand, summarizes the events of the season, and captures those happy moments that bring joy and satisfaction to most athletes.

This chapter examines ways to compile, distribute, and utilize an athletic handbook and a yearbook.

WHAT IS THE PURPOSE OF AN
ATHLETIC HANDBOOK?

An athletic handbook serves an athlete in many ways. Here are seven of them:

- To let athletes know what to expect.
- To offer specific guidelines for personal improvement.
- To help develop self-confidence and self-respect.
- To stress the importance of working harmoniously with others.
- To help develop a winning attitude.
- To help build determination, dedication, and discipline.

A school district may benefit if these items are included in an athletic handbook:

- District policies and regulations.
- Eligibility requirements, insurance information, and the procedure for taking a physical examination.
- Code of conduct for athletes.

Parents, too, may benefit if an athletic handbook carries a section outlining parental responsibility to the athlete, school, and community.

SHOULD EVERY COACH PROVIDE
A HANDBOOK FOR ATHLETES?

Whether or not a coach distributes an athletic handbook depends largely on school policy, philosophy of athletic director, or how the coach feels about issuing them.

Some school districts feel coaches should establish individual guidelines commensurate with the needs of their sport. Other districts believe a district-wide athletic handbook covering all sports should be issued by coaches. School districts hold different opinions as to what should be included in a handbook and who should assemble it. For instance, a school may delegate this responsibility to the athletic director or to individual head coaches. Most coaches prefer to use their own discretion in compiling athletic handbooks for members of their teams. Regardless of what direction an athletic department takes, one factor remains clear: All athletes should have a definite set of guidelines to follow throughout the season.

WHAT DETERMINES THE LENGTH
OF A HANDBOOK?

Usually the coach decides how long a handbook should be. There is no set limit for the number of pages a coach must include. However, a coach should keep in mind that a large, thick handbook bulging with extraneous material may do little more than gather dust.

Generally, a handbook should cover only those points that serve the best interest of the athlete and team. Again, the coach is in the best position to make this decision.

WHAT SHOULD A COACH INCLUDE
IN A HANDBOOK?

This varies greatly with each coach. In this section we'll examine samples from different athletic handbooks (basketball, baseball, softball, wrestling, and tennis) to see how coaches present their materials.

These coaches began with a letter of welcome from the athletic director.

Dear Athlete and Parents:

We are pleased to have your son/daughter as a member of one of our athletic teams. Athletics are an integral part of our educational system, and we are very interested in the part played by athletics in education. The athletic coaching staff believes that this part of our program can and does play a leading role in your son's/daughter's education. We know you are intensely interested in your son's/daughter's becoming an outstanding individual, and we assure you that this is also our primary goal.

Three of the important phases of a person's development are physical condition, mental condition, and moral attitude. Challenging team mates and opponents on a physical basis helps build confidence, courage, and condition.

Mentally, we can provide, through athletics, many experiences that have a direct carryover into life. First, accepting responsibility and carrying it through to a successful end. For example, competing before hundreds of people during a season, knowing that others are depending on him/her. Second, "the will to win." Athletics offers countless opportunities for a participant to experience success. Our desire is to see these experiences help an athlete succeed in later life. Third, it is important how we play the game. Fair play and sportsmanship are more important than winning at all costs.

We have enclosed this set of Athletic Eligibility Requirements and Code of Conduct in order that you and your son/daughter will become familiar with them.

This summary is for the benefit of you, your son/daughter, and the school. We hope that no one will be hurt because they are unfamiliar with the rules that govern athletics in our school.

If at any time the coaching staff can be of any service to you or your son/daughter, please feel free to call on us.

Very Sincerely Yours,

_____

(Athletic Director)

Eligibility Requirements (Part 1)

To participate in athletics a student must be eligible by the following rules of eligibility.

A. To be eligible an athlete:
1. Must be passing in all subjects but one, each grading period, quarter and semester grades count.
2. Must have been in school the previous quarter and semester and passed in all subjects but one.
3. Must have on file:
    a. Record of physical examination by a doctor during the *current school year.*
    b. Record of tetanus shot within five years.
    c. Parent Permit Sheet with parent's or guardian's signature for current school year.
4. Must not play on any outside team, in any California Interscholastic Federation approved sport, while playing on a school team.
5. Must present a clear Athletic Clearance Card to the coach before participating in any practice or contest.
    a. Athletes are responsible for all equipment issued to them listed on their Athletic Clearance Card. Equipment not returned at the end of the season must be paid for before the card is clear.
6. Professionals are not eligible.
    a. A professional is one who coaches or teaches athletics for compensation or one who competes:
        (1) For cash or merchandise or for any other compensation.
        (2) For a personal prize of any sort over $10.00 in value. This would apply to awards received from any source during the school year, September 1

to June 15. Such award cannot be cash or a gift certificate. It may be a suitably engraved medal, badge, plaque, picture certificate, or trophy.

    (3) Under an assumed name.

    (4) In a game or contest where any member or members of his team receives compensation.

7. Interpretations

    a. The following acts are violations of amateurism:

        (1) Competition in any sport under an assumed name.

        (2) Receipt, directly or indirectly, of any pay or financial benefit in consideration of, or as a reward for, participation in any sport in any public competition, or disposing of prizes for personal gain.

        (3) Acceptance of payment for loss of time or wages while participating in athletics.

        (4) Intentional violation of eligibility rules established by the California Interscholastic Federation, or by the school in which the student is enrolled.

        (5) Acceptance of material or financial inducement to attend a school for the purposes of engaging in athletics, regardless of the source of that material or financial inducement.

        (6) Receipt of payment for services as an official in any sport (see b-2 below).

    b. The following acts are not considered violations of amateruism:

        (1) Caddying for pay.

        (2) Recreation, playground, or camp employment of a public or semi-public nature. Officiating, if part of the several duties included in the job assignment, will not cause an athlete to lose amateur standing. Athletes serving as lifeguards or water safety instructors shall not lose their amateur standing.

8. Rulings

    a. An athlete is ineligible and deemed a professional if he or she participates in any tryout for a collegiate or professional team at any time during the school year (September 1 to June 15).

    b. Softball is considered the same as baseball as far as rules are concerned.

    c. Any boy who takes part in an exhibition of boxing or wrestling not under the direct control of his school will be barred from further high school athletic competition for one year from the date of the last offense.

d. High school golfers who compete in tournaments where money prizes are offered must file a declaration in writing, before competing, with the Secretary of the CIF Section, indicating whether they are competing as an amateur or as a professional. Failure to do so will be deemed cause for disbarment from further high school golf matches. This does not relieve the participant from complying with all other rules regarding amateurism.

e. An athlete who has reached his or her nineteenth birthday before September 1st is not eligible for high school competition.

f. A student who transfers from one school to another school without change of residence on the part of the parent or legal guardian, or court order, or board ruling, shall be ineligible in the second school for a period of time equivalent to one semester at the new school.

g. A student is entitled to athletic competition during a maximum of the first eight semesters at a four year high school, following completion of the eighth grade in any school.

Code of Conduct (Part 2)

I. All athletes are expected to obey the following Code of Conduct rules or be ineligible for athletics.

A. The athlete must be a good citizen of the school and the community.

1. An athlete who has been found delinquent or been placed on probation by the probation department, or a court, may be ineligible as long as he or she is on probation unless he or she has approval of the administration and probation department.

2. An athlete who conducts himself or herself in such a manner that in the opinion of school authorities his or her conduct would reflect unfavorably upon other students, the school or the community, may be declared ineligible.

   a. Conduct of athletes on campus.

      (1) Athletes will be well groomed and neat.

      (2) Athletes shall not use profanity.

      (3) Athletes shall not haze new students, fight, etc.

      (4) Athletes must have a good attendance record.
          (a) Must be in school the day of game or of practice.
      (5) Athletes should be leaders and help maintain proper conduct.
          (a) Should show respect of fellow students, faculty members, and administration.
      (6) Athletes will maintain proper standards of behavior in class and on the school ground.
      (7) No roughhousing or throwing towels in the locker room or shower.

b. Conduct of athletes while traveling to and from contests.
      (1) Athletes are expected to dress and conduct themselves in a manner that will reflect favorably upon the team at all times.
      (2) Athletes are expected to be on time.
          (a) Athletes should know what time the bus leaves for contests. Busses will leave as scheduled. Any athlete who misses the bus will not be allowed to play.
      (3) Athletes will travel to and from all contests in transportation provided by the school.
          (a) Athletes may be released to their parents only. The parent or parents must present to the coach a Release of Liability form signed by parent.
          (b) Athletes will behave on busses when traveling.

c. General Rules of Conduct of Athletes
      (1) Practice regulations
          (a) Athletes must attend all practices unless excused by the coach before practice starts or athlete is absent from school that day.
          (b) Practice will be held every school day unless otherwise notified.
          (c) Practice will usually start fifteen minutes after the close of school.
          (d) No athlete is to leave practice until dismissed by the coach.
          (e) Proper practice uniform will be worn every day.

(f)   No cleats or spikes are to be worn in locker room.

(g)   Hangers are to be removed from the locker room and placed on rack outside.

(2)   Uniforms

(a)   Athletes are responsible for all equipment and uniforms issued to them.

(1)   All equipment and uniforms must be returned to the coach clean and in proper condition at the end of a season or upon an athlete's leaving the team or school.

(2)   All equipment not returned must be paid for.

(b)   Athletes are to keep all equipment and uniforms clean. Practice uniforms should be washed each week.

(c)   School equipment is never sold. Anyone seen with school equipment in possession will be considered a thief.

(3)   Training rules

(a)   No smoking.

(b)   No drinking of alcoholic beverages.

(c)   Obey the specific rules of the coach.

(4)   Dropping or quitting a sport

(a)   An athlete who desires to quit must notify her or his coach as soon as possible.

(b)   An athlete who quits a sport will not be allowed to participate in any other sport during the same season without permission of the coach.

(c)   All equipment must be returned to the issuing coach immediately upon her or his quitting, or be paid for if lost.

Insurance And Physical Examinations (Part 3)

A.   Recent legislation requires that any student of any "educational institution" who practices or participates in any interscholastic athletic event, MUST be insured for $1,500.00 of Accidental Death Insurance, plus $1,500.00 of insurance covering the medical expenses of accidental injuries. Our school district will carry the Accidental Death Insurance.

Students will be excluded from extramural athletic activities if their parents are unable to assure the district that adequate insurance is in force which meets the requirements of this law.

B. Accidents must be reported promptly to the coach.

C. We would like to stress that the competitive athletic program is an extra-curricular activity which is voluntary on the part of those participating. There are certain risks involved that must be assumed by the students and the parents. The school will do everything possible to reduce the possibility of injury, such as providing adequate protective equipment, trained and qualified coaches, mouth-pieces, etc., but the school cannot be held responsible for injuries or the cost thereof, except in cases of negligence, and then only by court determination.

D. If you do not wish to assume the risk of injury and the cost thereof, your student should not participate in athletics. The school cannot be held responsible for injuries except by a court of law.

II. Physical Examinations

A. Physical examinations (and tetanus immunizations within five years) are required for all athletes each school year before they may participate. Each fall prior to the start of school, local physicians come to the school and provide these examinations free. If a student does not or cannot avail himself or herself of this public service, he or she must secure an examination and tetanus immunization at her or his own expense, before she or he may participate.

Now let's see how individual coaches handled specific items related to their sports.

Coaches' Message (Girls' Softball)

We believe softball is the most individual of all team sports. Each player has her own unique skill and is responsible for her own "part" of the whole team. The basic skills of throwing, catching, and batting are the same, but each player in each position must take those skills and develop them so that they become the best for that position.

We would also hope that each girl has fun while becoming an active part of her team.

Coaches' Welcome (Wrestling)

We the coaches wish to congratulate you on your decision to join our CHAMPIONSHIP wrestling team.

Our wrestling team has a proud history. We have more league, sub-section, and section team championships than all other sports combined in the history of our school.

In the past, our team has been complimented for being humble in victory and gracious in defeat: these compliments have been voiced by opposing wrestlers, opposing coaches, officials, school administrators, parents, and fans.

As you are now a member of a CHAMPIONSHIP team, you must do your share; that is, be an asset to the team—not a liability.

To be a champion you must be a man and a gentleman at home, in the community, at school, during matches and meets. This does not mean you cannot be a fierce competitor, instead, it means you are indeed a great competitor, competing within socially accepted rules and regulations.

Philosophy (Boys' Basketball)

Athletic competition is a great training ground for life. The lessons you learn on the court will be of value to you in more ways than you may ever know. Some of the most important areas, I believe, are fair play, sportsmanship, humility, success, failure, self-control, understanding, and patience. The game of basketball, like the game of life, must be a team game. There is no short cut to success. Success requires hard work and dedication.

Everyone should establish some goal for which to strive. The most worthwhile team goal is to be the league champions. If you make it a personal goal to do your very best, you'll experience an exciting event: a true feeling of satisfaction.

Coaches' Expectations (Girls' Softball)

We expect that you will:

1. Attend all practices unless excused by your coach.
2. Be at practice on time—practice begins at 3:00 sharp!
3. Not leave practice early without first checking with the coach.
4. Attend all games. Know when and where to catch busses.
5. Wear neat and suitable attire for practice.
6. Be responsible for taking care of equipment—yours and ours.
7. Always conduct yourselves as young ladies. Talking and chatter is part of the game, but know proper limits and conduct. Refrain from making personal or derogatory comments to fellow teammates, visiting team players, officials, coaches, or fans.
8. Always encourage each other to talk it up and hustle.
9. Always be a good sport whether winning or losing.

Parent Responsibility (Boys' Basketball)

The value of interscholastic competition and its overall effect on the athlete and school are too often clouded by the actions and words of thoughtless adults at an athletic contest. Parents have a responsibility toward their youngster and the school as the student body tries to display the best in sportsmanship during athletic contests.

Disappointment is a natural offshoot of a game that is lost, of a play that is unsuccessful, or the "breaks" that seem to go the other way. A person's ability to cope with this disappointment determines maturity, not the person's age.

To preface each season's competition these facts should be understood by both parents and athletes:

1. The score is recorded at all athletic events to determine a winner. Unless a contest is entered with the idea of winning, the competitive aspect and much of the value of an athletic program is lost.
2. When a boy reports for athletic practice at the beginning of a season there is no guarantee that he will be selected as a member of a team.
3. The coach must make the selection of players that he deems best for each position and that will develop into the best team. His opinion may not always agree with the opinion of others, but the authority vested in the coach by virtue of his position is the final word in team selection. An adult can only injure a boy or a team by derogatory statements about that team or the coach.
4. Because a boy makes first string for one game does not necessarily mean that he will be first string or even play for the balance of the season. A boy may be moved up at any time, within the policy of the school, and replace a first stringer if the coach considers that the boy is better and will strengthen the team.

General Policies (Girls' Softball)

1. Must attend school three periods on day of game.
2. Must participate in PE on day of game, if enrolled in PE.
3. Coach reserves the right to set reasonable dress standards for practice and games. No cutoffs.
4. Long hair must be pulled back off face for safety reasons.
5. Must wear uniform or gym clothes (if ok'd by coach).
6. Athlete is expected to be present at all games unless absent from school or excused by coach. If you are scheduled to play, you are expected to play.
7. The athlete is responsible for knowing what time bus leaves for game.
8. A school cut makes a player ineligible for the next game.
9. An athlete must wear shoes and socks.
10. Players must have the courtesy to check with the coach ahead of time if they cannot attend a game or practice.
11. Once moved up to varsity a player must participate at the varsity level during the rest of high school.

12. Any eligible students who wish to participate in a given sport will be allowed a try out period in order that they may be evaluated by the coach.

13. Once a player quits a team he or she must get permission from the coach of that team before participating in any other sport.

Special Safety Rules (Tennis)

1. Never jump over nets.
2. Never throw your racket.
3. Keep doors to courts closed.
4. Watch for sand on courts.
5. Immediately remove any obstacles from court.
6. Keep all equipment in one spot on court.
7. Always be aware of playing distance behind baseline.
8. Keep loose balls away from playing area.
9. Roll all balls when picking them up during practice sessions (to central pick up spot).

Winning Style of Play (Boys' Basketball)

Winning this year will depend on many different things. I'll mention a few:

1. We must out-hustle every team we play. This has reference to every aspect of the game.
2. We must be in better shape than any team we play. Our success will depend on it.
3. We must be opportunists. Every loose ball, every jump ball, every error by our opponents must be turned into a basket. This is the mark of a champion.
4. Our total game, offensively and defensively, will be based on pressure basketball. We will put pressure on our opponents until they crack. This, more than anything, will require one hundred percent effort from everyone. As soon as one man lets down we will collapse as a team. We may make mistakes, but never let us be accused of making a mistake because we weren't hustling.
5. The team that controls the boards usually wins the game. Without a doubt, the most overestimated abilities are height jumping and skill. The keys to rebounding are position and guts.
6. Defense pays off! You cannot always depend on having a good night offensively, but under no circumstances should you have a poor game defensively. Defense is work, but it pays off in victory.

Diet (Wrestling)

You should continue normal eating during wrestling season, in fact, eat more due to your increased activity.

If you wish to lose weight, the following ideas will prove useful:

1. If possible, stop eating fried foods. Eat the same foods, but broil or bake them.
2. Eat plenty of green vegetables.
3. Drink skim or low fat milk, if possible.
4. Eat very little potato, bread, and rice.
5. Skip desserts.
6. Drink fruit juice.
7. The hot lunch in the cafeteria is designed to put on weight. If you eat in the cafeteria, eat salads, juice, milk, soup, and so on.
8. Either take salt tablets or take a salt shaker and sprinkle all foods liberally with salt.

Playing Tips (Girls' Softball)

Here are ten suggestions for playing the outfield:

1. Throws to home plate should come in on first bounce.
2. Be mentally alert. Know what to do with the ball.
3. Play back so you can run up to meet the ball.
4. Never run backwards on your heels.
5. Call out loud for high fly balls.
6. Try for all balls hit in your area. Get together with other outfielders.
7. Get rid of the ball immediately. Try to keep the ball one base ahead of the runner.
8. Throw ahead of the runner.
9. Back up infielders. Back up each other.
10. Anticipate overthrows, back up those players.

When fielding ground balls charge toward the ball. Don't wait for it to get to you. Field the ball before making a throw. Use your body as a shield to guard the ball. If the ball comes to rest on the ground, pick it up with your bare hand.

Care of Equipment (Wrestling)

After receiving your equipment you are responsible for its care. If you lose it, you must pay for those items lost. If you do not want to accept this responsibility, do not join the wrestling team.

Your practice tights should be washed at least twice a week. Regular washing will enable them to last longer and will also be more hygienic to wear.

Your contest gear should be washed after each use. Wash it in warm water and soap. Do not add bleach. It may be dried in a dryer that has a "no heat" selection.

We suggest that you keep contest gear at home until meet days. This will cut down on your loss by theft. Leave contest sweats with a teammate or a coach during the time you wrestle in a match or a meet.

The rules of wrestling state that you have high top shoes; you will not be allowed on the mat with low cut shoes.

Requirements for Letter Awards (Boys' Basketball)

1. To be eligible for any award, the athlete must obtain a student body card, and must comply with all training regulations set down by the coach, the head of the department, and the principal of the school.
2. Letter awards shall be determined as follows: Basketball players shall participate in fifty percent of the quarters of all contests (any portion of a quarter played shall constitute a full quarter).
3. Note: The final decision for issuing athletic awards shall belong to the coach. Even if an athlete has not met the requirements for an award, he may be given the award upon the coach's recommendation.

Team Offensive Records (Varsity Baseball)

Here are the team's offensive records over the past fifteen years. Maybe you will be the one to break an individual record.

EVENT	RECORD	YEAR	ATHLETE
Homeruns	6	1967	Bill Turner
Triples	5	1971	Joe Chaves
Doubles	12	1970	Chuck Long
Base Hits	34	1975	Larry Howard
Runs Batted In	30	1978	Robert Guthrie
Batting Average	.543	1973	George White
Sacrifice Flies	8	1978	William Lew
Sacrifice Bunts	7	1972	Larry Nichols
Base on Balls	24	1969	Richard Morris
Stolen Bases	26	1968	Skip Collins
Runs Scored	31	1979	Bill Harris

Contest Schedule (Girls' Softball)

Sierra Foothill League
Softball Schedule
1977

Tues. March 22
Roseville at Marysville
Lindhurst at Placer
Nevada at Del Oro
Oakmont Bye

Thurs. March 24
Del Oro at Lindhurst
Marysville at Oakmont
Roseville at Nevada
Placer Bye

Tues. March 29
Oakmont at Nevada
Placer at Marysville
Lindhurst at Roseville
Del Oro Bye

Thurs. March 31
Nevada at Placer
Oakmont at Lindhurst
Marysville at Del Oro
Roseville Bye

Tues. April 12
Marysville at Lindhurst
Placer at Roseville
Oakmont at Del Oro
Nevada Bye

Thurs. April 14
Roseville at Oakmont
Del Oro at Placer
Nevada at Marysville
Lindhurst Bye

Tues. April 19
Placer at Oakmont
Del Oro at Roseville
Lindhurst at Nevada
Marysville Bye

Thurs. April 21
Marysville at Roseville
Placer at Lindhurst
Del Oro at Nevada
Oakmont Bye

Tues. April 26
Lindhurst at Del Oro
Oakmont at Marysville
Nevada at Roseville
Placer Bye

Thurs. April 28
Nevada at Oakmont
Marysville at Placer
Roseville at Lindhurst
Del Oro Bye

Tues. May 3
Placer at Nevada
Lindhurst at Oakmont
Del Oro at Marysville
Roseville Bye

Thurs. May 5
Lindhurst at Marysville
Roseville at Placer
Del Oro at Oakmont
Nevada Bye

Tues. May 10
Oakmont at Roseville
Placer at Del Oro
Marysville at Nevada
Lindhurst Bye

Thurs. May 12
Oakmont at Placer
Roseville at Del Oro
Nevada at Lindhurst
Marysville Bye

These examples show what items some coaches choose to include in their athletic handbooks. To get a clearer picture let's examine the outlines of four different athletic handbooks.

Wrestling Handbook

A. Welcome (Athletic Director)
   1. Eligibility Requirements
   2. Code of Conduct
B. Practice Sessions
C. Conditioning
D. General Information
E. Care of Equipment
F. Weight Control and Dieting
G. Challenge Day
H. Safety Factors
I. Contest Schedule

Tennis Handbook

A. Welcome (Athletic Director)
   1. Eligibility Requirements
   2. Code of Conduct
B. Uniforms
C. Traveling
D. Matches
E. Play Situations in Tennis
   1. Where to stand
   2. Choosing the right shot.
   3. Serving
   4. Returning the serve
   5. Rallying from the backcourt.
   6. Playing against a man at the net.
   7. Going to the net
F. Safety Factors

Softball Handbook

A. Welcome (Athletic Director)
   1. Eligibility Requirements
   2. Code of Conduct
B. Coach's Message
C. Uniforms
D. Practice Regulations
E. Training Rules
F. General Policies
G. Coach's Expectation
H. Play Situations in Softball

      1. Defensive play
      2. Overhand Throwing (with diagrams)
      3. Batting skills
      4. Baserunning techniques
      5. Playing the infield
      6. Playing the outfield
      7. Tips for the catcher
I. Contest Schedule

Basketball Handbook

A. Welcome (Athletic Director)
      1. Eligibility Requirements
      2. Code of Conduct
B. Basketball Philosophy
C. Conduct of a Basketball Player
      1. Be a gentleman
      2. Be a leader
      3. Be a student
      4. Be determined in all areas.
      5. Be a player
      6. Be a winner
D. Parent Responsibility
E. Requirements for Letter Awards
F. Contest Schedule

Handing out athletic handbooks doesn't guarantee that athletes (or their parents) will read them. So to emphasize the importance of following these printed guidelines, some coaches do these things:

1. Refer athletes to the handbook often. Continually stress the significance of following rules, regulations, and policies.

2. Require athletes to know and understand handbook information.

3. Insist that athletes have their parents or guardians read the handbook. Include a cover sheet like this:

> I have read the athletic handbook and understand
> its contents. If I have any questions, I'll
> contact _____ at
>   (Coach's Name)
>
> _____
> (Phone Number)
>
>   Date: _____
>   Athlete's Name: _____
>   Parent or guardian's
>   name: _____

A coach can get excellent results by not allowing athletes to participate until the cover sheet is signed and returned.

Tips for Putting Together a Successful Handbook

1. Plan ahead of time. Don't wait until the last minute to put handbooks together.
2. Solicit the help of others, i.e., student aides, student volunteers, team manager, and so on.
3. Attach an attractive cover, something that has visual appeal—humorous cartoon sketches or caricatures.
4. Keep everything attached in folders with fasteners. A stapled handbook usually falls apart the second time it hits the floor.
5. Personalize each handbook by putting athlete's name on the front cover. Many coaches wait until the final cut before passing out handbooks. In this way only members of the roster receive handbooks. Every athlete, however, receives information regarding team policies at pre-season meetings and practice sessions. Usually these are posted around the gym and locker room area.
6. Include a table of contents and number each page.
7. Include team records and outstanding achievements. These generate interest and encourage some athletes to try harder.
8. Present only pertinent information. Avoid loading the handbook with superfluous material. Keep the handbook brief, but concise.

Finally, it's a good idea to give copies of the handbook to the athletic director, principal, and district superintendent. Also, keep extra copies of the handbook around for those athletes who lose theirs.

What Is the Purpose of a Team Yearbook?

A team yearbook brings together information about everything that happened during the season; a gathering of humorous events and situations that athletes tend to remember long after the season ends.

A yearbook is a nice way for the coach to say thanks to athletes, and to those people who helped make the season a success. A yearbook, like a school annual, highlights many exciting events and gives athletes something to thumb through after they leave school.

What Should a Coach Include in a Yearbook?

This is strictly a matter of judgment. No two coaches think or act exactly alike. In fact, some coaches prefer not to hand out athletic handbooks or yearbooks—they say they are either too busy or simply not interested.

To get a better idea of what might go into a yearbook, examine the outline from a varsity baseball coach's yearbook.

VARSITY BASEBALL YEARBOOK

Introduction

This yearbook contains baseball statistics for every player on the varsity baseball team. Statistics on practice games, league games, and the Placer Tournament are included.

This booklet will serve as a remembrance for all players who participated this year.

Although statistical averages are indicators of one's performance, they are not the complete story. Such factors as player attitude, desire, and cooperation do not appear in these averages. These, I believe, are the most important items for consideration.

Special Coach's Message to   21
Athletes
(Letter of thanks to players
for their super effort.)

"Time Out"   22-26
(Cartoon sketches showing players
doing humorous things during the
season.)

The coach poured many hours into gathering statistics and information for the yearbook. Was it worth the effort? According to the
coach, yes. Several athletes and their parents personally thanked the
coach for the manner in which he presented the yearbooks at the baseball awards banquet.

Most athletes aren't turned off by thick yearbooks which illustrate
the fruits of a long, hard season. On the contrary, they show athletes
how well they've done and what specific areas need to be strengthened.
A yearbook serves as a great starting point for returning athletes.

What Are the Advantages of a Yearbook?

There are several benefits, but here are six major advantages:
One, a yearbook recognizes the efforts of all athletes on the squad.
Two, a yearbook shows athletes that the coach is interested in
sharing individual and team results with others.
Three, a yearbook makes a handsome keepsake for athletes and
their parents.
Four, a yearbook may encourage athletes to continue participation
throughout their school years.
Five, a yearbook provides easy access to statistical information;
it gives returning athletes a basis on which to improve.
Six, it provides key information for press coverage and college
coaches interested in recruiting athletes.
The advantages certainly outweigh the time and effort expended
by the coach. The only real complaint received by the baseball coach
came from a pitcher who thought his ERA (earned run average) was too
high!

Tips for Putting Together a Successful Yearbook

A coach should begin to gather information for a yearbook at the
start of the season. A last minute attempt usually fizzles because the
coach seldom finds the time to organize data and put it in publishable
form.

After each contest a coach should summarize the results, put them in respective folders (e.g., defense and offense), and store them in a safe place.

Shortly before the season ends it's a good idea for the coach to gather folders, paper, and willing typists to help put everything together. A yearbook should have an attractive cover, be held together with fasteners, and have the athlete's name appear on the cover.

Points to Remember

An athletic handbook serves to guide athletes throughout the season. It also outlines for parents, administrators, and athletes the goals and objectives of the program.

An athletic handbook should carry sections covering eligibility requirements and code of conduct. The contents, however, are usually determined by the coach, district policies, and needs of the athlete.

A well organized, attractive handbook adds a touch of class to the program. If a coach refers often to the handbook, athletes are more likely to take the handbook seriously. It's discouraging to see handbooks discarded soon after a coach passes them out. Therefore, a coach should do everything possible to stress the importance of reading and studying the athletic handbook.

A team yearbook summarizes the events of the season. A coach who spends the time organizing data and putting it together in a yearbook gives athletes an excellent overview of the season. It also convinces athletes that the coach appreciates their efforts.

A coach should distribute copies of the athletic handbook and yearbook to key personnel in the school district, i.e., the principal, athletic director, and district superintendent. These people should be aware of a team's progress at all times.

Finally, a yearbook encourages some athletes to improve their performances. It provides pertinent data for press coverage and recruiting college coaches.

QUESTIONS

1. In what ways do athletic handbooks serve the needs of athletes?
2. How can a school district benefit from requiring its coaches to distribute athletic handbooks?
3. Why is it important for parents or guardians to read athletic handbooks?
4. In your opinion, do you feel the school district should standardize athletic handbooks? Explain.

5. In your opinion, who do you think should decide what material goes into an athletic handbook? Explain.
6. What often happens to large, thick, athletic handbooks crammed with extraneous material?
7. What major points should be covered under "Eligibility Requirements"?
8. What major points should be covered under "Code of Conduct"?
9. Why do policies and procedures differ with each school district?
10. What can a coach do to encourage athletes to read the handbook?
11. What can a coach do to encourage parents to read the handbook?
12. What things can a coach do to insure the success of an athletic handbook?
13. Why do some coaches pass out yearbooks at the end of the season?
14. What items might be included in a yearbook?
15. How can a yearbook help a returning athlete?
16. What are three advantages of putting together a yearbook?

14

Bringing the Season
to a Smooth Finish

*He who stops being better
stops being good.*

Oliver Cromwell

The season doesn't end with the last scheduled contest. In fact, most coaches find the post-season very demanding. For example, a coach must collect uniforms, check equipment, inspect facilities, plan an awards program, and oversee activities. This requires the coach to keep moving at a brisk pace.

In this chapter we'll review how a coach can close the season on a happy note and make preparations for next year.

BUILDING FOR NEXT YEAR—NOW!

Most coaches realize that directing and maintaining an athletic program is a continuous task. This year's progress doesn't guarantee instant success for the coming season.

A coach who bounces from one sport to another has little time to concentrate on any single sport. Yet the manner in which a coach handles athletes during post-season can, to a certain degree, determine the outcome of future events.

It benefits a coach to follow the actions of athletes and stay in contact with them throughout the year. Here are nine suggestions to

205

help a coach communicate with athletes and encourage them to look ahead.

1. Maintain an open door policy. Talk with athletes about their interests and ambitions. Listen to their problems and, if possible, offer assistance. Let them know you have a genuine interest in their welfare.
2. Work with every athlete, not just two or three key players. Remember, today's reserve often becomes tomorrow's star. Let athletes know that you are interested in them as people, not just athletes.
3. Support their efforts in other activities by attending these functions.
4. Give athletes continuous encouragement. Offer specific guidelines for improvement. Let them know the part each athlete will play in future plans.
5. Listen to their concerns. Allow athletes to evaluate the program. A coach might pass out an evaluation form.
6. Reevaluate team goals. Adjust them according to the results of the Team Evaluation Forms.
7. Constantly sell, sell, sell. A program's success hinges on several critical factors. Player attitude and coaching dedication are two of them.
8. Always speak in positive terms. Build on the team's strong points. Play up those outstanding features that make the team go.
9. Be optimistic. Keep a fresh outlook toward the next season.

TEAM EVALUATION FORM

Sport _____
Date _____

1. List what you feel are the strengths of the program.
2. List what you feel are the weaknesses of the program.
3. List your recommendations for improvement.

Make sure athletes know these comments will be used to improve the athletic program.

Tips on Collecting Equipment and Uniforms

Collecting equipment and uniforms brings its share of frustrations to the coach. Athletes are famous for losing certain items or forgetting to turn materials in on time. The coach may feel a sudden urge to kill.

Murdering athletes, however, carries a stiff penalty and weakens the squad. So let's consider a less violent plan for easing the pain of collecting equipment and uniforms.

First, let's assume most coaches have a standard procedure for issuing equipment. Athletic departments usually require coaches to record on a check out sheet all equipment and uniforms that have been issued to athletes. Figures 14-1a and 14-1b list the items issued to athletes. The coach keeps these sheets in a binder and stores them in a safe place.

Here's a twelve point plan for collecting equipment and uniforms:

- Shortly before the season ends announce to athletes the exact times (days and hours) materials will be collected.
- Place an announcement in the daily bulletin to remind athletes to turn in their gear. Let the announcement run several days. Post reminders in conspicuous places around the gym and locker room area.
- Stress the importance of turning materials in on time.
- Make sure athletes fully understand the policies regarding the return of materials.
- Discuss with athletes any conflict that might interfere with the prompt return of materials.
- Have the team manager and volunteers help gather and store materials.
- The coach should personally inspect materials before accepting them. Student volunteers may not notice lost or damaged materials.
- Request each athlete to hand in materials personally. This eliminates the chances of materials being lost by other athletes. Fellow team members shouldn't shoulder the responsibility for one another's equipment.
- Know the exact amount to charge athletes for lost or damaged materials.
- Restrict an athlete from participating in another school sport until all items are either returned or paid for.
- If an athlete fails to turn in materials within a reasonable length of time, send a bill for lost items.
- If all else fails, contact the athletic director or appropriate administrator. The threat of disciplinary action usually does the trick.

Taking Inventory and Ordering Materials

Coaches shudder at the thought of taking inventory. It's a long, painful session which coaches must go through in order to make adequate preparations for the next year.

Inventory comes soon after athletes turn in their equipment and uniforms. A coach must know what items to repair or purchase.

In many instances, the head coach decides what the program needs, fills out purchase orders, and submits them to the athletic director who, in turn, passes them along to the principal.

Materials Checkout List			

Football

Hanger ___	Prac. Pants ___
Helmet ___	Prac. Jersey ___
Shldr. Pads ___	Game Pants ___
Hip Pads ___	Game Uniform ___
Knee Pads ___	Colored Jersey ___
	White Jersey ___

Basketball

Targer Hose ___	Game Shirt ___
Colored Jersey ___	Game Pants ___
Colored Pants ___	Socks ___
White Jersey ___	Prac. Shirt ___
White Pants ___	Prac. Short ___
Warm up Shirt ___	Sweat Shirt ___
Warm up Pants ___	Sweat Shorts ___
Knee Pads ___	

Baseball	**Wrestling**	**Hockey**	**Tennis**
Jersey	Hanger ___	Skirt	Coat
Socks ___	Prac. Tights ___	Shirt ___	Pants ___
Pants ___	Head Gear ___	Brief ___	Shirts ___
Hat ___	Tights ___	Socks ___	
Belt ___	Uppers ___	Sweat Shirt ___	Dress ___
Slid. Pads ___	Shorts ___	Sweat Pants ___	Sweat Jacket ___
Sanies ___	Shirt ___	Prac. Shirt ___	Prac. Shirt ___
Sw. Shirts ___	Pants ___	Prac. Short ___	Prac. Short ___
Pitch. Jack ___	Game S P ___	Shin Guards ___	Windbreaker ___
Prac. Pants ___	Game S S ___	Stick ___	

Volleyball	**Softball**	**Gymnastics**	**Soccer**
Game Shirt ___	Game Shirt ___	Leotard ___	Shirt ___
Game Short ___	Game Pants ___	Kickpants ___	Pants ___
Kneepads ___	Sweat Shirt ___	Socks ___	Socks ___
Prac. Shirt ___	Sweat Pants ___	Sweat Jacket ___	Sweat Pants ___
Prac. Short ___	Hat ___	Sweat Pants ___	Sweat Shirt ___
Sweat Jacket ___	Socks ___	Prac. Shorts ___	
Sweat Pants ___	Windbreaker ___	Prac. Shirt ___	

Badminton	**Cross Country**	**Swimming**	**Golf**
Dress	Sweat Shirts ___	Swim Suit ___	Shirt
Racket ___	Sweat Pants ___	Sweat Shirt ___	Jacket ___
Prac. Short ___	Running Shirt ___	Sweat Pants ___	
Prac. Shirt ___	Running Pants ___	Cap ___	
Windbreaker ___			

Track	**Practice Equipment**
Sweat Shirts ___	Sweat Shirts ___
Sweat Pants ___	Sweat Pants ___
Game Shirt ___	Practice Shirts ___
Game Shorts ___	Practice Shorts ___

FIGURE 14-1 Materials checkout list

The following suggestions can save the coach embarrassment later on:

1. Keep accurate records. Be able to account for team materials.
2. Make sure team materials are locked in a safe place.
3. Know exactly what materials the team will need for next season.
4. Find out how much money is available for ordering new materials. If there isn't enough money to replace old, worn out uniforms, a coach needs time to plan a fund raising activity.
5. Check out several sporting goods suppliers before placing orders. Select the best and safest equipment money will buy.
6. Always follow district policies when purchasing materials. When in doubt, ask somebody. A baseball coach, for example, found himself in hot water after he ordered baseball hats for his team from a supplier not recommended by the school district. When the hats arrived the coach was ordered to deliver them to a local merchant. The players had to buy their hats from the local dealer.
7. Follow up on purchase orders. Make sure they are sent out on time.
8. When orders arrive be careful to check the contents with the package slip. If everything appears in order, return the package slip to the district office for payment.
9. Store materials in a secure area.

End-of-the-Year Awards

Issuing athletic awards requires sound judgment on the coach's part. Before an award has any real value, two things are necessary: 1) It must be earned by the athlete; 2) It must be presented by the coach in a sincere manner.

Let's see how some coaches handle awards.

Letter Awards

To earn a letter award an athlete must play a specified length of time in league contests or be recommended by the coach to receive one.

Some coaches give letter awards to every athlete on the squad. These coaches believe that any athlete who regularly attends practice and supports the squad deserves to receive a letter. Regardless of how a coach feels about issuing letters, athletes should know what it takes to earn a letter.

Individual Awards

Individual awards act as an incentive for many athletes to excel, to do the best job they possibly can. These awards are intended for those athletes who turn in outstanding performances. Here are some typical examples:

Defensive Player Award

Offensive Player Award

Most Outstanding Athlete Award

Most Improved Athlete Award

Most Valuable Player Award

Not all coaches agree on who should select the winners for these awards. Some coaches feel their athletes should act as judges; others believe the coach is best qualified to make the final decision. If athletes make the decision, the coach can guide them by reminding athletes that an award should be based on total performance, not on one or two outstanding events. A major objection to letting athletes vote is that the outcome often parallels a popularity contest; that is, the most popular athlete on the team receives the Most Outstanding Athlete Award.

Coach's Appreciation Award

It's difficult to describe the "perfect" athlete, the one outstanding individual a coach labels as "the pinnacle of superlative." After all, such an athlete may come around only once in a coach's career.

A "perfect" athlete, to many coaches, is the person who gives one-hundred and ten percent, seldom complains, attends every practice, makes personal sacrifices for the team, and has outstanding athletic ability.

Some coaches feel that these exemplary individuals deserve a special award, one that recognizes the four D's—determination, dedication, desire, and discipline. Furthermore, since these are personal awards made on rare occasions, most coaches buy them with their own money.

Championship Awards

Winning a championship brings its share of busy work for the coach. For example, the soccer team wins the league championship. Excited athletes anticipate receiving their awards on time. Therefore, a coach must check to see that awards have been ordered and will arrive on time for the awards program. Holding an awards program without awards is like fishing without any bait. You go through the motions but come up empty-handed.

Coaches want their athletes to experience complete satisfaction. In order to avoid disappointment, a coach should do these things:

- Make up a list of athletes who will receive awards. Go over the list of names. Make sure nobody is left out.
- Submit the list to the person in charge of ordering athletic awards.
- Confirm that the awards have been ordered.
- Allow sufficient time for delivery.
- If possible, schedule the awards program after the awards arrive.

Competitive Drill Awards

Practice sessions spring to life when coaches include fast-action competitive drills that emphasize a "champion."

Coaches who use competitive drills not only help athletes to recognize their weaknesses and strengths, but give them something to look forward to at the end of the season—small trophies or plaques—which the coach presents at the awards program.

Special Fun Awards

Special fun awards go to those athletes who turn in humorous performances during the season. For example, a baseball player losing a shoe while rounding first base or a tennis player swinging at the ball and losing the racquet.

These, of course, are tongue-in-cheek awards which the coach announces at the close of the program. The awards themselves frequently take the form of whistling and jeering from fellow athletes. The coach may say something like . . . "And now it's my pleasure to announce the winners of the following awards: Lost Shoe Award—Bill Walters; Broken Bat Award—Steve Ramirez; Hanging Curve Ball Award—Joe Davidson." And so on.

A coach, however, may wish to spice up the presentation by giving each winner a token of remembrance. The Lost Shoe Award, for instance, may be an old, worn out tennis shoe with the following inscription:

If found, please return to Bill Walters. He refuses to play in his street shoes.

Letter of Participation

Many school districts present each athlete with a Letter of Participation. These letters recognize the athlete as an active team member. They are usually passed out, along with awards, at the awards program. Often these letters carry the signatures of the student body president, school principal, and coach. Therefore, the coach must remember to sign these letters prior to the awards program. A last minute autograph party shows a lack of organization and tends to snuff the spirit of giving.

All-League Selections

Usually coaches from every school in the league get together at the end of the season to select an all-league team. During this meeting coaches have an opportunity to "push" deserving athletes from their squads. A few coaches may disagree with the final selection, but at least they've had a chance to speak and be heard.

Unfortunately, some coaches miss the meeting. They either mail in their choices or send them along with another coach. In either case, a coach owes it to the team to support deserving athletes.

The all-league selection meeting often brings surprising results. A baseball coach, for example, had the best catcher in the league on his team. The athlete hit well over .300 and led the league in home runs. However, after the last game of the season (an away game), the athlete rode home with friends without permission. As a result, the coach officially kicked the boy off the team.

The athlete's coach requested other coaches not to consider his catcher for all-league honors since the boy was no longer a member of the squad. They didn't. And, unfortunately, the athlete lost out on a gratifying experience.

When selecting an all-league team a coach should keep these things in mind:

- Study the record of each candidate. Listen to what other coaches have to say. Weigh everything before making a decision.
- Support only those athletes who merit recognition.
- Avoid letting prejudices against certain coaches affect your choices.
- Make positive statements about every candidate. A derogatory remark may hurt an athlete's chance of being selected.
- Use your best judgment when casting your final vote.

SETTING UP THE AWARDS PROGRAM

Athletic awards programs vary sharply from district to district. In fact, coaches in the same district often hold different opinions about how a program should be handled. The decision is influenced by district policy, coach's philosophy, desires of athletes, desires of the athletic department, squad size, time of year, availability of facilities and services, and the expense of financing the program.

A coach may elect to work directly with the administration or may independently organize the event with assistance from athletes and their parents.

Let's look at several possibilities and examine the advantages and disadvantages.

The All-School Athletic Awards Assembly

The school sets aside a certain time for all students to attend the athletic awards assembly. Students meet in the gym or auditorium and watch as athletes receive their awards.

Advantages

- All athletes receive their awards at the same time.
- Coaches don't have to make special plans for holding their own programs.
- Athletes are honored before the entire student body.
- The school makes all of the arrangements.

Disadvantages

- Coaches receive a limited time to present athletic awards.
- The program often becomes a long-drawn-out affair.
- Poor acoustics lead to hearing difficulties.
- A crowded gym or auditorium encourages student unrest.
- There is extra work for the maintenance staff.
- Many parents are unable to attend.

Most large schools find it impractical to hold an all-school program. Therefore, as might be expected, coaches are usually better off planning awards programs to fit their individual needs.

Special Athletic Awards Rally

As in the all-school assembly, students gather in one area to view award ceremonies. Usually the band plays while cheerleaders and pom-pom girls perform. The advantages and disadvantages parallel the all-school assembly, with one major difference: there's more stimuli to activate the adrenal glands of students.

Sports Award Banquet

An athletic department may prefer to hold a sports award banquet three times during the year—fall, winter, and spring. For instance, an athletic awards banquet held in late fall would recognize such sports as football, soccer, and cross country. A winter sports awards banquet might honor basketball players, wrestlers, and volleyball teams. The spring awards banquet could be held to honor baseball, track, and gymnastics athletes.

Advantages

- Several coaches, along with the administration, can work together in planning the banquet.
- An evening banquet would allow parents and friends to attend.
- Everybody brings their own utensils and food. The school, in many instances, provides the drinks.
- Only those people invited would attend.
- Expenses could be held to a minimum.
- Coaches would receive more time to honor their athletes.

Disadvantages

- Agreeing on a time and place suitable for everyone.
- Some people leave before the ceremonies are over.
- Occasionally a food shortage occurs. There are always those who fail to bring enough.
- Finding volunteers to set up the banquet and clean up afterwards.
- Some coaches dominate the program by spending too much time presenting awards.

Team Sports Night

Some coaches prefer to hold an awards program for their athletes only. As an example, basketball coaches may organize a potluck dinner for athletes, the athletes' girlfriends, parents, and relatives. This would include the freshmen team, junior varsity, and varsity squads.

Each athlete takes home an information sheet (Figure 14-2). When athletes return these sheets, coaches finalize their plans for the program.

Advantages

- The entire program centers around a single sport.
- Parents and coaches become better acquainted.
- The teams celebrate together and share in each other's success.

Disadvantages

- Some athletes fail to turn in banquet information sheets on time. This, of course, makes planning difficult.

Basketball Awards Night

Are you proud of your son's athletic achievement? If so, show your support by your presence at his awards dinner.

When? Monday night, April 21, 1980

Time? 6:30 P.M. (We will eat at 6:30 sharp)

Where? Roseville High School P.T. Building

What to bring? Everyone should bring plates and eating utensils in addition to the following:

Varsity—hot dish and salad for at least 8 persons.

Jr. Varsity—Hot dish and dessert for at least 8 persons.

Frosh—Hot dish and rolls for at least 8 persons.

. . . .

DRINKS WILL BE PROVIDED

If parents cannot attend, please sent the items mentioned above with your son.

YOUR SON MUST BE PRESENT TO RECEIVE HIS AWARD

We need to set up the correct number of tables, so please return the bottom portion of this letter to school with your son by Thursday, April 17, 1980. We invite you to bring your families.

— —

Detach and return to one of the coaches by April 17, 1980.

I will   will not   attend _____'s awards dinner.
  (circle one)   (Student Name)

There will be _____ members of my family attending, including my athlete.

                              _____
                                      (Parent Signature)

FIGURE 14-2 Basketball awards night

- Sometimes more people attend than expected.
- An unhappy parent might use this occasion to voice objections.
- Finding volunteers to help prepare tables and clean up afterwards.

Individual Team Awards Dinner

A coach may wish to keep the awards ceremony simple by holding a dinner at a local buffet or pizza restaurant for only one team, say the varsity baseball team.

The coach calls ahead and reserves a space. People who attend "pay as they go." After everyone finishes eating the coach comments about each athlete, the team's success, and future aspirations. Then the coach hands out awards.

Advantages

- The coach doesn't have to send home information sheets asking parents to bring food.
- The program isn't restricted to the school grounds.
- Usually a limited number of people attend and ceremonies don't last too long.
- People wait on themselves and order their own food.
- There are no tables to set up or messes to worry about afterwards.

Disadvantages

- Not all people like pizza or buffet restaurants.
- Sometimes slow service leads to agitation.
- Other coaches and athletes in the same sport (freshmen or junior varsity) feel left out. Their absence from the awards program suggests that their efforts aren't appreciated.

These are only a few ways coaches close out their seasons. Some coaches favor holding potluck dinners at their houses or hosting an awards day picnic. As a rule, most coaches stick with tradition and do the same thing every year.

Regardless of how coaches choose to handle their awards programs, they should remember to do certain things. They are:

1. Plan well ahead. Check with the administration concerning use of facilities.
2. Make sure athletic awards are ready to be distributed.
3. Choose a time convenient for most people.
4. Invite key personnel to attend the program, i.e., principal, athletic director, district superintendent.
5. Start and end the program on time.
6. Be organized. Keep the program moving at a steady pace. Have an agenda and follow it.
7. Be sure to recognize those people who helped make the season a success.
8. Thank those who helped organize the awards program.
9. Give a special thanks to parents and friends for attending.
10. Say only positive things about athletes. An awards program is no place for a coach to downgrade athletes, especially in the presence of their parents.

Several years ago during an awards program a thoughtless coach accused his athletes of "falling apart" causing the team to plunge into third place. As he handed out awards, he criticized several athletes for quitting at critical times during a contest.

After the program ended several irate parents complained to the school principal about the coach's negative attitude and how his comments embarrassed them in front of others. The principal talked to the coach on the following day. He mentioned how the coach's presentation upset some of the parents. The conversation went something like this:

Principal: "You know, you really stirred up a hornets nest last night."

Coach: "How do you mean?"

Principal: "Well, I had parents ready to string you up for some of the caustic remarks you made about your players."

Coach: "Hey, I'm not going to lie to them. Parents should know when their kids fail to do the job."

The principal asked the coach to refrain from criticizing athletes in front of their parents. The coach, feeling betrayed by his principal, responded by saying that awards programs are a stupid waste of time, and that from now on he would let the office staff distribute athletic awards.

11.   If possible, present each athlete with a yearbook. It's a classy way to conclude a season.
12.   Invite the local press. It's a good way to let others in the community share in the team's success.

Post-season Team Activities

Many coaches like to stay in contact with their athletes during the off season. They host social gatherings like pizza parties, house parties, or arrange for coaches and athletes to attend professional sports contests. Again, a wise coach will follow the guidelines of district policy before organizing special events.

Some coaches put on contests that pit their athletes against faculty members or the alumni. These gatherings help generate funds for the athletic program.

A training program such as weight lifting also brings athletes together in the off season. Athletes not participating in other sports have an opportunity to stay active and ready themselves for the coming year. These activities require sound organization and strict supervision by the coach.

Post-Season Coaching Activities

Two or three coaches may be contemplating a much needed rest at the end of the school year. But there are those who, like marathon runners, cover miles and miles of territory. They seldom settle in one place too long.

These coaches continually strive to upgrade their athletic teams by pouring energy into programs that will ultimately attract more athletes. Some of these programs include summer sports camps, summer or winter recreational leagues, coaching clinics and workshops, and special youth athletic programs.

Many coaches spend their time attending college courses for personal improvement, enrichment, or for moving across on the salary schedule. Some coaches concentrate on securing a degree or special credential.

Coaching, as stated earlier, places a high demand on the services of those working to strengthen the athletic program. Dedicated coaches learn early that long hours and personal sacrifices are part of the job.

A few coaches accept the challenge of outlining individual prescriptions for their returning athletes; they list the specific activities and skills that these athletes need to stress during the off season. This time-consuming task, if handled intelligently by both coach and athlete, can turn mediocre players into outstanding performers.

TO COACH OR NOT TO COACH

Many coaches, at different times in their careers, question their decision to coach. Serious thinking, however, usually occurs when a coach begins to tire or develop a new interest.

To continue to coach, or not, is a difficult decision because for many coaches the smell of a gym or the sound of a referee's whistle jars loose a few memories of exciting moments in coaching.

Some coaches quit for a year or so, suffer withdrawal symptoms, and return with a fresh outlook. Other coaches, feeling slightly embarrassed for telling others "you've seen the last of me," sneak back into the picture by assisting another coach. Then, like the wave of a magic wand, they're riding the range again the next year.

The Sacramento Bee Newspaper, Sacramento, California, recently ran a story concerning a teacher who had coached boys for eleven seasons before retiring to spend more time with his family. Last year he helped the girls' basketball coach during the final eight games of the season. Now he's coaching the girls' basketball team full time.

Why did he return to coaching? According to the article, the team needed a coach and since the school's principal gave him his first teaching job, he felt that he owed the principal something. Also, the girls behavior impressed him. "This group of girls is a lot of fun to be around," said the coach. "Every away game this year, people came up to me and commented about how nice the girls looked and how mature they were. The girls look sharp when we go somewhere to play."

Without a doubt, coaches face a tough challenge preparing athletes to cope in a competitive society. For many coaches the rewards outweigh the disappointments; for others the responsibility for guiding young athletes becomes overpowering.

Today's high school coach must contend with crowded facilities, limited budgets, and transportation problems. Yet with a strong, positive attitude and a desire to make each year better than the one before, a coach can build a highly competitive program and can help develop outstanding young athletes. Regardless of how many contests a coach wins or loses, he or she will not have to apologize.

Points to Remember

The demands on a coach's time remain long after the season ends. Equipment needs to be collected and stored, repaired or replaced, and facilities must be carefully inspected.

Plans for the coming year must be made months in advance. A coach, in order to capture and hold the interests of athletes, needs to stay in contact with them during the off season. It's imperative that the coach lend a hand in helping athletes plan future goals.

A coach should give athletes every opportunity to evaluate the athletic program. A Team Evaluation Form can help a coach pinpoint trouble spots and make the necessary adjustments.

A coach can ease the pain of collecting uniforms and equipment by soliciting help in advance, establishing and following a definite plan, and publicizing the event. The key to collecting materials is to keep it simple.

Organizing athletic awards programs requires patience, intelligent planning, and work on the part of the coach. How a coach plans an awards program often rests on such factors as squad size, team interest, and the coach's attitude. If the team had a disastrous season, they may wish to skip the program altogether. An enthusiastic coach, however, will use this opportunity to inspire athletes by highlighting the strong points of the season and by encouraging those athletes who show future promise.

There's little doubt that coaching is a tough, demanding job. It tests an individual's stamina, desire to succeed, and understanding of self and others. Coaching, like many other activities, carries its share of disappointments and thrills. Fortunately, for many people, the rewards exceed anything else.

QUESTIONS

1. How does the post-season present a challenge for the coach?
2. Why is it important for a coach to work with athletes during the off-season?
3. What is meant by maintaining an open door policy?
4. How might a coach allow athletes to evaluate the program?
5. What are the advantages of allowing athletes to evaluate the program?
6. What steps can a coach take to maximize the success of collecting equipment and uniforms?
7. Why is it necessary for the coach to take inventory?
8. What problems face coaches when they have to order supplies and equipment?
9. How can a coach minimize the problems of ordering supplies and equipment?
10. In your opinion, what should an athlete do in order to earn the following awards: Letter Awards, Individual Awards, Coach's Appreciation Award, and All-League Selection?
11. Why do some coaches buy athletic awards with their own money? Do you think this is a good idea? Explain.
12. What is meant by the four D's?
13. How do athletes develop each of the four D's?
14. How can a coach increase the chances of athletic awards arriving in time for the awards program?
15. How do awards inspire some athletes to improve?
16. What is the purpose of issuing Letters of Participation?
17. What problems do some coaches face in deciding which athletes should make the all-league team?
18. What are several advantages and disadvantages for each of the following programs: The All-School Athletic Awards Assembly, Special Athletic Awards Assembly, Sports Awards Banquet, Team Sports Night, and Individual Team Awards Dinner?
19. What things should a coach keep in mind when planning an awards program?
20. How can post-season team activities help athletes?
21. How can post-season coaching activities help a coach to grow professionally?
22. What are the advantages of outlining individual prescriptions for returning athletes?
23. What factors help a coach decide whether or not to continue coaching?
24. Why do some coaches come out of retirement shortly after quitting?
25. In your opinion, what major obstacles will coaches face in the next few years?

REFERENCES

1. Adams, Samuel. "Coaching Certification: The Time Is Now." *USSA News* Vol. 3, No. 4, (1979), pp. 1-3.
2. "Coach And Student Interest Keep Workshops Total Growing." *The First Aider* Vol. 49, No. 4, (1979), p. 17.
3. "Common Athletic Injuries" (Muscle Soreness). *The First Aider* Vol. 49, No. 3, (1979), p. 14.
4. *Cougar Crier Newsletter.* Del Campo High School Fair Oaks, California. March–April, (1980), p. 9.
5. Dirksen, Jay. "The Dilemma of 'Overtraining'—The Energy Crises In Sports." *Sportsline* Vol. 2, No. 2, (1980), pp. 3, 8.
6. Frazier, Charles S. "Coaches Legally Accountable To Athletes." *Coach & Athlete* April, (1978), p. 14.
7. Frazier, Charles S. "Sports Litigation: The New Attitude." *Coach & Athlete* May–June, (1979), pp. 11, 14, 19.
8. Garrick, James G. "Sports Medicine." *Pediatric Clinics of North America.* Vol. 24, No. 4, (1977), pp. 737, 739, 742-743, 745-746.
9. Hemmer, John C. "Motivational Techniques In Track And Field." *The Coaching Clinic* Vol. 17, No. 3, (1979), p. 2.
10. Hilgard, Ernest R. "Introduction To Psychology." Second edition. New York: Harcourt, Brace, and Co., 1957, p. 269.
11. Hoehn, Robert G. "The Coach As A Psychologist." *Scholastic Coach* Vol. 40, No. 8, (1971), pp. 78, 90-91.
12. Hoehn, Robert G. "Champ Or Chump Drill." *Athletic Journal* Vol. 50, (1970), pp. 30, 100.
13. "How To Raise Funds For Your School." *ASCO, Inc., Fund Raising Catalog/Guide* (1980-81), p. 4.
14. Jones, Duane. "Winning Edge Through Organization." *The Coaching Clinic* March, 1978.
15. Kazmaier, Richard. "The Naked Truth About Sports." *Scholastic Coach* Vol. 47, No. 3, (1979), pp. 26, 27, 88.
16. Lane, Mike. "Teaching Methods In Coaching." *Coach & Athlete* Jan.-Feb., (1978), p. 10.
17. Masin, Herman L. "Writing For Publication (One More Time)." *Scholastic Coach* January, 1979.
18. *NEA Reporter.* "Teacher Burnout." Vol. 18, No. 6, (1979), pp. 5, 10.
19. Rainey, Ron. "Organize Your Practice." *The Coaching Clinic* Nov.-Dec., 1978, pp. 20, 24.
20. Snow, Glen and Sendre, Ron. "Starting A Training Program At The High School Level." *The First Aider* Vol. 49, No. 8, (1980), pp. 1, 6, 7.
21. "Sports Survival Facts." *American Sports Education Institute* 1980.

22. Tener, Morton. "Making Practice Sessions More Efficient With P.E.R.T." (Program Evaluation And Review Technique). *Coach & Athlete* March, 1978, p. 22.
23. *The Collegiate Commissioners Association.* "Manual Of Football Officiating (For Six Man Crews)" 7th edition, 1980, pp. 5, 6.
24. Welker, William A. "Organizing Daily Practice Session." *The Coaching Clinic* February, 1978.
25. Whiddon, Sue. "The Coaching Dilemma In Girls' Interscholastic Sports Program." *Coach & Athlete* Vol. XXXX, No. 5, (1978), pp. 12-13.

Index